ARCHITECTS TODAY

ARCHITECTS TODAY

KESTER RATTENBURY
ROBERT BEVAN
KIERAN LONG

LAURENCE KING PUBLISHING
in association with
HARPER DESIGN INTERNATIONAL
an imprint of HarperCollins*Publishers*

LAURENCE KING

Published in 2004 by Laurence King Publishing Ltd
71 Great Russell Street
London WC1B 3BP
United Kingdom
Tel: + 44 20 7430 8850
Fax: + 44 20 7430 8880
e-mail: enquiries@laurenceking.co.uk
www.laurenceking.co.uk

Published in North and South America by:
Harper Design International
an imprint of HarperCollins*Publishers*
10 East 53rd Street
New York, NY 10022
Fax: +212 207 7654

Note on dates
Where relevant, the dates given
for buildings in this book are
for the year of completion.

This book was designed and produced by
Laurence King Publishing Ltd, London

Library of Congress Control Number: 2004105159

A catalogue record for this book is available
from the British Library

ISBN 1 85669 369 4

Project managed by Philippa Baker
Designed by Simon Osborne
Picture research by Peter Kent

Printed in Singapore

Contents

'Bizarre omissions, weird inclusions' – we can hear you muttering now. Any book that attempts to take a broad look at the peculiar world of contemporary architects and architecture is asking for trouble. The usual safe alternatives are books featuring the work of favoured practices, written by their acolytes, or slim volumes on the most currently fashionable architects. The result is a factionalized, specialized publishing sector, which makes it difficult for the student or casual reader to find any sensible overview of what is happening out there. Using, with all its oddities, a gazetteer format – trainspotting meets criticism – we thought it was worth putting our heads above the parapet and naming names, however jumbled and contentious a grouping they may form.

This book aims to be an introduction to the world's most influential living architects. But as a selection, it also attempts to describe the broad range of ethos, style and tactics at the forefront of the architectural world. Our criteria for inclusion, in addition to a pulse at time of going to press (sadly some have already died since, though their influence remains powerful), were that the architects should be currently practising and highly influential at international or regional level or with a particular renown in an area of architecture. These are architects who have changed the way in which their contemporaries and successors think and practise.

This means that we have included the extreme, the eccentric and the controversial at the expense of the eminent practitioner who operates within a well-established tradition. Many world-class high-tech architects, for example, are not in the book, and we ended up omitting almost all the neo-classicists we originally wanted to include, because they were working within a tradition whose key exponents were either already included or long dead.

At the same time, we have also had to deal with the tricky issues of fashion and changing times. We have deliberately included a few people whose influence was mammoth in their day but who are almost unheard of now even though they continue to practise; we would like to have included more. And we have had to choose fairly critically from the mass of young practices currently making a big noise on the international scene. With three authors, there was an instant majority on particularly contentious decisions – the only really scientific part of the process. But we also went on adding and dropping throughout production, partly in response to events, partly on the basis of continuing arguments on the merits of each architect, and partly to adjust the overall picture we are inevitably presenting. If we did it again tomorrow, we would be bound to have a slightly different list. Every time.

This book is fundamentally journalistic with only a toehold in academia. This allows for condensed, easy-access writing, mixing fact, opinion and ideas in a very tight space. But we have also tried to give some sources and references for the reader who wants to take things further. Our idea was that this should be something like a spotter's guide to the various breeds of architects in all their showy plumage rather than an in-depth natural history. The various entries should allow readers to develop their own understanding of the often mythologized species.

Introduction

Main picture: Public
Library, Usera, 2003

Top right: Valdemingómez
Waste Treatment Centre,
Madrid, 2000

On the opening page of their 1997 monograph *Areas of Impunity*, Iñaki Abalos and Juan Herreros printed a picture of a pair of hands dealing tarot cards onto a dark table. The cards can be taken as a critique of functionalism and Postmodernism, or as a statement of intent for the practice. They demonstrate humans' superstitious desire to make order visible in the random and also remind us of the Jewish joke: 'Want to make God laugh? Tell him your plans.'

Design, for Abalos and Herreros, is something that is revealed in the impotent fumblings of the human race – as much in a card trick as in ivory-tower academia. Their work to date has been characterized by their wonderful, playful writings as well as their built work, and these writings lie somewhere between manifestos, diaries and essays.

Born in 1956 and 1958 respectively, Abalos and Herreros began working together in 1984 in Madrid, where they were involved in the last throes of the 'movida madrileña', a scene in which they were somewhat idiosyncratic participants. Described by Alejandro Zaera as 'always somewhat less neat and tidy than was normal', they were an individual presence even then, more interested in mildewed tomes by old engineers than the architectural pornography of international publications.

Work such as the Gordillo House (1996), to the north of Madrid, takes their teacher Alejandro de la Sota's 'architecture of pure technique' and enhances it with the use of off-the-peg products. This interest in industrial methods of building is demonstrated throughout their work, from the drawings for the Villa FG in Madrid (1999), which could be folded to make a paper version of the house, to their huge project for the Valdemingómez Waste Treatment Centre, Madrid (2000), which is a veritable cathedral of rubbish, slowly turning a landfill site into a public park.

They have also tackled public buildings, including the charming corrugated plastic of the Village Hall in Colmenarejo (2000), and the Public Library in Usera (2003), an elemental building in concrete, sitting on a low podium that forms a public park. This building could, perhaps, be mistaken for the work of one of the older generation in Spain – Rafael Moneo in particular – but the details still speak of the architects' abiding concerns. A most pleasing detail is the interior finish, with walls covered in silkscreened wallpaper – a reference to Andy Warhol, by whom they are much influenced.

Abalos and Herreros are interested in an architecture that acts on the senses rather than one that signifies meaning. This does not prevent them from using decoration liberally, however, and their design for the new urban Coast Park in Barcelona (2004) prints giant pictures of fish onto the ground. New directions are still appearing in their work.

'It is often our phobias that are the best guide,' they write in the essay 'A Fragile Skin' (1997), taking a psychological condition as the agent for creative work. While this might seem reductive, Abalos and Herreros seem to have found a way of ignoring the semioticians and the technocrats while still making an architecture that is both intellectually rigorous and materially sensuous.

Abalos & Herreros

a

Top left: Painting for
Peckham Library

Main picture: Hôtel du Département
des Bouches-du-Rhône (the 'Big
Blue'), Marseilles, 1993

Top right: Peckham Library,
London, 2000

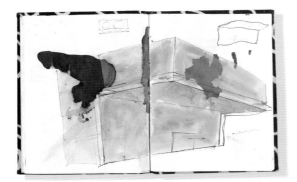

In 1990 a maverick forty-two-year-old with only small buildings and unbuilt projects to his name beat all-conquering Norman Foster in the competition for a local government building in Marseilles. The massive redesigns that ensued, to meet budget and political deadlines, were followed closely in the UK as the young office boomed, tottered and regained its footing, taking the world stage with the triumphant opening of the abrasively romantic building – the 'Big Blue'.

Born in 1947, Will Alsop remains more of a maverick than his worldwide success might suggest. He studied at London's St Martin's School of Art and the Architectural Association, and was taught by Archigram and Cedric Price, famous for their radical, experimental thought, tough structures and anti-aestheticism. Through and beyond early partnership with John Lyall, Alsop became famous for his paintings – huge, colourful, abstract interpretations of his projects, made spontaneously and worked up later.

His articulated, transformer-like structures – later known as 'blobs on legs' – emerged from more revolutionary work: his 1989 proposal for heavy-mechanical opening flower structures on the Garonne River in France (unbuilt) or his Berlin City of Objects (also unbuilt) (1992). 'No Style No Beauty' was an early slogan. A visitors' centre at Cardiff of 1990 (a plywood tube wrapped in polythene) and a lifting bridge and control building at London's Canary Wharf (1991) showed how these ideas would transform into buildings.

Despite its many redesigns, the Marseilles building is a powerful manifestation of the original idea: the early eco-principles of the atrium and blocks; the articulation of the 'Déliberatif' (as Alsop calls the council chamber) and the 'fish' in the foyer; the structural toughness of the X-grid legs. Its transformer-aged Modernism somehow echoes Le Corbusier's Unité d'Habitation in the same town. And the beautiful, Yves Klein ultramarine ties it into the dazzling craggy industrial land and seascape of Marseilles.

Alsop's verdigris Peckham Library in London (2000) scooped the UK's Stirling Prize in 2000 against the stiffest competition of any year (Norman Foster's Canary Wharf Station; Caruso St John's exquisite Walsall Gallery). His deep-blue-tiled North Greenwich Underground Station (1999) was the most delicious of all the Jubilee Line stations with which London overhauled its transport image. Major international projects continue to grow.

Alsop's image as a great artist-architect remains greater outside his native territory. He is part of a European world in which culture and power are not antithetical. At home, he has maybe built too much, with too much concern for sheer shape-making, to be seen as a true apostle of Archigram or Price. But if the UK views his relaxed painting technique with wry amusement, he retains the respect of the art world: he is a Royal Academician, working annually with Bruce McLean, and won the competition for a new arts complex at London's influential Goldsmiths College. His conceptual–Expressionist paintings and sketchbooks are increasingly impressive in their own terms and fetch respectable prices. Outside the UK he is a vindication of Englishness, with his clever, lyrical, tough, wry, big projects.

a

When something is described as awe-inspiring, the tendency is to think big. While Tadao Ando's buildings do indeed inspire awe, there is nothing grandiose about his work, which at its heart is about relating the body to its immediate surroundings and to the natural world beyond.

Born in 1941, Ando is a poet in concrete who learnt as a child how to work in three dimensions in timber from a carpenter who lived across the road from his Osaka home. The lessons have been invaluable: Ando's superb handling of the wooden shuttering for moulding concrete ensures his buildings' silky perfection – some moulds are even varnished internally to create the ultimate finish. The bolt-holes in the shuttering that stud his unadorned walls have become a trademark.

Ando has won nearly every architecture award going, but he does not even have an architecture degree. After starting out as a boxer he trained the hard way, working in local architects' offices, travelling and observing the traditions of his Japanese home and the Western architectural canon overseas. He saved for weeks to buy a volume on Le Corbusier, tracing and retracing the drawings until the pages were blackened, and later named his dog after the master. Louis Kahn and Frank Lloyd Wright were also great inspirations.

When he set up his practice in 1969 his initial works were in timber but it was his first tiny row house in concrete, the unassuming Azuma House in Osaka (1976), that put him on the map – 'the point of origin for my subsequent work' – creating a quiet internal world accessed through a doorway that is a mere slit in the façade.

In a series of religious projects in Japan – the Church on the Water at Tomamu (1988), the Church of the Light in Osaka (1989) and the Shingonshu Honpukuji Water Temple, Hyogo (1991) – religious awe and awe before beauty are brought together without pomposity. Concrete interacts with the elemental qualities of light and water: the shadow of a crucifix across a pond, the play of light through a simple cross aperture, the experience of stepping down through a lotus pool to a vermilion meditation space that ignites at sunset.

It has been observed that there is something of the temple in the ascetic calm of all Ando's buildings (apart from his own studio – a five-storey galleried madhouse around a central space from which he delivers his homilies). This is true of his numerous museum projects – the circular court of the Naoshima Contemporary Art Museum, Kagawa (1992), and the contemporaneous Kumamoto-prefectural Forest of Tombs Museum, Kumamoto – a building type that lends itself to the sacral. For all its serenity, his work is an attempt to resolve the conflict between the self and the business of the social world and architecture is his method of manipulating that relationship. He has defined architecture as 'the box that provokes'.

Since the early 1990s he has been working internationally – France (Meditation Space, UNESCO), UK (Piccadilly Gardens Regeneration, Manchester), Italy (Fabrica, Benetton Communication Research Centre), Germany (Vitra Seminar House) and the US (Modern Art Museum of Fort Worth) – but he remains firmly rooted in his home town Osaka and the lessons of his childhood.

Tadao Ando

a

Top left: Ron Herron's
Walking City, 1964–73

Top right: Mike Webb's
Cushicle, 1966

Bottom: Peter Cook's
Instant Cities, 1968

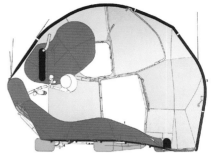

Contentious and troublesome, Archigram are extraordinarily influential. Whether to include them in this book has been hotly debated. Were they ever really architects? Are they still practising? It depends what you mean by practise. Since the 1960s they have extended the language of architectural thought and expression, overturning its boundaries and conventions. Without building a single project (as a group, at least), they have arguably had more impact on architectural ideas than anyone since Le Corbusier.

Archigram was originally a magazine – architecture meets telegram – formed in the early 1960s by the newly qualified David Greene and Peter Cook to publish work that broke the straitjacket of international Modernism, reinventing technology and form. They co-opted Mike Webb, whose furniture design they admired, and the slightly older Warren Chalk, Ron Herron and Dennis Crompton from London County Council's architects department, who kept coming second in competitions – a sure sign of good work.

The magazine was a home production that gained worldwide circulation through Cook's neighbour, critical historian Peter Reyner Banham, who called Archigram 'short on theory, long on fun'. Using new printing techniques, fusing graphics and collage (much more difficult before photocopiers), technology and Pop Art, their fantastical drawn projects provided some of architecture's most famous, influential and provocative images.

They proposed new ways of living, overthrowing the 'form follows function' Modernist dogma to explore the possibilities of new technologies: serviced lifestyles via pods, capsules, add-ons, serviced clothes, massive mobile megastructures, robots and circuses. They were rebellious, idealistic, consumerist, optimistic – architecture's Beatles.

Ron Herron's famous Walking City (1964–73), is in fact a misnomer. The first drawing, 'Cities: Moving', is a massive bubble containing all the elements of city life, unconnected to its environment and serviced via huge plug-in tubes (often misread as legs). Peter Cook's Instant Cities (1968) propose entertainment towns adapted or formed by serviced balloons and temporary structures. Mike Webb's Drive-in Housing (1966) explores the car and popular lifestyles; his Cushicle (1966) and Suitaloon (1968) look at serviced clothes. David Greene's Rok-plug, Log-plug and LAWUN projects (all 1969) explore the relationship of technology and landscape. All allow changed behaviour and make normal fixed buildings redundant.

The group split in the early 1970s but they still sometimes describe Archigram as current. The surviving members – Cook, Greene, Crompton and Webb – collected the RIBA's Royal Gold Medal in 2002. Archigram's influence is remarkable – through both their projects and their later teaching, based at the London schools, where they set up a hotbed of experimental activity that continues to do battle with the professional orthodoxy. This book is full of their pupils. Some members have built – Ron Herron's Imagination Building in London (1989), Peter Cook's Kunsthalle in Graz (2003). But Archigram's non-building is an essential part of their influence. The ideas, uncompromised by the pragmatics of building, remain open to interpretation by the massive range of practices who have been influenced by them.

Archigram

a

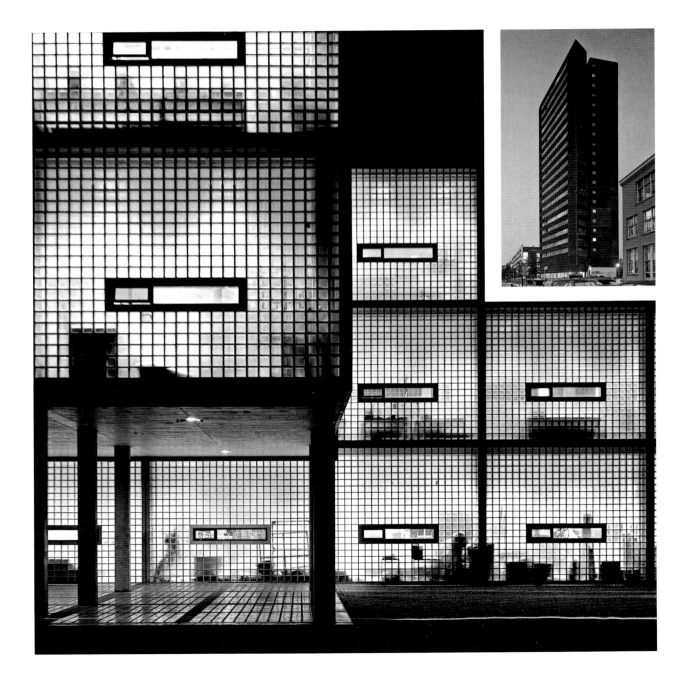

Main picture: Academy
of Arts and Architecture,
Maastricht, 1993

Wiel Arets is one of those architects whose touchstones are cosmetically diverse and yet depressingly familiar. In an essay in his 2002 monograph his influences turn out to be Jean-Luc Godard, Masai tribespeople, Luis Barragán, Adalberto Libera's Villa Malaparte in Capri, bamboo scaffolding in Hong Kong, the Mets' baseball stadium in New York, a printed circuit board and the work of Richard Serra. There cannot be an architecture student in the world who has not heard these mentioned in a lecture somewhere, usually by someone trying a little too hard to show a rounded view of the world.

But despite the identikit references, Arets' work has always been highly tectonic and very coherent. Born in the Dutch-German border town of Heerlen in 1955, Arets graduated from Eindhoven University in 1983, establishing Wiel Arets Architect & Associates in his home town a year later.

His buildings are usually compositions of geometrical shapes, from the regimented proportions of the Academy of Arts and Architecture in Maastricht (1993) to the freer stacking of boxes that makes up his 1997 police station in Boxtel, the Netherlands. His design process has produced a characteristic visual style that usually includes spectacular drawn perspectives on sepia-tinted paper. These, together with his trademark massing models, have drawn comparison with the methods of Tadao Ando and Giorgio Grassi.

Arets has almost certainly never regained the heights of his first major building, the Maastricht Academy. The project refurbished the existing school of art and created two dramatic extensions in glass block and concrete, linked by a concrete footbridge. Critic Kenneth Frampton saw the building, with its bridge connecting workshops and a public core, as an updating of the design of the Bauhaus in Dessau. The bridge is also a gateway to a former city-centre industrial area that has since been transformed into a residential neighbourhood.

In his other work, the rigour of Arets' material approach leads to some Kafkaesque moments. His police station in Vaals (1995) is arranged around a series of corridors. In one waiting area for the interview rooms are two pre-cast concrete chairs, strangely out of scale and almost floating in the air. The detention cells also make no concessions to a touchy-feely image for the police, walls of raw, streaked concrete and a postage-stamp-sized window being the main features.

Arets' work can come across as right-wing and austere but his uncompromising materiality shows an immense sureness when dealing with high buildings. It is difficult to see how the KNSM Island Apartment Tower in Amsterdam (1996) will not, one day, be considered a classic.

The jury is probably still out on whether Arets will be remembered for more than a few of his buildings. His commitment to teaching (he was dean of the Berlage Institute in Amsterdam between 1995 and 2001, and has held a dazzling array of professorships) and his prolific production should guarantee him a place in the top echelon of contemporary architects, even if work on the drawing boards at the turn of the century – including a cathedral in Ghana – does not look the most inspiring of his career.

a

Top left: Atlantis
Condominium, Miami, 1982

Top right: Westin Hotel,
New York, 2002

Bottom right: The
Palace, Miami, 1982

Philip Johnson called Arquitectonica 'the gutsiest team in the business. Ever since the Pink House of 1978 they have fought the front line of avant-garde design.' Arquitectonica themselves say they have 'never reneged on the principles of Modernism, but pushed it forward'. Now a huge international corporation with offices in Miami, New York, Los Angeles, Paris, Hong Kong, São Paolo, Shanghai, Lima, Manila and Buenos Aires, Arquitectonica is a curious fusion of the avant-garde and absolute driving commerce – right up Johnson's street.

Theirs is not quite a familiar career path. Married with six children, Laurinda Spear, born in Miami in 1950, and French–Italian Bernardo Fort-Brescia, born in Peru in 1951, used to work for the ultimately avant-garde Rem Koolhaas before setting up their own firm in Miami in 1977. Many of their first projects bear marks of Koolhaas's early work – the axonometric drawing of their Palace scheme, for instance, looks like an out-take from the Dutch architect's Delirious New York project. But unlike most of Koolhaas's hugely influential protégé-collaborators, Arquitectonica have built projects all over the world that are thoroughly enmeshed with the market – and absolutely massive.

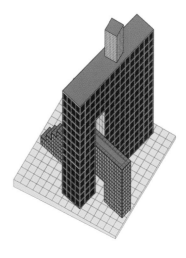

Their breakthrough was the Pink House (1978), for Spear's father, on Biscayne Bay, Miami Shores – probably their most classically modern building. Painted in shades of pale to saturated pink with shifting proportions, it is orthogonal, with an architectural promenade taking in outside stair, ramp, internal two-level 'street' and enclosed pool. It is one of their most popular projects. And one of the smallest.

The Palace (1982), a condominium on Biscayne Bay, is a three-dimensional collage – a thin slab cut right through by a huge red stair that itself forms another massive residential block. The Atlantis Condominium in Miami (1982) has a hole in it, the gap forming a 'sky court' half way up the building with red spiral stair, tiny pool and palm tree. Sky courts caught on and Miami had found a firm that could produce its trademark 'tropical internationalism'.

But if Miami loved this playful, full-on commercialism it was not alone. The Banco di Credito, Lima (1988), had a jogging track roof and lap pool, a heliport and a communications centre. The US Embassy in Peru (1995) was a huge cartoon monolith, its high-security façade patterned with windows of silver and gold. Hong Kong got a huge urban complex, Festival Walk (1998); the Banque de Luxembourg a new headquarters (1994); Dijon a performing arts centre (1998), Fukuoka a housing complex, Nexus World (2000) – all playing with shapes, all highly coloured (Arquitectonica are good at making mirrored glass look fun), and all immediate, confident icons. Even New York, in many ways one of the most restrictive building environments, let them put up the massive Westin Hotel and entertainment complex (2002), its silver half split from its bronze half by what has been called a meteor crashing into Times Square.

It can sound rather queasy – the knowing, critical element that we like in our avant-gardes turned over at full volume to the mass market. But Arquitectonica's fans assure us that their projects work against all the odds.

Arquitectonica

a

18-19

Top left: Cultural Centre,
Marion, 2001

Top right: Storey Hall, RMIT
University, Melbourne, 1996

Bottom: National Museum
of Australia, Canberra, 2001

Judging by their design for the National Museum of Australia in Canberra (2001), Ashton Raggatt McDougall's work is the architectural equivalent of dance music, sampling other architects' work with a bouncy freedom that is infectious but puzzling. The museum looks at the cultural history of the 'Lucky Country' – which does not seem so lucky from an Aboriginal point of view. ARM were not scared of the controversy inherent in these questions of Australian identity, and their 'quoting' of Daniel Libeksind's fractured Berlin Jewish Museum has obvious resonances – although Libeskind was not best pleased. The museum and the associated Institute of Aboriginal Studies also incorporate sections of Le Corbusier's Villa Savoie (painted black instead of white) and Sydney Opera House (by way of Aldo Rossi and James Stirling among others). It is as audacious and in-your-face as ARM's previous work.

The Melbourne-based practice was formed in 1986 by partners Stephen Ashton, Howard Raggatt and Ian McDougall (born 1954, 1951 and 1952 respectively) and, despite the populist veneer to the work, they have been driving an Australian architecture that is about ideas rather than a pragmatic or poetic response to landscape. They are out to prove that Australia's cultural 'cringe', which has seen a dearth of great public architecture, can be overcome. Their work ranges across all sectors – educational, commercial, housing – but it is cultural projects that have given them the profile and freedom to make their voice heard. And boy do they shout.

Their 1996 reworking and extension to Storey Hall, at the RMIT University in Melbourne, carried their name overseas. It is like an extraordinary green chameleon, transforming a neoclassical building into a gallery and auditorium encrusted with a scaly internal and external skin, informed by an exploration of mathematical and computer-based models.

More recently, a cultural centre for the city of Marion, South Australia (2001) has used the place name literally to organize the buildings: the M and the A are angular folded elements that run through the building; the R is a curvaceous metal-clad *porte-cochère*. By the time you get to the N (a free-standing sculpture of steel trusses) the conceit is wearing a bit thin. Anyone looking for subtlety should look elsewhere. Their scheme for St Kilda Library in Melbourne (1993) creates a new façade in the form of a large stone book, complete with leaves. This is Postmodernism writ large.

ARM do have their quieter moments, however, and have taken a more subdued approach to another monument of national importance, the Shrine of Remembrance war memorial in Melbourne, where they are excavating the hill on which the neoclassical temple sits to create a visitors' centre and galleries of remembrance. The practice has also been responsible for some intelligent housing and masterplanning schemes, including the ongoing regeneration of Melbourne's extensive docks area.

Despite, or perhaps because of, the nudge-nudge quotations and jokes, the Australians have taken the practice and their clever work to heart, even if the conservative establishment are not happy with ARM's architectural outspokenness. Two of their schemes have even made it onto postage stamps. Lick that.

Ashton Raggatt McDougall

Top left: Hydra Pier,
the Netherlands, 2002

Top right: Los Angeles West
Coast Gateway, 1988

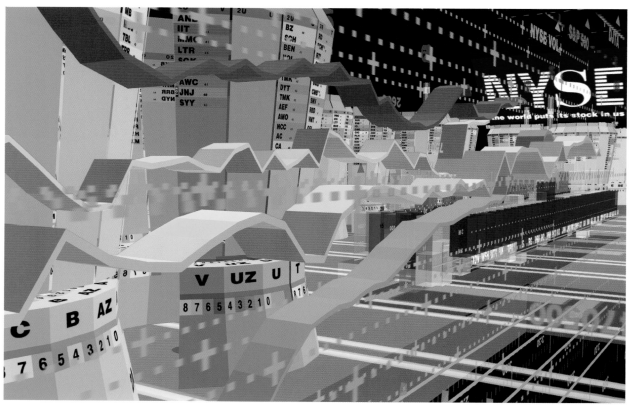

Bottom: 3DTF, New York
Stock Exchange, 1999

Asymptote is a mathematical term meaning 'a curve approaching a given curve arbitrarily closely'. This explanation could be read in a variety of ways. Is Asymptote's work just a collection of arbitrary curves?

Run by husband-and-wife team Hani Rashid and Lise Anne Couture, the practice is at the apex of the so-called blobmeister architects at Columbia University in New York even though they have completed just one building – the small Hydra Pier for the Floriade Garden Festival in the Netherlands (2002). Their prolific work in digital media and their zeal in writing, lecturing and teaching means that their profile in contemporary architecture is high.

Rashid was born in Cairo in 1958, but his family fled war-torn Egypt for Toronto, where he was brought up with his brother, furniture designer Karim Rashid. Couture was born in Montreal in 1959 and trained at Carleton University, Ottawa, and Yale. Founded in Milan in 1987 to undertake work on the edges of normal architectural practice, Asymptote moved to New York in 1989 when Couture joined Rashid as a partner. Their work includes digital installations, computer-generated environments and three-dimensional information modelling as well as buildings, interiors and urban design.

Their earliest work, a prize-winning project for an ideas competition for the Los Angeles West Coast Gateway (1988), proposed a steel cloud building accommodating galleries, cinemas, theatres, parks and libraries, its skin and form adjusting according to the frequency of traffic passing below. It was an early expression of an obsession with the potential of technology to create responsive environments.

The Archigramesque model of the cloud contrasts strongly with Asymptote's later work, which has become all sinuous curves and lines. They quote their influences as Andre Bloc, Eric Mendelsohn, Konstantin Melnikov, Bruno Taut, Frederick Kiesler, Georges Maciunas, Marcel Duchamp and John Cage. This wide range of designers and artists now seems a little obsolete. Asymptote's frame of reference necessarily consists of its own work, which is the cutting edge of fashionable thinking about virtual space.

A 1999 commission to design a virtual environment for the New York Stock Exchange produced the 3DTF (three-dimensional trading floor), one of the first large-capacity virtual environments. The model brings together information from disparate corners of the stock exchange, providing real-time information in an accessible way, and is intended to prefigure the stock exchange's movement towards a completely virtual environment.

A project under development for a very different institution, the Guggenheim Foundation, creates another virtual environment, this time made to exhibit art. The plan is for a genuinely navigable on-line museum that could change its shape according to visitor patterns, exhibiting both conventional art (photography and such) as well as internet art and the Guggenheim's digital collection.

Asymptote's reputation seems to be on an unstoppable rise but they are now realizing more buildings and the market for virtual environments is still unclear. They are set up for a fall in some senses, but they are young enough to be allowed a few mistakes. They have avoided them so far.

Asymptote

a

Top: Wall-less House,
Nagano, 1997

Bottom left: Atsushi Imai
Gymnasium, Odate, 2003

Bottom right: Temporary
housing, Kobe, 1995

Shigeru Ban has made a high-profile career out of convincing the world that he is just a modest guy who would rather be left alone to do his work. A self-publicist of remarkable proportions, Ban, until recently, was known principally as the architect who made buildings out of paper. Now his work seems to have entered another phase, and his shortlisting for the World Trade Center competition in 2002 means that his name is likely to be mentioned in connection with more high-profile jobs.

Ban was born in Tokyo in 1957 and studied at two of America's most influential schools – Sci-Arc in California and Cooper Union, New York. He worked in Arata Isozaki's office before setting up on his own in 1985.

Despite making the world's first permanent building using paper tubes as the main structure (Library of a Poet, Zushi, Kanagawa, Japan, 1991), it is for his Takatori Church in Kobe (1995) that Ban is justly famous. After the devastating Kobe earthquake in 1995, he created an oval enclosure of fifty-eight 5-metre-long paper tubes that could seat eighty people. The building was a huge success, not least because Ban designed it to be constructed by local people, giving a sense of ownership to the community. From this success, he went on to design shelters for the homeless in Kobe, also with paper structures, and a paper refugee shelter for the UNHCR (1995), piloted in Rwanda as a sustainable and easy-to-construct basic shelter for displaced people.

His non-paper constructions are sometimes less spectacular, such as the depressingly orthogonal 9 Square Grid House in Kanagawa (1997). The acclaimed Wall-less House, Karuizawa, Nagano (1997), though, is stunning, dug into a steeply sloping site and completely without internal partitions. The ground of the house runs up at the back of the plan to help bear the load of the ceiling slab and roof, leaving only three 55-millimetre columns at the front of the plan. This gives almost uninterrupted views out to the countryside around the house.

Ban returned to the theme of his early work – pavilion and exhibition design – with his Japanese Pavilion at the Hanover Expo in 2000. This quite extraordinary structure, designed in collaboration with the legendary German engineer Frei Otto, created an undulating roof, clad in white plastic and supported by a structure of paper tubes and ladders. Hanover Expo was a flop in terms of visitor numbers and Ban's pavilion suffered badly from construction delays, cost overruns and a dreadful exhibition design that obscured views of the paper structure. However, the building was a great leap forward in paper technology and provided a sustainable solution to the ecologically questionable phenomena that are expo pavilions.

The mustachioed Ban is on the up and up, and has finally shaken the tag of paper architect with a succession of buildings such as the steel and concrete factory at Hamura, Dengyosya, Tokyo (1993), the timber and glass Tazawako Station, Akita (1997) and the Atsushi Imai Gymnasium in Odate, northern Japan (2003), with its laminated plywood dome. It remains to be seen whether his now global fame will erode the idealism that has characterized his career thus far.

Shigeru Ban

b

Main picture: Stadium
for the Olympiapark,
Munich, 1972

Bottom left: West German
Parliament Building, Bonn,
1992

Bottom right: Kindergarten,
Stuttgart-Luginsland, 1991

Günter Behnisch is probably the most important name in post-war German architecture, and yet his work's only characteristic is its diversity. Behnisch & Partners, in its many incarnations, has never had a house style imposed; partners, assistants and collaborators have been given a remarkable amount of freedom throughout the firm's history.

Born in Dresden in 1922, Behnisch served as a submarine commander in the Second World War and spent two years in a British prisoner-of-war camp before returning to Germany to study architecture and working for five years with Rolf Gutbrod. He then set up his own practice in Stuttgart and worked during the 1960s on a prefabrication system that promised to provide a quick and clean way of reconstructing war-damaged Germany. Although the system was used successfully at an engineering school at Ulm (1963), Behnisch became disillusioned after seeing the unimaginative way it was applied by local authorities and builders.

But by this time, the Behnisch office had been transformed, having won the job that is probably still its most famous – the Olympiapark for the Munich Olympics of 1972. The stadium, with its cable-net roof, may be the greatest ever designed, and is often largely credited to legendary German engineer Frei Otto. The design was originated by the Behnisch office, however, with important assistance from Otto, and engineered by Heinz Isler.

Rarely has an architectural project had as much symbolic importance for a nation as the Olympic Park in Munich. The Berlin Olympics in 1936 had used typically axial architecture to demonstrate the strength of the Nazi regime and the superiority of the Aryan race. The Munich Olympiad was intended to demonstrate the polar opposite – the liberalism of the German people, the inclusiveness of German society and a sense of informality. Although the tent structure is the icon of the event, the landscape strategy was almost more important, creating a series of slopes that encouraged repose and reflection and that later became a permanent public park. This interaction with landscape became a theme of Behnisch's work, as in such projects as the University Library at Eichstätt (1987) and the State Insurance Agency at Schleswig-Holstein (1997).

In 1983 Behnisch was chosen to design the new West German Parliament Building in Bonn (1992), which grew from an initial project for a new entrance foyer to a whole new office building and debating chamber. Lit from above by a glazed roof shielded with a system of shades and louvres, the chamber represents one of the first convincing uses of motorized louvres, which prevent direct sunlight from entering the interior.

The creative independence within the office has been to good effect, and it is no accident that Behnisch & Partners has been an incubator for some of the more important offices in Germany. Diversity is not always a good thing, though, and there have been moments that some critics would probably rather forget (the 1991 kindergarten at Stuttgart-Luginsland, which looks like Noah's Ark dropped from a great height on a sylvan countryside). But the work continues to push boundaries technologically and environmentally while remaining formally eclectic.

Günter Behnisch

b

Top left: Model of Borromini's
San Carlo alle Quattro Fontane,
Lugano, 1999

Top right: House at Riva
San Vitale, 1973

Bottom: Casa Rotonda,
Stabio, 1982

Mario Botta's career has straddled the two most powerful generations of twentieth-century architecture. Born in Ticino, Switzerland, in 1943, he has a CV to die for. A pupil of prominent theorist Tita Carloni, he worked for both Le Corbusier and Louis Kahn during their time in Venice in the 1960s. He also studied under Carlo Scarpa while at the Venice architecture school, and found himself in an ideal position to assimilate into the strongly region- alist tendencies of Ticino a host of international influences, particularly drawing on the Italian Neo-Rationalism of Aldo Rossi and Vittorio Gregotti.

Botta's early work was quite extraordinary. His iconic house at Riva San Vitale (1973) is a concrete and brick tower in a spectacular setting, referring to the vernacular tradition of 'rocoli' summer houses in the region as well as serving as a marker in the landscape – an important aspect of much of Botta's work. The house looks both monumental and hermetic and openings in the fabric of the building are chosen to coincide with choice views of the landscape.

His first public buildings were heavily influenced by Kahn's work in Venice and had a strong attitude to the urban realm. His design for Zurich Central Station (1978), made in collaboration with his close contemporary Luigi Snozzi, proposed a bridge over the railway tracks – described by critic Kenneth Frampton as a 'viaduct megastructure' – linking two areas of the city with an elevated, tree-lined route, and providing restaurants, shops, offices and parking.

Botta is perhaps now best known for the strong stylistic features of his buildings – striated materials (most often brickwork), and the drum form that has recurred throughout his work, from his Casa Rotonda in Stabio, Switzerland (1982), to the San Francisco Museum of Modern Art (1995). SFMOMA's geometric forms step back in a kind of ziggurat with a truncated cylinder rising through the middle. The subtlety with which Botta manipulates natural light in this building had critics in paroxysms of delight and brought comparisons with his old mentor Kahn. It is perhaps more strongly symmetrical and referential than Kahn's work, though, with all of Botta's classical influences on show.

Perhaps the most delightful of his buildings is the most anomalous: in 1999, Botta designed a 33-metre-high, full-scale model of Borromini's San Carlo alle Quattro Fontane church in Rome. The model was assembled from 35,000 wooden planks held together by steel cables and fixed to a steel frame. This strange apparition was placed on a raft in the lake at Lugano, Switzerland, to commemorate the four-hundredth anniversary of Borromini's birth, also forming a job creation scheme for the unemployed. Screaming out for interpretation as a defining piece of Postmodernism, the project is stunningly beautiful as an object and perhaps should be left at that.

Botta, whose career began as an apprentice when he was fifteen, is still relatively young, and is an important figure already. There are signs that his work is returning home, with low-key projects such as a winery in eastern Italy, and it will be interesting to see whether this powerful stylist can make his architecture relevant to the post-minimalist generation.

Mario Botta

b

Concrete-spined and glass-winged, Santiago Calatrava's engineering-led
architecture has taken flight over the last two decades. From the first his
career spanned at least two countries: he was born near Valencia in 1951
and trained there at art then architecture school before studying engineering in Zurich, where he opened his first practice in 1981. His early buildings
were in Spain and Switzerland, including many of the fine bridges that
have become something of a speciality. These and the competition-winning
Stadelhofen Railway Station in Zurich (1990) established his reputation
as an engineer who could sculpt the lightest of forms. The Zurich station's
characteristically canted columns and delicate canopies defined a direction
that was to reach fuller expression at his TGV station in Lyons (1994), nicknamed 'the bird' for its swooping wings.

　　　It was the geometrical rigour of the historical buildings he studied
in Valencia that led Calatrava to Switzerland and engineering. Geometry, he
has said, is fundamental to an understanding of architecture: 'the language
of geometry is as important as the language of structure.' This mathematical
framework has been married to a love of the sculptural potential of concrete
and of forms from the natural world. The motto 'natura mater et magistra'
– nature is both mother and teacher – has, says Calatrava, guided all his
work. Oriente Railway Station, built for the 1998 Lisbon Expo, shows this
tendency in full flower. The bone-like flying bridges and buttresses of the
concrete underground section rise up into daylight to support a filigree of

Santiago Calatrava

C

Top: TGV Station,
Lyons, 1994

steel and glass shading the train platforms above. It is almost Expressionist. Calatrava works in parallel with the high-tech tradition, touching it at points but pursuing a more sensuous path that has its antecedents in the tree-like tracery of Gothic churches.

Although for a long time he rarely designed enclosed buildings, preferring canopies and bridges, Calatrava's recent work has included all building types, handled by offices in Valencia, Zurich and Paris. These capture space in the same way as his open structures. At the 2001 extension to the Milwaukee Museum of Art, 'wings' appear again in the form of the steel-ribbed arc of a *brise-soleil* that shelters the building. This is the first of a string of US projects (an inspired scheme to complete New York's Cathedral of St John the Divine remains unimplemented) that includes a terminal at Dallas Fort Worth Airport and a Catholic cathedral in Oakland, California.

It is in Valencia, however, that Calatrava has been given free rein with the commission to build the City of Arts and Sciences, a sprawling and stunning cultural complex. The first building to be completed was a planetarium (1998) set like the pupil in an eye-shaped structure (an abiding Calatrava obsession). This has since been joined by the 220-metre-long spine of the Science Museum (2000). The Palacia de las Artes, when completed, will contain auditoria for the performance of plays, concerts and opera. The complex is a vast expression of Calatrava's sculptural skills rather than his technical restraint and it is immediately obvious that it could be only his work. This is an architect who is not afraid to have a signature style – and he writes it all across the 36-hectare site.

Canadian Adam Caruso (born 1962) and Briton Peter St John (born 1959) are standard-bearers for an architecture that has less currency in the UK than in mainland Europe. They are deadly serious, making austere but intellectually allusive buildings influenced by late Modernist heroes Alison and Peter Smithson and by a strain of Swiss architecture that prizes craftsmanship and the primacy of the architect in the construction process.

Based in London, the practice had its big break in the heady days of the National Lottery in the UK, when hundreds of millions of pounds were spent on new cultural facilities. Their success in the competition for Walsall New Art Gallery (2000) put them and the building's blighted locale – more of a suburb of Birmingham than a town in its own right – on the world map. Those in the know had been waiting for them to win something substantial. Their early careers, working for influential teacher Florian Beigel and subsequently for Arup Associates, and their strong performance in competitions for the Yokohama Ferry Terminal and the Nara Convention Hall, both in Japan, suggested that something special was to come.

They did not disappoint. Walsall emerged as the most important building in England in maybe twenty years, produced with an incredible quality of construction. The gallery seems to contain within it the gamut of British architectural references, feeling by turns like a castle, a manor house and a working-class terrace, with a series of galleries of beautifully tuned, almost domestic scale. Above all, it provided a civic façade with windows presenting specific views – editorializing Walsall and reconstructing it as 'a Black Country San Gimigniano', as critic Rowan Moore put it.

Caruso St John is old school made new. The practice, usually grouped in the 'archtitecture of the everyday' movement or with conceptual minimalists Herzog & de Meuron, is at the other end of the spectrum from the media junkie architects that glory in the mess of the Postmodern city. Peter St John, when talking about his teaching, says: 'With our students we end up asking ourselves...what is one's attitude to urbanism, because there seems to be so little one can admire now.'

Their work is diverse. Projects for set-piece galleries like Walsall are offset by refurbishments – a new contemporary arts centre in an old industrial building in Cardiff currently on the drawing board is a potential mini-Tate Modern – signage, housing competitions and their scheme for the reconstruction of a Baroque public square in Kalmar, Sweden (2002). Their project for an acoustic ceiling for the Barbican Concert Hall in London (2001) saw them come up with a system of burnished red reflectors for the ceiling that engaged with this historical interior without obscuring the dramatic concrete construction.

Something of a hiatus in their practice occurred after Walsall when, for all the adulation, new work at a large scale was not forthcoming. Now they are moving into gear again, with the competition for the Cardiff building won, Bethnal Green Museum of Childhood completing, and the Gagosian Gallery in London about to begin. They deserve more major public buildings.

Caruso St John

C

Top right: River and Rowing Museum, Henley-on-Thames, 1997

Bottom left: Palace of Justice, Salerno, 2004

David Chipperfield is one of the UK's most successful architectural exports, which is fortunate because his spare yet luxurious and thoughtful Modernism has been constantly overlooked in his home country. Chipperfield has had to build his reputation in Germany, Japan, Spain, Italy and now the US. This is perhaps because his work does not fit into the in-your-face showmanship of the UK's high-tech architectural establishment, which has provided such a service to the commercial world. Chipperfield's work – in concrete, glass, stone and timber – is, by comparison, much more subtle.

That said, he is a respected player within the UK architectural scene. He was a founder of the short-lived but influential 9H architecture gallery and has been mentor to a healthy crop of young British practices, who have steadily emerged from his office. He is also a much sought-after visiting critic at schools of architecture around the world.

Born in 1953 in London, Chipperfield trained at the Architectural Association and worked for Douglas Stephen, Richard Rogers and Norman Foster. These credentials have equipped him with a technical know-how that he uses as a tool rather than as a stylistic end in itself. He established his London practice in 1984 (in a much-praised office building of his own design) but, after failing to make much headway in the UK, opened an office in Tokyo in 1987 on the back of a variety of high-end projects including shops for Issey Miyake and a design showroom in Kyoto. The Japanese move was a natural one for Chipperfield, whose work, with its clean lines, unfussy details and faith in smooth expanses of natural materials, has always incorporated a Zen-like quietude. His approach can superficially look minimalist but this is really the result of Chipperfield's functionalism.

Commissions in Germany and Spain started to flow in but none of any significance in the UK, which for a nation of shopkeepers can be rather sniffy about architects who have made their reputation serving the ephemeral world of restaurants and boutiques. His UK break was the award-winning River and Rowing Museum in Henley-on-Thames (1997), which reinterpreted timber boathouse vernacular in a contemporary way. A fit-out by another practice, however, has prevented it from becoming a good example of the totality of Chipperfield's vision, which extends to furniture and other interior products.

His sensitivity to tradition has, in recent years, won him a number of important ongoing projects in Europe, including the masterplanning and reordering of Berlin's Neues Museum and its related institutions and the extension of the San Michele Cemetery in Venice, which involves building a new island in the lagoon. He has also won competitions to build a court complex in Salerno, Italy, and the Davenport Art Museum in Iowa. With offices now open in the US and Germany, Chipperfield is taking on the role he deserves on the international stage. Even back in the UK, his profile is on the rise with commissions to design the British Film Institute (presently bogged down within the two-decade-long struggle to rebuild London's South Bank arts precinct) and a new headquarters building for the BBC in Glasgow. He may yet, like Alvar Aalto, be a prophet in his own country.

David Chipperfield

Top: Parcel 25 Housing, the
Hague, 1992

Bottom left: Het Baken Tower
project for Deventer, 1999

Bottom right: Hague Housing
Festival Masterplan, 1987

Kees Christiaanse has quietly become the power behind the throne of Dutch architecture. His office, founded in 1989, has tackled some of the highest-profile urban-design schemes in the Netherlands, hosting buildings by all that country's finest architects and many from abroad.

Like many of the big names in Dutch architecture, Christiaanse worked the significant part of his early career at Rem Koolhaas's Office for Metropolitan Architecture, being made a partner in 1983 at the age of thirty. His earliest success as an independent was his masterplan for the 1987 housing festival in the Hague, which proposed a new urban quarter consisting of 550 new dwellings in thirty-six new buildings. This immensely confident plan was undertaken with the light touch of a much more experienced architect. All the buildings were placed on a 40-metre-wide strip and read as a set of objects in a territory. The only strictures he placed on the design of the individual buildings were the type of dwelling and a maximum building envelope. Beyond this the architects involved had a free rein. What was most intriguing was Christiaanse's choice of architect. The project ushered in many practices whose experience was then limited – MVRDV, Mecanoo, Architecten Cie, Neutelings Riedijk – and juxtaposed them with old masters such as Peter Eisenman, Bernard Tschumi and Henri Ciriani, all of whom have an immense influence on Christiaanse's work.

The project also set the tone of the architects who designed mass housing in the Netherlands during the 1990s on the so-called Vinex sites. From 1993 to 1996 Christiaanse was 'artistic director' of the Dutch Building Department, allowing him to continue the work begun on a smaller scale in the Hague housing festival. His practice is responsible for the Langerak site of the Leidsche Rijn Vinex near Utrecht (1995) and the 1,000-hectare Lelystad South area of the Flevoland Vinex (1999) among many others.

Although he may be best known for his urban planning, Christiaanse is also a prolific author of housing buildings, with a strongly geometric brand of late Postmodernism akin to that of his contemporaries Sjoerd Soeters and Wiel Arets. His Parcel 25 housing in the Hague (1992) manages to cram eleven different dwelling types into a block that has only forty-four units in total, wrapping the whole in an eclectic skin reminiscent of high-Modernist social housing, and his large block on the Java Island experimental housing development in Amsterdam (1998) elaborates a more abstract language of geometrical rigour and scaleless exteriors.

Later work, such as the proposed Het Baken residential tower in Deventer, designed in 1999, promises to take Christiaanse in a more sculptural direction. The abstraction of his buildings is generated by a belief that they should not be designed to accommodate a specific use, but should have the 'architectonic character and dimensional grandeur' that invites inhabitation. A strong pragmatist, Christiaanse once said that 'you should always have at least three valid reasons for drawing a curve'. He has not yet found those reasons, and will no doubt continue to design his highly geometric but programmatically loose buildings and urban plans for some time to come.

Kees Christiaanse

C

Top left: St Antoine Hospital
kitchen building, Paris, 1985

Top right: Archaeological
Museum, Arles, 1993

Bottom left: Noisy II,
Marne-la-Vallée, 1980

Bottom right: Museum
of the Great War, Peronne,
1992

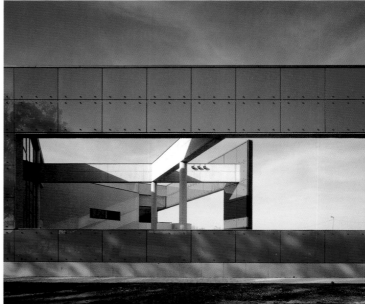

A central figure in French architecture through both his teaching and his buildings, Henri Ciriani is a determined torch-bearer for the Modernist tradition in France, keeping the flame of Le Corbusier alive. Today he is known outside France for two important cultural projects – the Museum of the Great War at Peronne (1992) and the Archaeological Museum at Arles (1993) – but housing and urbanism were his primary architectural focus for decades and made his name.

Ciriani was born in Lima in 1936 and trained at the architecture faculty there before working in the municipal architecture department, where he was in charge of a series of public housing projects. He also designed a number of private houses before moving to Paris in 1964. In his adopted home he became involved in the design cooperative Atelier d'Urbanisme et d'Architecture (AUA), where he worked on experimental living projects that pursued Modernist social and spatial objectives, including the early 1970s Villeneuve housing scheme in Grenoble. However, it was his own practice's housing scheme, Noisy II (1980), for the new suburb of Marne-la-Vallée outside Paris, that really put him on the map in France. (The site also brought Ricardo Bofill's neoclassical megastructures to the world's attention.)

Although his houses may be characterized by an orthogonal and rational modularity and openness, this is achieved within protective enclosures that mediate between the street and the home – an advance on Modernist housing schemes, which presented themselves defenceless to the outside world. Where Le Corbusier sought to 'kill the street', Ciriani has been interested in remaking it in a contemporary way. Public and private realms are delineated by layers of separation made up of balconies, terraces and other devices, leaving inner courtyards secure and protected.

His work at Marne-la-Vallée, which marked a move away from the megastructure housing solutions of the previous decades to more humane and urbane projects that are integrated into the city, has been hugely influential on the following generation of French architects. Ciriani's neo-Modernist group includes architects Edith Girard, Michel Kagan and Pierre-Louis Faloci.

The concerns explored there are evolved in later housing developments around Paris and in the Netherlands. His St Antoine Hospital kitchen building in Paris (1985) carefully maintains the street line with cut-outs and a framing device at the upper levels that forms a screen to the building behind. This approach is perhaps most pronounced in his museum at Arles, where the core of Corbusian galleries is protected by a triangular perimeter wall finished in an intense blue glass through which elements project on *pilotis*. The height and slenderness of the perimeter's profile make the wall seem symbolically protective rather than defensive and hostile. At Peronne, however, despite the Corbusian white concrete and *pilotis*, the protective enclosure becomes more of a bastion, relating to a nearby castle and to the museum's purpose as a memorial to events at one of the most murderous fronts in the First World War.

Henri Ciriani

C

Bottom: Drawing for Nautilus
Restaurant, Schiphol Airport,
Amsterdam, 1993

Top right: Powerhouse:: uk,
London, 1997

Centre right: Centre for
Popular Music, Sheffield, 1999

In 1983 James Stirling, vastly respected as both architect and teacher, tried to fail every student in one of the teaching units at London's high-flying Architectural Association for being insufficiently architectural. The other teachers sat the meeting out until Stirling went home, then passed the students. In the shock waves this sent through the teaching world a new star – or star maker – was born.

The transgressive teachers set up a magazine and forum to promote their ideas. *Narrative Architecture Today* (*NATO*) was a variant of theoretical explorations of architectural event, led by Nigel Coates, Catrina Beevor, Martin Benson, Peter Fleisig, Robert Mull, Christina Norton, Mark Prizeman, Melanie Sainsbury and Carlos Villanueva, but called 'Nigel And The Others'.

Coates – born in Malvern in 1949 and educated at Nottingham and the AA – was indeed the frontman, partly because of his media verve, partly because of his memorable drawings. Glorious, bonkers, comic-book sci-fi fused with sweet little architectural sketch, they described a world of sprawling, visceral, phallic forms, fully and vibrantly inhabited, where teacups and chairs were at least as important as structures, services or spatial sequence. Untrammelled architectural forms mixed with an exuberant urban commercial world just then coming into view. They grabbed architectural theory and took it out shopping and clubbing.

Depending on where you stood in the generally repressive London of the 1980s, Coates (who formed Branson Coates in 1985 with Doug Branson), with his consumer-end-up, messy creativity, was either curio or tidal wave. The drawings (as of the Nautilus Restaurant, 1993), models and exhibitions – like 'ArkAlbion' at the AA (1984) – gained cult status. So

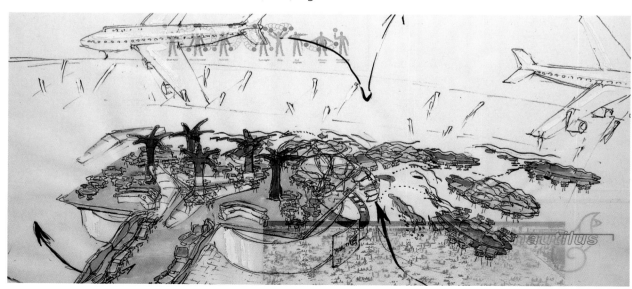

Nigel Coates

did the much-published Caffé Bongo in Japan (1986), where Coates lashed an aircraft wing to the front of a building, its interiors bursting with such paraphernalia as aircraft parts, espresso machines and pointy bras.

By UK standards, Coates' big buildings were not long coming – and a bit disappointing. His glassware, ceramics, temporary pavilions, events, furniture and interiors – like the Jigsaw clothes shops (1988–96) – were generally better received than buildings like the Sheffield Centre for Popular Music (1999), with its four metal drums, or the extension to London's Geffrye Museum (1999). But if his phallic designs – for example, the blatant 'Habitable Bridge' proposal (1996) – were criticized as real proposals, they certainly pulled the punters, as did his 'Erotic Design' show in London (1997), his Body Zone at London's Millennium Dome (2000) and his Oyster House prototype (1998) – a 'hamburger on stilts' said critic Hugh Pearman, who hated it but admitted it made the Ideal Home Show worth visiting.

So though they are still pretty frequent, maybe Coates' buildings are not the point. As 'bad boy of British architecture' he is a classic English eccentric, but heading into the world of popular commerce. His part-fantasy *Ecstacity* book (2003), narrating the culure of global congestion, was a major return to form. As architectural entrepreneur, he has promoted a new generation: his 'Powerhouse:: uk' (1997) was a showcase for Brit-Arch, housed in an inflatable version of his Sheffield building, set cheekily on London's precious Horse Guards Parade. With this and his professorship at the tiny but prestigious Royal College of Art, he has figureheaded a shift in the way a whole section of the young design community works.

C

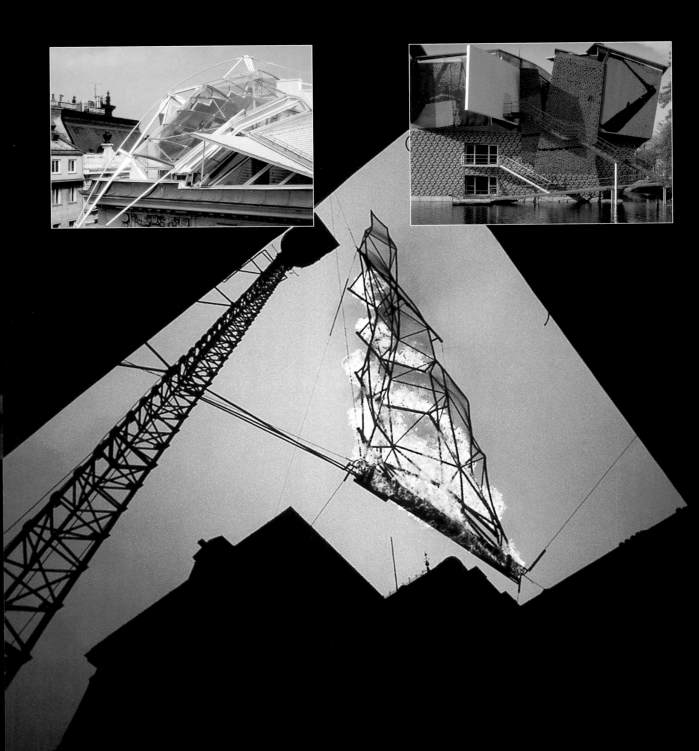

Main picture: Architecture
Must Burn installation,
Graz, 1980

Top left: Lawyer's Office,
Vienna, 1989

Top right: Museum exten-
sion, Groningen, 1994

Coop Himmelb(l)au

'Architecture Must Burn!' proclaimed Coop Himmelb(l)au in 1980, igniting their huge, 50-metre, steel 'wing' installation in the courtyard of the Technical University at Graz. And burn it obediently did, breaking all the windows in the surrounding buildings. They wanted 'Architecture that bleeds, that exhausts, that whirls and even breaks. Architecture that lights up, that stings, that rips and under stress tears.'

Coop Himmelb(l)au (parentheses added in the 1990s) were once textbook iconoclasts. Wolf D. 'Wolfy' Prix and Helmut Swiczinsky formed Coop Himmelb(l)au – 'Not a colour, more of an idea' – in Vienna in 1968 (they are older than they look, born in the early 1940s in Vienna and Poland). Advocates of architecture-as-rock-music (Prix is the proud owner of a Gibson guitar), they spawned controversial installations with familiar components juddering into built forms like a building pile-up. Hostile public reaction in Vienna to such gentle, classic 1960s projects as living capsules and bubbles drove them, they claimed, into more aggressive work. 'Our architecture is...like a wild animal in a cage,' they said, and 'The tougher the times, the tougher the architecture' – among other things, Coop Himmelb(l)au are lords of the really masterly slogan.

It was the 1980s that defined Himmelb(l)au, as their prolific jagged forms became Deconstructivist icons. Their design process was based on the partners working closely together, setting nothing down until 'the whale was ready to leap', then drawing frantically, simultaneously developing models based on body gestures, and converting it all directly into built form. Their 1989 Lawyer's Office, a shiny, warped, eagle-insect form perched on the roof of a formal Viennese nineteenth-century block, took their work to the world stage and is still their definitive project.

For their museum extension in Groningen (1994) they worked from their second office in Los Angeles, computer-linked to the shipyards cutting the rusty steel: 'Le Corbusier promised it, we did it.' But their jagged dyna-mism was becoming less subversive, their expanding workload forming part of the Deconstructivist drift into the establishment mainstream – about which they are flagrantly unrepentant. Their slogans – 'Get rid of thinking about clients, get rid of thinking about money, get rid of thinking about codes' – were replaced by equally outspoken manipulation of clients and building regulations: 'Now we are conventional architects, quoting Corb, clients are starting to believe us.'

If Archigram are architecture's Beatles, Coop Himmelb(l)au have always laid claim to be the Rolling Stones. There is some truth in this – great lyrics, sharp rock, big bucks. Coop Himmelb(l)au's skewed, jagged forms are now flagrantly the progressive face of part of the establishment. The locations of their worldwide practice (their third office is in Guadalajara) certainly have rock-star appeal. Their big buildings – like the huge UFA Cinema in Dresden (1998) – look, well, partly like their earlier work and partly like the institutional work of the 1970s that they used to hate so much. They are, after all, in the business of selling records – sorry, archi-tecture. And they still have 'Gimme Shelter' as their telephone hold music.

C

Top left: Gandhi Memorial, Ahmadabad, 1963

Top right: Kanchanjunga Apartments, New Bombay, 1983

Bottom left: British Council Building, Delhi, 1992

Bottom right: Madhya Pradesh State Parliament Building, Bhopal, 1996

Charles Correa was born in Hyderabad in 1930 to a family of Portuguese descent from Goa – a mixed personal heritage that is reflected in his work. He has sought to elide modern and Western models with traditional and even spiritual values in his long career in post-independence India.

After training in the US (including a spell under Buckminster Fuller at Massachusetts Institute of Technology) he returned to Bombay in 1956 and set up his own practice two years later. Rather than serving his most wealthy countrymen, Correa rolled up his sleeves and began looking for solutions appropriate to the masses. This included the planning and design of massive new towns across India such as New Bombay, a city for two million people of which he was chief architect between 1970 and 1975. His engagement with issues of growth and the needs of low-income groups led to his 1985 appointment as chair of India's National Commission on Urbanization.

Correa draws lessons from the pragmatic 'architectural' solutions of rural builders and slum dwellers' shacks in their response to climate and everyday necessity. The 84-metre-high Kanchanjunga Apartments tower in New Bombay (1983) may be built for wealthy inhabitants but it incorporates elements of old bungalow design, with verandas that allow in breezes but form a protective layer. Double-height terraces carve slices out of an almost Brutalist concrete slab of a building.

But it is his singular cultural and institutional buildings for which Correa is best known. His Madhya Pradesh State Parliament Building in Bhopal (1996) is a notable successor of Louis Kahn's sublime Dacca National Assembly and Le Corbusier's internationalist Chandigarh but is worlds apart from these in being firmly grounded in a specifically Indian culture. It remains open to external influences but without having them thrust upon it from the outside by globalization and undifferentiated solutions. The circular lower chamber sits under a dome inspired by a Buddhist *stupa*, and its *parti* is generated from the Vedic mandala symbol, but some of the interiors are positively Soanian in their mannered use of controlled natural light. Shades of James Stirling's later polychromatic work are a brushstroke away in projects such as the 1992 Centre for Astronomy and Astrophysics at Pune, but this would be a superficial reading – again, it is the mandala that is the guiding order of the centre's dusty pink courtyard buildings.

Both these schemes suggest a predilection for sharply cut openings in smooth expanses of wall and this is also true of the British Council Building in Delhi (1992), reached through a sequence of sandstone screens sliced with openings and incorporating a vibrant mural by Howard Hodgkin. Correa has an Indian ability to place colour where it is not expected but seems right.

As Correa has progressed, the traditional has gained the upper hand over the Modernist. The wonderful pavilions and courtyards of the Gandhi Memorial, Ahmadabad (1963) have given way to a more intrinsically Indian idiom. The National Crafts Museum, New Delhi (1990), may perhaps exaggerate this tendency in its incorporation of artefacts from vernacular buildings but the museum as a whole reads as a traditional village complete with spine street.

Charles Correa

Top left: Wooden Building
Housing, Dublin, 2000

Bottom left: Technical
Library, Cork, 1996

Right: Samuel Beckett
Centre, Trinity College,
Dublin, 1993

De Blacam & Meagher are, along with O'Donnell & Tuomey, the godfathers of contemporary Irish architecture. Shane de Blacam, born in 1945, and John Meagher, born 1947, formed the practice in 1976. Their previous experience informs their work today. De Blacam worked for Chamberlain Powell & Bon on the Barbican Centre in London, and for Louis Khan in Philadelphia after his training in Dublin and Pennsylvania. Meagher trained at Dublin College of Technology before spending a year in Finland at the Helsinki School of Architecture in 1971.

Their work is characterized by a strong interest in natural materials, particularly timber, that sometimes draws attention away from their deeply rationalist and typological architecture. Their work has both helped to form the confidence of the Irish architectural scene today, and has fed from that confidence, and in recent years they have produced some buildings that are icons of the resurgence of urban Irish architecture.

Two timber-clad buildings in Dublin remain their most famous. The first, the Samuel Beckett Centre at Trinity College, Dublin (1993), shows a strong interest in a rationalized vernacular, with its timber cladding and pitched roof, topped with a ventilation chimney. Comprising an entrance hall and lecture hall on the ground floor and studio theatre and dance space above, the building won awards on its completion, and its timber cladding has now weathered in places to a silvery hue that refers to the masonry of the buildings it adjoins.

Their second most-published project is the Wooden Building housing in Temple Bar (2000). Although de Blacam & Meagher is not one of the famous Group 91 practices who designed the many cultural institutions in this area of Dublin, this landmark residential building is one of the finest contemporary buildings in the city and one of the highest, with a strongly vertical element facing the street and sheltering an internal courtyard. From the courtyard the building is a magical collage of natural materials. The tower itself looks taller than it is, being sited on a steeply sloping street with its top levels stepping out slightly from those below.

Housing has been a strong theme of De Blacam & Meagher's work. Two other notable projects in Dublin – their apartments on the corner of Werburgh Street and Castle Street (2003), which won the Royal Institute of Architects in Ireland Housing Medal in 2003, and their barrel-vaulted mews houses in Waterloo Lane (2002) – continue their interest in urban accommodation on complex urban sites.

Although the practice is masterful in an urban context, it has also produced some fine rural buildings, including the Chapel of Reconciliation at the Catholic shrine at Knock, Ireland (1990). This white chapel recalls the churches of Alvar Aalto or Jørn Utzon, and shows the strong influence of Scandinavian architecture in their work.

De Blacam & Meagher's *oeuvre* has now extended to corporate offices – the 2002 Esat Headquarters in Dublin – and educational buildings – the technical library at Cork University (1996). It seems that they will continue to maintain a high critical profile.

De Blacam & Meagher

d

Giancarlo de Carlo was born in 1919, and is one of the few living architects who is linked to the trailblazing Modernists of the Congrès Internationaux d'Architecture Moderne (CIAM), and the group that superseded it – Team X. With fellow members Alison and Peter Smithson, Aldo van Eyck, Ralph Erskine and others, de Carlo came up with some of the earliest critiques of Modernism years before Postmodernism, attacking the CIAM view of architecture (formulated by Le Corbusier et al.) as autocratic and functionalist. In its place the group attempted to reassert an architecture by the people and for the people, exploring how buildings could be designed through the participation of their users.

Despite the fact that his built works are fewer than they should be, de Carlo is one of the giants of twentieth-century European architecture. This is the result of his deeply held political beliefs, forged in the political instability of 1940s Italy. After seeing active service in Greece during the Second World War, de Carlo was involved in coordinating partisan activity for anti-Fascist groups in Milan between 1943 and 1945. This experience and an interest in the anarchist movement helped him to dissolve the paradigms that defined modern architecture throughout most of the twentieth century. In an interview in 1970, de Carlo said: 'Method and experimental curiosity, rigour and imagination, coherence and chance, rationality and irrationality are not irreconcilable opposites. They are poles of that oscillating dialectical reality which is the essence of life.'

His early work includes an apartment block in Sesto San Giovanni (1950) and a housing scheme for Baveno (1951). The 1950s also saw de Carlo begin in earnest his work as a writer and critic, becoming involved in Ernesto Rogers' *Casabella* journal and launching his studies on the city of Urbino, which became a key part of the *Team X Primer* (1968), one of the group's most important works. This critical discourse continued later with the publication of his journal *Spazio e Società*, which he edited for twenty-five years until 2001.

De Carlo is most closely associated with the city and university of Urbino, where he has worked on masterplans and individual buildings for around half a century. His work there, exemplified by the Magistero Building (1976), is a reaction against the Modernist architecture that was tearing the heart out of cities across Europe in the 1950s and 1960s. The Magistero is a great amphitheatre, lit by skylights, occupying a whole city block but retaining an intimate scale and permeability and a contextual perimeter, and it is highly influential among the later critical regionalist school of architects. The Urbino work – including the Collegi dei Cappuccini (1983) and the Law Faculty (1966) – continues, along with large plans in San Marino, Pistoia and Florence.

Although de Carlo can be seen as a contextualist, his urbanism is politically and socially radical and in tectonic terms should not be underrated. As a generation of architects rediscovers the work of Team X, expect to see de Carlo's architecture referred to more and more as an example of what is possible when society and the fineness of the urban grain are the objectives.

Giancarlo de Carlo

d

Top left: French Pavilion for
the Venice Biennale, 1995

Top right: Banque Populaire
de l'Ouest, Rennes, 1990

Bottom: Motorway
viaduct and service
centre, Nantes, 1995

'Too much English' said architect Francis Soler of Odile Decq and Benoit
Cornette's two buildings for the Banque Populaire de l'Ouest in Rennes,
the project that took them onto the international scene. And indeed, both
couple and buildings did have strong English tendencies. The buildings have
been variously linked with both Norman Foster and Zaha Hadid, fusing a
high-tech love of engineering – which France never had – with some of
the dramatic formal dynamism of Hadid – which it never picked up. And
the couple dressed in resolute Goth-punk garb – then out of fashion in
the UK but never fashionable in France. All this helped to put them straight
on the international conference circuit and to establish a powerful international reputation. In an era when Deconstructivism was still a series of
paper projects, a few tiny pavilions and a mass of theory, they had built
two buildings that, if not really Deconstructivist, certainly evoked its formal
dynamism and drama – without any interference from theory.

Decq and Cornette come from Rennes in Brittany (he was born in
1953, she in 1955), where Decq studied architecture and Cornette medicine.
Decq dropped out of her course, moving to Paris and the experimental UP6
school. Cornette followed and trained there too once he had finished his
medical studies. Decq set up in practice immediately, with Cornette first an
assistant, then partner. They developed their work using beautifully made,
highly coloured models, sometimes formed by pick-up-sticks random form-
ations, and the computer graphics then entering the world scene.

Intriguingly, many early projects were for banks – a tiny Credit
Agricole cashpoint facility in Mayenne in 1983, a Credit Mutuel interior
(1987) – until they won their first social housing project, Rue Manin in Paris
(1989), with its typical use of tight volumes, open and dramatic circulation
and comfortable, light interiors. But the BPO (1990) was the big one. The
administration building, with its illusory, shimmering glass wall creating a
dramatic entrance screen, made the headlines. Its social centre showed a
cosier use of expressive form.

The project established a series of other commissions, like their social
housing at Rue Ernestine, Paris (1995). Their scale shifted quickly from small
exhibitions such as 'Hyper-tension' in Grenoble (1993) to a masterplan for
the Porte de Gennevilliers in Paris (1994). Best known of their many later
projects is probably their motorway viaduct and service centre at Nantes
(1995), where they took the brief for the building – which they slung under
the viaduct – as an excuse to redesign the viaduct itself, thus harnessing
their project to the dynamic of the car – what critic Clare Melhuish calls
their 'slick dynamic refinement'. They won the Lion d'Or for their design
for the French Pavilion at the Venice Biennale in 1995.

In 1998 the architectural world was shocked when Benoit Cornette
was killed in a car accident in which Odile Decq was also injured. Decq's
recovery and continuation of the high-profile practice – one of France's
most glamorous and hardworking – her international presence as teacher
and speaker and the continued power and popularity of the work is a testament to the positive, proactive, direct drive their work has always had.

d

Xaveer de Geyter is yet another protégé of Rem Koolhaas's Office for Metropolitan Architecture, but has reasonable claim to be one of the best of them. Born in 1957, this Belgian architect spent ten years in the office of the Dutch master, and was project architect on some of OMA's most iconic projects, including the Villa dall'Ava in Paris and the Zeebrugge sea terminal competition. He was known in the office for his urbanism, and his input on projects such as Melun Senart 'new town' in Paris won him many admirers.

Xaveer de Geyter Architecten was founded in Brussels in the early 1990s and has become a practice on the model of OMA, carrying out wide-ranging research into urban matters while producing radical buildings. De Geyter's first two projects were villas in Belgium, one at Mariakerke (1990), and the second in Brasschaat (1991). The latter made his reputation and confirmed that his practice would continue the spatial experimentation of his OMA years. The building is an inversion of a Corbusian villa, entered by vehicle at roof level, with access to the house down a ramp divided by partitions and bookcases in a range of different materials.

Very quickly for a young architect de Geyter was able to win major projects and turn them into widely published and influential buildings. The success of Brasschaat led to a scheme for twenty-two houses in Amsterdam (1994) in the Borneo-Sporenburg area, where some of Europe's most high-profile architects have been building. Perhaps his best-known project is his Chassée Park apartment complex in Breda in the Netherlands (2003) where, as part of a development plan by OMA, de Geyter designed five residential towers. With their spectacular cross-braced façades the towers owe as much to the commercial architecture of Chicago as to apartment typologies.The Janus-faced buildings change from different viewpoints, each having one white-enamelled brick façade that reflects the light and contrasts with the other façades, clad in green and black concrete panels. The elegant towers meet the ground with a grace enhanced by a landscaping project by West 8.

De Geyter's urban work has included a project for the 200-hectare Schaerbeek shunting yard north of Brussels, now ongoing. This scheme proposes greening huge areas of the city to create parks and landscapes that penetrate the city centre, creating coherence in a part of the city that is blighted by its former industrial uses.

Ongoing projects include the extension of the city into the sea in Monaco; buildings for Ghent University; a building at the Paju Book City in Seoul; a mixed-use urban study at Ilôt Saint Maurice near Rem Koolhaas's masterplan in Lille; and a hotel in collaboration with Belgian designer Maarten Van Severen in Nîmes.

De Geyter's star is undoubtedly rising. The publication of his book, *After-Sprawl: Research for the Contemporary City* in 2002, asserted his credentials as the provider of solutions for the acute urban problems of the Netherlands, Belgium and beyond. In his built work, he is working on major projects, particularly in Ghent, where in 2001 he opened an office with Stephane Beel. Buildings on site there include a university and a new train station, which will confirm him as one of Belgium's pre-eminent talents.

Xaveer de Geyter

d

Top: Corrugated Duct
House, 1998

Bottom left: Vertical
Smooth House, 1997

Bottom right: Gallery MA
installation, Tokyo, 1996

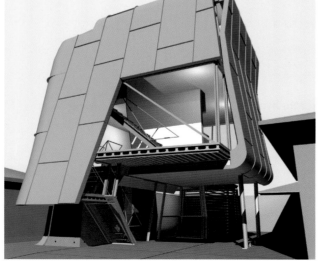

A latter-day Sir Gawain bearing a banner of sea-foam green (Pantone 3375) in search of the holy grail of the continuously folded surface, Neil Denari is one of those modern myths who has achieved world influence through...it is hard to say what: the third prize in the 1989 Tokyo Forum competition? A long-anticipated book? A small exhibition space in Tokyo? Some great computer imaging? Probably mostly the latter. Denari's prodigious unbuilt projects are notable for their spectacular contemporary aesthetic: the folded surface, proposed by Gilles Deleuze et al., beautifully rendered into part-space-age, part-Brutalist, part-found-technology schemes, with a deeply specific palette of colours. They suggest the absolute buildability of the aesthetic fold – a device intended, somehow, to revolutionize our lives.

Denari keeps guitars in his studio – one of his defining myths. He was born in 1957 in the Texas Dallas-Fort Worth 'Metroplex'. His father worked on experimental aeroplanes and Stealth Bombers are a key influence. He trained as an architect in Houston and at Harvard and worked for Aerospatiale, one of Europe's largest aviation contractors, before moving to Los Angeles. There he became a key figure in the West-Coast scene with its experimental digital shape-making expertise and untroubled adoption of European cultural theory. He was briefly director of Sci-Arc, masterminding the move downtown before leaving over its internal politics.

Denari is not really a 'theoretical' architect. His long-awaited book, *Gyroscopic Horizons* (1999), largely a fabulous collections of images, is also a bran tub of popular critical goodies (Deleuze, Jean Baudrillard et al.) but he is definitely referring to rather than advancing these arguments. His buildings, he says, 'do not have excessive theoretical values based on their forms and geometries' – unlike others we could name – but adds: 'instead, the work attempts to pry open a logical space between the ends of scenario-based architecture and geometry-as-content architecture.' Phew. Catch that?

Anyway, it looks great. There is a Brutalist luxury to the sumptuous computer and physical models and the spiced-up technical drawings. Denari is interested in James Stirling, and there are bits of Archigram and aerospace machinery in such unbuilt projects as the Vertical Smooth House (1997), with its wraparound green envelope; the Corrugated Duct House (1998), with its techno-sculptural serviced ceiling; and the inward-looking Japanese Prototype House (1993). The same techno-smooth, hybrid aesthetics are applied to tiny built installations with more simple polemic concerns. The lovely Gallery MA installation in Tokyo (1996), is an 'unfolded world map', the smooth, continuous wraparound surface forming ceiling, walls, floor, screen, desk – all discreetly branded with big-name logos.

So far, most of Denari's questions about the way we live have remained just that – questions. The actual projects are perfectly recognizable things like houses, superbly formally achieved. The only big fish to bite are the ongoing Arlington Museum of Art in Texas, where the real brief is for a fit-out and extension of the local white Modernist museum (formerly J.C. Penney), and a Microsoft retail store in San Francisco. Denari's plans to draw a major project out of these will be right in the fashionable centrefold.

Neil Denari

d

In the intense rivalry between Melbourne and Sydney, the latter is regarded as something of a brash *nouveau riche* party town, while Melbournians see themselves as more cultured, with more depth and intellectual engagement. The split is evident in architecture too; it is a rare practice that can conquer both cities. But Denton Corker Marshall can probably claim to have come closer than most. Although their heart remains in Melbourne, DCM have brought something of Sydney's shiny, boisterous commercialism to their home town, while exporting Melbourne's gridded rationalism to unruly Sydney and beyond.

Partners John Denton, Bill Corker and Barrie Marshall (born 1945, 1945 and 1946 respectively) were all educated in Melbourne, graduating in the late 1960s and forming a practice in 1972. They were quietly (as far as the world outside Australia was concerned) ploughing a mainstream Modernist furrow until their work exploded across Australia and South-East Asia in the late 1980s. They gained international plaudits for their Australian Embassy in Tokyo (1990) – an intensely crisp and finely detailed piece of architectural diplomacy – and in Melbourne for the Adelphi Hotel (1992), where an audacious rooftop swimming pool projects, glass-bottomed, over the parapet so that swimmers float giddily many storeys above the street. The project also illustrates DCM's defining devices: the grid, the cantilevered plane or blade, and slender pole supports and battens.

These stick-like poles are planted everywhere: in barcode battens at the Adelphi; in a 450-metre-long plantation supporting the swooping

roof and entrance blade of the Melbourne Exhibition Centre (1996); and on a titanic scale as a motorway gate to the city (the 1999 Citylink Gateway project). Over in Sydney, the blades have been employed to good effect on top of Governor Philip Tower (1993), one of a pair of skyscrapers that has DCM's Museum of Sydney (1995) at its feet. The tower has a grid of stainless-steel blades as its crown in the same proportions as the divisions of its façade and re-emerging at the base as *pilotis*.

DCM are a successful commercial practice with offices in Hong Kong, Indonesia, Vietnam, Poland and London, where they have finally struck gold (after years of making it only to millennium project shortlists) by winning the Stonehenge Visitors Centre competition (2001). At first sight, the scheme bears little resemblance to the practice's earlier work, gouged into the landscape as it is, like an unearthed monolith, revealing itself as a building layer by layer. Yet this layering can be seen in many earlier projects where the 'real' building is only reached after first passing through an outer screen or façade. Approaching the Kyneton House, Victoria (1998), across the windswept grasslands of Australia's sheep country you are faced with a vast concrete bunker wall that hunkers down into the ground. Beyond this screen, though, a courtyard leads to the house, which opens up to views below an oversailing roof supported by more slender columns.

Both Stonehenge and Kyneton suggest an exciting new direction for a practice that, for rather longer than is good, has been rapidly expanding the more commercial end of its *oeuvre*.

Denton Corker Marshall

d

Left: Louis Vuitton Tower,
New York, 1999

Top right: Cité de la
Musique, Paris, 1995

Centre right: Hautes-
Formes affordable
housing, Paris, 1979

Bottom right: French
Embassy, Berlin, 2001

Christian de Portzamparc has certainly contributed to the making of his own myth. Boyish good looks, smouldering dark eyes and his trademark raincoat and fedora make him as near as architecture gets to a pin-up. Born in Casablanca in 1944, he moved to Marseilles with his parents when he was just a few months old, training in the 1960s at the Ecole des Beaux-Arts in Paris, where his early influences were the canonical Modernist names, particularly Le Corbusier.

De Portzamparc was one of a generation of French architects who benefited from François Mitterrand's Grands Projets in the 1980s and 1990s. He had produced an eclectic body of early work, his most important project probably being the Hautes-Formes affordable housing in the 13th *arrondissement* of Paris, completed in 1979 with Giorgia Benamo. The award in 1985 of the Cité de la Musique, a huge complex comprising concert halls, a museum and offices completed in 1995, was a coup and the project made de Portzamparc's name. The building is arranged around two large streets, from which all the facilities are accessible, a product of de Portzamparc's concept of buildings as fragments of the city around them. The west façade, however, with its monumental curved form and reflecting water pools, resembles strongly a watered-down version of Le Corbusier's Chandigarh Assembly, a building not known for its integration with the urban context.

It is somewhat revealing that de Portzamparc became the first (and so far only) French laureate of the Pritzker Prize, architecture's richest honour, at the age of just fifty. His work is nowhere near as challenging or influential as that of Jean Nouvel, and his Corbusian form-making and addiction to corporate-style atriums (as at his Opéra Dance School in Nanterre, completed in 1987, or the large, arcing internal street at the Cité de la Musique) do not suggest a truly individual voice.

Having completed extensions to the Palais des Congrès in Paris and the Palais de Justice in Grasse (both 1999), his practice made a quantum leap with the headquarters tower for Louis Vuitton in New York (also 1999). The folded façade was genuinely a radical break for curtain-walled office towers in Manhattan, dealing with the massing of the building and helping to temper the problem of reflection that plagues tall glass buildings. The practice worked carefully with New York's zoning laws, setting back the upper floors to create the tallest building in the area at twenty-three storeys, topped by a dramatic three-storey room looking towards Central Park. Although the interiors were designed by other architects, the job took de Portzamparc into the league of architects who can handle large corporate commissions in the US.

More recently, de Portzamparc has been commissioned to construct the Luxembourg Philharmonic building, the French Embassy in Berlin and the extension to the Pathé Tushinski Cinema in Amsterdam, indicating that, while he remains a house architect for French institutions, his influence is becoming more international. Despite his relative youth, he is a French architect of the old school, with a formal vocabulary that appeals to and reassures his many public clients.

Christian de Portzamparc

d

Main picture:
Schauspielhaus,
Basle, ongoing

Top right: Swiss
Embassy, Berlin, 2000

There is a long and noble tradition of family dynasties in architecture and particularly of sons following their fathers into the profession. Architects marry other architects and then give birth to more architects.

One of the most significant father-son teams has been the Basle-based practice of Diener & Diener, founded by Marcus Diener in 1942 but taken over and transformed by his son Roger Diener in 1980. The younger Diener was able to turn an unknown practice into one of the most respected names in Europe with an architecture of rigour, austerity and material literacy, second in profile only to Herzog & de Meuron in its native land.

Before taking over the practice, Roger Diener studied at the Swiss Federal Institute of Technology (ETH) in Zurich, the alma mater of most of the big Swiss names around today. In the 1980s, Diener & Diener completed several residential buildings of quality but not outstanding merit in and around Basle. These included St Alban-Tal housing (1986) and the Hammer 1 residence (1981), with its rendered upper three floors and grand two-storey entrances, which hint at a historicist interest.

Soon the work moved away from housing and the practice found success with its first major cultural building – the Gallery Gmurzynska in Cologne, Germany (1990). Built for a Swiss client, the art gallery – a shocking red timber object on a podium of red brick – was a departure for the practice and, despite its modest size, had a big impact on their profile. This was not the only objective, and the modulation of the two main volumes and the full-height slot windows in the façades make it an object of intrigue rather than bombast.

Commissions since the early 1990s have become more prestigious and larger in scale, including the controversial extension to the Swiss Embassy in Berlin (2000) and two ongoing projects: the extension to the Museum of Modern Art in Rome and the Rosengart Museum in Lucerne. Diener & Diener have also worked on a more urban scale, with their housing at the Ypenburg Vinex project near the Hague (2003), and their victory in the 2001 competition for a new university in historical Malmö, Sweden.

The greatest concentration of their work is still in Basle, with an array of buildings completed in the 1990s. These include the Vogesen School in west Basle, completed in 1996, and the Kohlenberg office, completed in 1995 – a simple composition with offset glazed openings which forms the corner of an urban block. One of the most provocative and well-published of their Basle projects is the Schauspielhaus, a new theatre and performance venue won in competition in 1997.

Roger Diener has exerted a big influence in architectural education as a professor at the ETH in Zurich and visiting professor at Harvard University Graduate School of Design, the School of Architecture in Vienna, the Academie van Bouwkunst in Amsterdam, and the Royal Danish Academy of Fine Arts in Copenhagen. In collaboration with such big names from Swiss architecture as Marcel Meili and Jacques Herzog, Diener has also founded Studio Basel, a practice-based system of educating students that has been influential in approaches to architectural education in Europe.

Diener & Diener

d

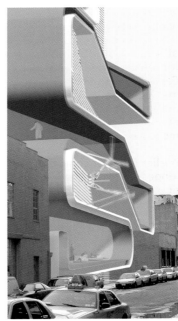

Visitors to the Swiss Expo 2002 were required to don raincoats and hats
to view Diller + Scofidio's Blur Building. It was not leaky: the whole building
was one wonderful leak. The pair created an artificial cloud hovering above
a lake, where 31,400 needlepoint jets gently emitted tiny droplets to form
a ghostly and magical mist that enveloped visitors.

New York husband-and-wife team Elizabeth Diller and Ricardo
Scofidio inhabit that fuzzy grey zone that exists between architecture and
art, between creating 'real' buildings and designing experiences that illuminate the meaning of architecture. They have been described as 'Duchampian
guerrilla architects' because of their early penchant for seizing vacant lots
and erecting art-architecture installations. These days, however, they are
more likely to receive a substantial grant from an art museum for their
deliberations or even to build actual, usable buildings.

Scofidio is a native New Yorker, born in the city in 1935; Diller,
born in 1954, arrived as a child from Poland. Both studied at Cooper Union
in New York, and both taught there until Diller took a post at Princeton in
1990. As might be expected of a cerebral couple, it is the theories and ideas
whirling around academia that continue to inspire them, and their research
and teaching is as important as their practice, which they set up in 1979.

It was their 1989 Slow House project that first marked them out as
superstars in architecture's avant-garde. The scheme was a seafront holiday
home for an art lover that meditated on the idea of a 'view' as framed by
human intervention. The crescent-shaped house culminated in a picture

window but this was preceded by a screen projecting the view from the window so the visitor would see the 'artificial' view before the 'real' one.

The Slow House was never built but still made its mark and a series of installations followed such as 'Interclone Hotel', an advertising campaign for a fictional hotel chain (1997), and 'The American Lawn' exhibition at the Canadian Center for Architecture (1998). Cameras, screens and electronic media, notions of surveillance and tracking movement, are a recurring motif in their work, as in their scheme for the Brasserie in New York's Seagram Building (2000), where surfaces peel away and video cameras project the movements of diners.

More recently, commissions have come for buildings. The Eyebeam Atelier (due for completion in 2006) in New York's arty Chelsea district is a looped and folded edifice twelve storeys high which, when completed, will house a digital arts school, with shades of cutting-edge Dutch architecture or the work of Foreign Office Architects. Other substantial ongoing commissions include the Institute of Contemporary Art on Boston's waterfront and a masterplan focused on the Brooklyn Academy of Music (in collaboration with Rem Koolhaas).

The pair may have said that they never intended to form a professional architectural practice in the conventional sense but they certainly seem to be heading that way. It remains to be seen whether they can fully jump the gap from a work of art to a functional building. The signs are promising though.

Diller + Scofidio

d

Left: Stonehouse,
Carinthia, 2002

Top right: Documentation
centre, Nuremberg, 2001

Bottom right:
Zentralsparkasse Head-
quarters, Vienna, 1979

'I would prefer it if architecture critics and art historians just wrote poems about my work' says Günther Domenig. And, obligingly, on the eventual completion in 2002 of his twenty-year project, the Stonehouse in Carinthia – part house, part school, part bird, part earthquake, with metaphor laid on metaphor – some friends and critics did. The best was by eminent word-smiths Coop Himmelb(l)au: 'Breathing hard, he stood in the ring/ His head bowed into the problem's paper breast/ He landed hooks of concrete/ swings of steel/ and uppercuts from the details' shoulders...He always was before his time.'

He was indeed. Born in Carinthia in 1934, Domenig is both father of the Graz School – an extraordinarily powerful architectural community for such a small city – and a proto-Deconstructivist a good ten years ahead of the field. He studied in Graz but immediately rebelled against the com-placent commercialism of contemporary practice.

His Zentralsparkasse Headquarters (1979) broke this mould, with its melted-looking articulated façade – like a knight's gauntlet slipping off – and huge abstracted 'hand' inside. It is extraordinary in any light, not just for breaking orthogonal forms but for its overt metaphorical intentions and its location in a banal suburb of repressive Vienna. And this was the edited version.

The Z-bank was the best known of a portfolio of fiercely expressive buildings, overloaded with meaning and physically ferocious in their explo-sive forms: the visceral multipurpose hall for the convent school in Graz (1977), the Olympic swimming pool pavilion and restaurant for the Munich Olympics (1977), the Funder Factory, Carinthia (1988). But the second project that defined Domenig's career was the Stonehouse, which he started in 1983, apparently with no plan of ever completing it.

The site was inherited from Domenig's grandmother, and childhood memories fuse with a personal invented myth in the project: mountains splitting and erupting a river of stones (shown in extraordinarily sexual drawings), and 'the bird' that Domenig frequently refers to as a mysterious mythical beast. These forms appear repeatedly in early drawings, fusing with the programme – part house, part architectural school, a place for twenty-five people to work and hold discussions. A spiral plan erupts out of the ground with disrupted working spaces and sleeping 'baskets' clinging to it, and a slipped cube of a meeting space. Entrance is through a 'ravine' walkway with broken handrail, leading out towards the lake – the take-off ramp for 'the bird'. Certainly not in traditional stone but in metal and con-crete, the edges are, Domenig claims, sharp enough to draw blood.

In Domenig's third key project, the meaning needed no working up. His 2001 documentation centre in the Congress Hall of the buildings used for Nazi Party rallies in Nuremberg slashed a linear steel and glass circulation tract through the building, ending in a lookout over the huge space. Guerilla architecture rather than outright war, one critic called it, but powerful enough for its difficult task. Himmelb(l)au's ferocious fighter analogy works well.

d

No architect has had such an influence on the development of recent
Indian architecture as Balkrishna Doshi. His career, like that of fellow
Indian Charles Correa, has been a gradual journey from the international
to the local without losing sight of either. Until, perhaps, now.

After attending the J. J. School of Art in Bombay he was, like
many Indian architects of his generation, educated overseas (in London).
On graduating, he worked with two of the seminal figures of Modernism,
Le Corbusier and Louis Kahn, on their respective projects in Chandigarh
(where he became senior designer for the new city) and Ahmadabad.

Doshi was born in Pune in 1927 but has had a long attachment
to Ahmadabad, where he set up private practice in 1962 and where he
has been instrumental in developing a multidisciplinary educational complex, founding its highly respected architecture and planning school, which
he also designed (1966) in his environmentally appropriate, vaulted and
open-to-the-elements Indian–Corbusian fusion style. He also set up the
Vastu-Shilpa Foundation for Environmental Design, which investigates
low-cost housing and planning initiatives.

The influence of Corb and Kahn permeated his work for many years, notably in the airy barrel vaults of his Sangath Design Studio in Ahmadabad (1981) or his own 1959 house in the city. Sangath means 'moving together through participation' and the studio was conceived as a design laboratory integrating arts, crafts, engineering and philosophy, becoming an umbrella from which he has disseminated his ideas.

In recent years, however, Doshi has, like Charles Correa, become more deeply engaged in finding a specifically Indian form of architectural expression. One result of this quite staggering style shift is the Hussain Doshi Gufa Gallery (1993), on the same educational campus as his earlier work in Ahmadabad. The white mosaic-clad roof is an organic landscape of seedpod forms that draws on Hindu mythology for its inspiration. It is both bizarre and beguiling and looks to have more in common with Ushida Findlay's *oeuvre* than anything produced by the Modern Movement. Buddhist cave temples have informed the circles and ellipses of the interior, which, like the roof, has been formed by spraying concrete onto a metal mesh to form a moulded plastic space. Even the floor curves. Computer-aided design has been matched with craft construction techniques.

This new direction is not consistent, however. The National Institute of Fashion Technology, Delhi, completed a year later, moves in a completely different direction. It is organized around internal courtyards surrounded by blocks of accommodation and bridges, which act as both connections and catwalks. Areas of mirrored glazing in steel framing, one deliberately askew, sit alongside a stone wall built to look like a ruin. Where this is going next is anybody's guess. It is hard not to feel that Doshi has become lost in his dream of bringing past and future together.

Balkrishna Doshi

d

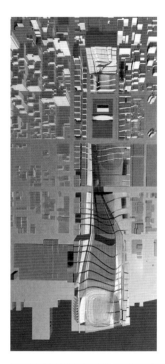

Peter Eisenman is an ambiguity wrapped up in a riddle. His famously impenetrable paper architecture and writings and his rarer buildings have been identified as 'anti-architecture', as architecture as an ever-changing text, or as an attempt to remove the author (the architect) from the process. Eisenman spent years exploring how to create a building that would be unencumbered by the expectations brought to it by doing away with the dictates of contextual baggage or a programme. Through his close relationship with philosopher Jacques Derrida, Eisenman has been at the forefront of the Deconstructivist movement in architecture, drawing on linguistics, psychoanalysis and literary theory to analyse the apparent objectivity and unity of Modernism and reveal the subjective human desires beneath. To his critics, his musings are obscurantist – a severe case of Emperor's New Clothes.

The consummate intellectual New Yorker (big specs, big bow tie, big hair), Eisenman was born across the Hudson in Newark, New Jersey, in 1932. As a bright spark he studied at Cornell, Columbia and Cambridge, UK, returning to New York to establish his Institute for Architecture and Urban Studies in 1967 and its influential journal, *Oppositions* (now defunct).

Since the late 1960s Eisenman's principal contribution has been to architectural theory and education but he has also designed a series of houses: House I (1970) through to House X (1978) in locations throughout the US. Rather than responding to his clients' specific needs, Eisenman created an experience for them to inhabit. The resulting buildings 'deconstructed' a typical Modernist box, pulling apart its planes, playing with gaps, edges and Cartesian grids. In House VI, this went as far as slicing a slot down the middle of the marital bed and putting a staircase on the ceiling. The houses were certainly visually new and exciting but rather than revealing a repressed 'deep structure' they had Eisenman written all over them.

In 1980 he formally established a practice in New York and began to build at a larger scale. Faced with a number of existing buildings when designing the Wexner Center for the Visual Arts at Ohio State University (1989), he inserted a new gridded spine between them – a displacement – and manipulated the context by rebuilding in fractured, almost cartoon-like form the brick bastions of an armoury that used to exist on the site. An arts faculty for the University of Cincinnati (1986) similarly claims a space between existing buildings in a series of sliding planes. In his attempt to abandon the rules Eisenman realized that he had created a set of new ones. Either there would always be something outside the text of a building or his textual creations had supplanted the bother of building at all.

More recently he has turned to computers as a way of removing the polluting author from the design process, letting the machine generate the form – an approach that comes dangerously close to the anti-humanism that so alienated him from high Modernism. A product of this phase is his topographic megastructure proposal for the reshaping of Manhattan's West Side. It will, of course, remain on screen. Other projects will be built, like Staten Island Institute of Arts and Sciences – both museum and ferry terminal. Its interlocking ellipses mark it as a building of the computer-aided design age.

Peter Eisenman

e

Until ten years ago, Arthur Erickson was the most famous living Canadian architect. He has now been comfortably superseded by Frank Gehry, but it was he that brought Modernism to Canada, and he is enjoying something of a renaissance after spending much of the 1990s in the wilderness.

Born in Vancouver in 1924, Erickson worked as a Japanese interpreter in India and Malaysia during the Second World War. His route into architecture was prompted by US Modernist legend Richard Neutra and inspired by the first published pictures of Frank Lloyd Wright's Taliesin West. Erickson studied at the University of British Columbia and McGill University in Montreal, where he was schooled in the European masters of the International Style. He retained a devotion to the poetic intuition of Frank Lloyd Wright, however, although he turned down a chance to study with him, electing to travel for two-and-a-half years – the buildings of Egypt and the Lebanon remain important for him today.

His big break came in 1963 when he won the competition for Simon Fraser University campus in Burnaby, Vancouver, in collaboration with Geoffrey Massey. The practice was all but unknown but Erickson managed to build the huge project in just two years, creating a vast, orthogonal vision in concrete, with grand Modernist loggias and a gridded plan.

The apotheosis of this approach is his Government Offices and Courthouse complex in Vancouver (1979), a remarkable urban block that presents accommodation within an envelope, allowing the public to interact with and move through it. A ziggurat of gardens, pools and terraces covering the roof, designed in collaboration with landscape architect Cornelia Oberlander, makes this one of the most successful Modernist complexes in North America, standing as a plausible institutional building as well as knitting with the urban fabric of Vancouver.

Erickson's office grew to be one of the largest in Canada, winning prestigious public buildings. The Canadian Chancery in Washington, DC (1989), has been both loved and reviled in equal measure since its completion. The design again incorporates large external and internal courtyards and terraced planting, but its cool Modernist rectangles clashed with the prevailing historicist tendency in architecture at the time.

Erickson has fought Postmodernist historicism every step of the way. He is a disciple of Le Corbusier still and his attitude to architecture has changed little since the 1960s. In a recent interview he trotted out all the usual Modernist maxims. 'The early Modernists reduced everything to absolute essentials, they got rid of the idea of style,' he says. 'Concrete is a wonderful material; to cover a building with stone is to disguise its truth.' However, his later work shows a slightly eccentric but confident eclecticism. His National Museum of Glass in Tacoma, Washington State (2002), incorporates a metal-clad cone that punches through the low podium of Modernist concrete blocks.

Erickson has won almost every honour there is to win in North American architecture, and there is surely the chance of a few more yet, even if his work is somewhere outside the Zeitgeist.

Arthur Erickson

e

Top left: The Ark,
London, 1991

Bottom left: Egstrom
House, Liso Island, 1956

Right: 'Byker Wall',
Newcastle, 1982

Ralph Erskine's groundbreaking participatory architecture and eclectic modernity were hugely influential in the 1970s and 1980s, part of a break away from didactic Modernism in a world struggling with the aftermath of *tabula rasa* planning. Born in Mill Hill in 1914 and educated at Quaker school and Regent Street Polytechnic, he worked briefly on Welwyn Garden City before setting out with bike, rucksack and tent for Sweden in 1939.

Struggling for work during the Second World War, he was given a free site at Lissma and built himself and wife Ruth a tiny 'box' cabin where the woodstack helped insulation and the bed was hoisted up during daytime. He moved house and office to Drottningholm Island in 1946 – his community practice voted on whether to take projects – adding another studio in a Thames barge, brought perilously across the North Sea. This was sailed away for working summer holidays bearing office and families.

Erskine's love of Modernism (Louis Kahn, Frank Lloyd Wright and, surprisingly, the ruthless Mies van der Rohe) is widely adapted to extremes of user choice and climate, giving each project a highly recognizable, idiosyncratic form. The Egstrom House on Liso Island (1956) is built from sheet metal from its owners' factory; the Molin House in Lidingö (1947) is covered with plants for its landscape architect client. Huge projects, involving users wherever possible – factories, offices, churches, town centres – are as distinct. He is specifically noted for design of the space around buildings – an often disastrous area in early Modernism. Astonishingly prolific in old age, he built the Ark in London's Hammersmith (1991), reintroducing the 'office landscape' to London's new office-as-playground building type, and worked on London's Millennium Village (ongoing).

Erskine also pioneered what was to be eco-architecture, expressing the ecological superiority of passive local construction over high-serviced internationalism. His love of chimneys, sun-reflectors, shutters, drainage channels and cable-supported balconies gives his buildings their sometimes sculptural, sometimes awkward, always highly characterful animation.

But his community projects – many in Sweden, others in the Arctic, Israel, Africa and England – are the best known, famously the rebuilding of the working-class Byker area of Newcastle (1968–82). Local people were deeply involved in the retention of buildings, the greater proportion of houses to flats, the programme of works and the gardening. Erskine's on-site office – painted with his trademark balloon (his answer to the Modernist aeroplane) – also gave out seeds and gardening advice. The 'Byker Wall' of flats wrapping to form a sheltered southern environment for the houses, the deck access, personally chosen balconies and coloured brickwork (local colour is key in Erskine's work) became the closest thing community architecture could have to an icon.

Not everyone liked these eclectic aesthetics: 'It looks as if a tidal wave of sheddery and pergolation has broken over the lower terraces' said Reyner Banham of the Byker Wall. Yet to have combined such pioneering practices – community and ecological architecture – with a distinct if contentious style is an enormous achievement.

Ralph Erskine

e

Top left: TV AM,
London, 1982

Top right: Embankment
Place, London, 1990

Bottom left: Clifton
Nurseries, London, 1980

Bottom right:
Kowloon Ferry Terminal,
Hong Kong, 1996

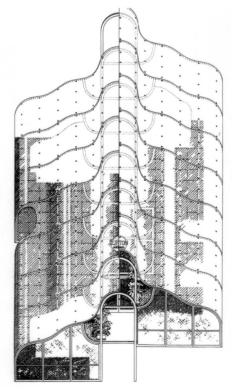

Terry Farrell has one of the most peculiar of architectural careers. Wild swings of critical opinion have moved him from hero to demon and back. Born in 1938 in Newcastle, he studied architecture and city planning at Durham and Pennsylvania. As co-founder of Farrell Grimshaw Partners in 1965, he was a darling of the UK 1960s–1970s revolution, with funky, clip-on, lateral thought. Their Sussex Gardens housing, London (1968) was a 1960s classic with its proto-high-tech, spiral-stack bathroom pod tower outside the existing building and the total remodelling of circulation and spaces inside, plus pull-out furniture on a trolley.

When FGP painfully split, Farrell was reborn as the friendly face of UK Postmodernism. Playful and inventive projects like TV AM in London (1982), with its built-in logo and eggcup finials, or the clever, pop-on technology of Clifton Nurseries in Covent Garden, London (1980), were hits, combining architectural invention and wit with popular taste. Then he became hero of the conservation and community movements with clever reuse and redevelopment plans for a block of threatened buildings in London's Seven Dials (1976). Then came 'alternative' proposals for big developments like the hugely controversial Mies van der Rohe Mansion House scheme in London (1983).

So in the factional UK of the 1980s and 1990s, the sudden appearance of huge Postmodernist office buildings was seen as shocking treachery. Postmodernism had been seen as a voice for democracy against developers: Farrell seemed to have sold it down the river. In fact, Farrell was never part of the style-ethic factionalism into which the UK had split. His wide-ranging thought adopted a different approach to every project and every situation, and, increasingly, an unfashionably inclusive love of style.

The first big offices, most notably Embankment Place, London (1990) – a huge, almost Metabolist office palazzo over Charing Cross Station with some expert shifts of urban scale from river view to side street – were followed by a period when he built almost nothing in the UK. He worked instead in Hong Kong and the Far East, where his buildings got even bigger and even more Metabolist in their combination of huge Expressionist forms with a detailed, urban scale, as in the yellow, amphibian-like Kowloon Ferry Terminal building (1996). Hugely popular in Asia, when Farrell returned to the UK – with projects like The Deep aquarium in Hull (2002) with its Expressionist forms, or witty, Soane-inspired remodellings as in the Dean Gallery in Edinburgh (1998) – critics no longer knew what to make of him.

But Farrell's portfolio of work never fitted the critics' labels: he was doing contextual late Modernism at the height of his 'high-tech' phase. His shrewd urban design has continued and developed throughout his career: he became a major influence on the rethinking of existing urban fabric. Many of his early arguments on energy, reuse of buildings, urban design and enlightened commercialism were way ahead of their time. The breadth of his work has often meant he is a victim of his own stylistic changes. In many ways, he remains the light-footed lateral thinker of FGP days, always open to change.

Top left: Brunel Rooms,
Swindon, 1995

Top right: Blue House,
London, 2002

Bottom: Kessels Kramer
Advertising Office,
Amsterdam, 1998

For people who have resolutely embraced the aesthetic of commerce, dissed the idea of starving in a garret and upset three-quarters of their peers with their adaptations of famous, populist and unfashionable architectural styles, Fat have signally failed to sell out. The very young, very controversial art–architecture collaborative will probably be the most hotly disputed inclusion in this book. Many people loathe them. But their cult following has brought work in the ultra-cool Netherlands, a big-league international lecture and exhibition circuit, and a small, powerful, furiously debated body of built work, some of it up before the protagonists hit thirty.

Fashion Architecture Taste was set up in London in the 1990s in an overt challenge to the absolute orthodoxy of Modernist good taste. After an early fling with blobby experimentalism – their Anti-Oedipal House (1993), which separated parents and children – they hotly and loudly rejected the endless, gloopy computer shape-making passing almost every-where for radical thought.

Operating on the art world's terms (and on shoestring budgets), they remain emphatically collective and anti-hierarchical, distributing art works (some by famous contemporaries) free from card dispensers at the 1995 Venice Biennale or on shopping bags in London's Carnaby Street (1999). Their influences are extremely wide – from Robert Venturi to the Situationists, Mannerism to the Arts and Crafts, Archigram to commercially inspired Pop Artists like Jeff Koons. In architecture, such tactics are shocking to the narrow, sacrosanct conventions of good taste. Fat steal, copy, collage and make overt references to all kinds of high and low architecture; reusing, rescaling, recolouring; remaking their sources in the wrong materials. Their first projects were interiors – the Brunel Rooms nightclub in Swindon (1995), with its running track, swimming pool, garden shed and lounge made a then-shocking new leisure landscape.

More challenging still was the Kessels Kramer Advertising Office (1998) – a conversion of a nineteenth-century Amsterdam church. The client selected a range of big playground furniture from a faxed 'catalogue' of sketched suggestions. The meeting rooms are in a bought Russian fort with fake diving board, the TV space in a gold *Baywatch* tower, the library in a sawn-up garden shed. It is an extraordinary senso-spatial overload – difficult to take but adored by the clients and visitors.

The iconographic manipulations gain subtlety when moved into a whole building. The house that one of Fat's directors, Sean Griffiths, built for himself in London's East End (2002) is at first sight a cartoon house, baby blue, with child's-drawing windows and doors in front of an office block (it is an office for Griffiths's partner as well as their home). The cut-out tree in the wall and Amsterdam gable skyline are less obvious. The façade forms a deep window wall in which internal circulation runs round a fireplace. There are references – Edwin Lutyens, Adolf Loos, Venturi – as subtle as anyone's. Fat's critics were only marginally won over by this surprisingly sweet mani-festo. But locals immediately adopted it as a beloved landmark. Venturi, advocate of the boring, called them 'Not boring – but in a good way'.

Main picture: Hedmark
Cathedral Museum, Hamar,
Norway, 1979

Bottom right: Glacier
Museum, Fjaerland
Fjord, 1991

To Sverre Fehn, within every person there is an architect, animated from the moment he or she cuts a path through nature, treading down grass and bending back bushes. It is this dialogue with nature and the human reshaping of it that is, for Fehn, the beginning of human culture, and it is this that is at the heart of his architecture.

Fehn's story is that of the quintessential Modernist architect. He was born in Kongsberg, Norway, in 1924 and attended Oslo's architectural school, where he came under the influence of his architect mentor, Arne Korsmo, just as the sentimental Nordic romanticism of the pre-war era was giving way to the Modern Movement. When he graduated in 1948 he established an office in Oslo and won the competition to design the Lillehammer Museum. Then, in the early 1950s, Fehn and his musician wife spent time in Paris, where he met Le Corbusier and those in his milieu such as Alvar Aalto and Fernand Léger, and became active in the Congrès Internationaux d'Architecture Moderne. Like Le Corbusier (but actually on the advice of Jørn Utzon), he travelled to North Africa to look at the more elemental and cubist forms of its vernacular architecture.

Fehn, however, has not pursued an international career in the International Style. He returned to Oslo and developed his particular Nordic brand of Modernism, with a heightened sensitivity to the light, materials and natural world of the region. In this, rather than for reasons of style, he is rightly compared to Aalto. In fact, the notion of style would appal a Modernist such as Fehn, who argues that the only architectural signature should be 'anonymous'. Buildings should emerge from a 'rightness' with regard to their place in nature and a faith in the contemporary rather than historical models. His work strives for the stillness of being 'in the moment'.

However, Fehn has also said that 'his most important journey was perhaps into the past', when he was designing the Hedmark Cathedral Museum at Hamar, Norway (1979). Here he carefully interlaced a contemporary structure of concrete and frameless glass with the ruins of a medieval bishop's palace, acknowledging but connecting the temporal differences in a manner that recalls Carlo Scarpa's seminal Museo Castelvecchio in Verona. 'Only the manifestation of the present can bring the past to life,' he has said.

Since Hedmark, Fehn has built a number of sublime private houses that fuse with the Norwegian landscape as at the Bodtker houses – a pair of homes for two generations of a family, which use formal linked square plans set on the orthogonal and diagonal without the setting being ignored or the geometry feeling forced. Unsurprisingly, though, it is his public buildings that have brought him attention. The 1991 Glacier Museum at the Fjaerland Fjord is, in its abstracted angular shapes, in the spirit of the glacier that rides above the building, vertical slots between its elements recalling the glacier's own fissures.

For an architect who has made such a poetic contribution to the architectural canon, Fehn is scandalously unknown outside architectural circles. But then star-architect status is irrelevant to someone who would rather be anonymous.

f

Main picture: Yokohama
International Port
Terminal, 2002

Bottom left: Belgo Zuid,
London, 1999

Top right: Computer drawing
for Yokohama International
Port Terminal, 2002

There is a dream that every young and ambitious architect shares: to win
a genuinely anonymous architectural competition for a huge project that
allows him or her to express in unadulterated form their view on architecture. These competitions come along a handful of times in a generation.
In 1995, when the two partners were thirty and thirty-two and had just
small domestic buildings in their portfolio, Foreign Office Architects won
the competition to rebuild Osanbashi Pier in Yokohama, Japan, as a major
port terminal. Their spectacular computer-drawn entry, intended as a research
project as much as a realistic proposal, was chosen over 660 others from 41
nations by a jury that included Rem Koolhaas, Toyo Ito and Arata Isozaki.

    This astonishing win was a dream ticket for husband-and-wife team
Alejandro Zaera-Polo and Farshid Moussavi, but all did not go well initially.
The client was unnerved by the jury's choice and withdrew from the project,
hoping that it would be quietly dropped. Only in 1999, on the eve of football's World Cup in Japan, was the project revived.

    FOA was founded in 1992 when Iranian Moussavi and Spanish
Zaera-Polo were both working for Koolhaas's Office for Metropolitan
Architecture in Rotterdam. Moussavi's education was at London's Bartlett
School of Architecture, then at Harvard, where Zaera-Polo also studied
after completing his diploma at the Escuela Tecnica Superior in Madrid.

    During the hiatus of the Yokohama project, the practice served
its apprenticeship with a collection of domestic, commercial and theoretical
projects as well as teaching at London's Architectural Association, UCLA in
California and the Berlage Institute in Amsterdam. An early client was the
Belgo restaurant chain, for whom FOA built three restaurants in the UK and
New York in 1998 and 1999. The most spectacular of these was in Notting
Hill, west London, where the timber-lined overlapping shells of the high
roof hint at the spectacular structure of the Yokohama project.

    The port terminal is a new piece of topography for the coastline
of Yokohama. The timber-clad roof is an undulating public park, with
entrances to the terminal through depressions and cuts in the landscape.
Inside, the building is entirely column-free, made of prefabricated steel
girders that were transported to site by barge and craned into position.
The origami-like ceiling was created in collaboration with one of Japan's
leading structural engineers, Kunio Watanabe.

    Though so young, FOA has already been hugely influential in
its computer-generated, landscaped architecture, and is at the heart of a
group of practices interested in architecture designed using computers to
suggest new spatial configurations. They worked with three of these like-
minded practices in their 2002 proposal for the World Trade Center reconstruction – UN Studio, Greg Lynn and Reiser & Umemoto – which gained
much publicity but was unsuccessful. One fear is that FOA might never
again get the chance to build on the scale of Yokohama. But their next
slew of substantial projects includes a new theatre complex in Torrevieja,
Spain, a new building for retail chain Selfridges in Bristol, UK, and a huge
new business park in Barcelona, among others.

Foreign Office
Architects

f

Top left: Willis Faber &
Dumas, Ipswich, 1975

Centre left: Stansted
Airport, London, 1991

Bottom left: Sainsbury
Centre, Norwich, 1978

Right: Hongkong and
Shanghai Bank, Hong
Kong, 1986

As far as some critics are concerned, Lord Foster of Thames Bank is a victim of his own success. And what a success that is. One of two architects (with Richard Rogers) who stormed from the beleaguered UK 1960s avant-garde to the top of the world premier league, Foster is – astonishingly in the UK – hugely commercially successful, on the rich list and a peer to boot. That may be what the critics do not like.

Foster's practice started with Richard Rogers and their wives as the hip Team 4 – pioneering high-tech, celebrating and heroizing the new world of lightweight technology. When Foster and Rogers split, their takes diverged. Foster's first independent icon was the gorgeous Willis Faber & Dumas 'Black Piano' in Ipswich (1975), with its slinky, reflective walls and rooftop, kidney-shaped garden. But it was the Sainsbury Centre at the University of East Anglia (1978) – a high-tech shed as Parthenon in an English landscape – that defined his direction. Foster made high-tech classic.

In 1986, while Britain struggled to support home talent, Foster was completing the most expensive building in the world. The Hongkong and Shanghai Bank in Hong Kong, with its earthquake-proof cross-bracing and vast, public-access underbelly daylit by mammoth sunscoops, was glamorous and tough, tackling environmental, civic and architectural issues on a grand scale. It was one of the great projects that launched the UK profession into unprecedented popularity and world fame.

At Stansted Airport (1991) – finally! A UK public client! – Foster's love of flying produced aviation romance. This big aircraft hangar, dappled with sunshine and high-tech shadows, simplified complex circulation into the clearest possible plan. This was Foster's heyday. At home, his foot was in the establishment's door (the Royal Academy's Sackler Gallery, 1991). His own, elegant Battersea Thames-side office and penthouse (1992) became a landmark for the cognoscenti. Abroad, the commissions got bigger: the elegant Carré d'Art in Nîmes (1993); the Commerzbank eco-office in Frankfurt (1997); the world's biggest construction project, Hong Kong Airport, Chek Lap Kok (1998). The workload boomed and main-tenance of quality became essential. Tales of staff employed to check the aesthetic rigour of items in the office fridge were apocryphal.

By the late 1990s, Foster's commissions were ubiquitous, prestigious – notably, the rebuilding of Berlin's Reichstag (1999) – and newsworthy. Most dramatically, London's Millennium Bridge (2002), linking St Paul's to Herzog & de Meuron's Tate Modern, wobbled and had to be closed and damped down. No egg stuck to Foster's Teflon exterior but the critics had cooled: Foster had not just gone establishment, he was the establishment.

His plain, grey, classical Modernism is so prevalent it is often judged by its failings, not its extraordinary worldwide successes. Critics lament the fun of Willis Faber, the technological daring of the Hongkong Bank, the purity and wit of the Sainsbury Centre, or the absolute rigour of detailing and proportion of his pure classical phase. The avant-garde, of course, has long overtaken him. And why not? Foster has nothing left to prove. He has already conquered the world.

Norman Foster

f

To anyone not into architecture's extraordinary, impenetrable discourse, the theoretical hype surrounding Tony Fretton's work can act as a smokescreen, hiding some of Europe's most exquisite and influential architectural work by one of the key exponents of the 'architecture of the everyday'. The buildings themselves are much more eloquent.

Born in 1945, Fretton set up Tony Fretton Architects in 1982 after graduating from the AA and working (including a spell at big commercial firm Chapman Taylor) on projects from commerce to community – a mixture that is at the core of his work. His first major project was the exquisite Lisson Gallery (1990), a private gallery designed in specific relationship to its scruffy setting in inner-city London. Subverting the boutique minimalism of the age, Fretton drew and redrew the façades of the neighbouring down-market shop fronts, reducing them to a pure, perfect distillation to form the gallery façade. The symmetry is shifted on the upper floors so as not to overpower the gallery's slimmer neighbour – a Renaissance trick, Fretton says – and the huge, varied windows set the art against the playground yard opposite. Far from feeling overworked, the Lisson feels perfectly casual – like an exquisite small-scale warehouse with a sense of some kind of history.

The Lisson established Fretton as an excellent designer of location-sensitive arts spaces. At the Sway Centre in Hampshire (1996), the gallery spaces are tucked into the silhouette of old stables by digging out a new low-level courtyard, evolving a sharp, abstracted relation to the vernacular, also evident at the Quay Arts Centre on the Isle of Wight (1998). Sometimes his buried references have comic touches, as in his scrapped scheme for an art gallery in Hoxton Square, east London (1998), with its spiky haircut – a system of rooflights – and overscaled windows.

Fretton's Red House (2001), for wealthy patron Alex Sainsbury, applied these techniques to pure wealth with more contentious results. An enviable budget and Chelsea location allowed red stone, bronze-on-wood windows and glass handrails – a balance of sparseness and luxury that many found uneasy. So far Fretton is more admired for rich-to-poor than rich-to-rich. Where the Lisson's elegance and sensitivity in relation to its less literate neighbours was described as politically radical, the subverted minimalism of the Red House can seem to be talking itself out of a job as much as evolving a new hidden elaboration.

But it may have helped finally, after decades of tiny projects, to move Fretton to a different league. Although he was beaten by Herzog & de Meuron for London's Laban Centre, Fretton has now worked on an important London public gallery at Camden Arts Centre (2003). His success in 2003 in the competition for a new British embassy and residence in Warsaw takes him into the international arena. For all its uneven reception, the Red House may have pulled Fretton from behind the veil of adoring theory into the clear light where his buildings – their highly intelligent, beautiful manipulation of proportion, form and material; their play of vernacular and buried iconography; their exploration of sheer aesthetic response – can be clearly seen.

Tony Fretton

f

'I can do radical architecture, but I am not radical,' Massimiliano Fuksas told critic Jeremy Melvin, putting his finger on the central dilemma of his work. Fuksas is both joker – the wild card who critics thought was having a laugh, who plays successfully with the establishment – and the critic who directed the Venice Biennale to 'Less Aesthetics, More Ethics'. All things to all men, in fact. It may attract criticism but it certainly keeps the critics on their toes.

Fuksas was born in Rome in 1944 of Lithuanian, German and French parentage, taught by Manfredo Tafuri, and worked briefly for the Surrealist painter Giorgio de Chirico – an impressively rich and contradictory background. He set up practice in Rome in 1969, with a Paris office in 1989, and became Italy's part of the European new wave of maverick, iconoclastic, expressive post-Postmodern architects, which also included friends and sometime collaborators Will Alsop and Jean Nouvel.

From his early work, this playful variance was easy to see. His town hall in Cassino (1990) was dubbed 'Pat Garrett and Billy the Kid' – plainish with an 'explosion of life' on top. His Palazzetto dello Sport, Anagni (1988), with its famous slipped portico, teased Postmodernism as much as it used it. Interestingly, Fuksas became well known for his cemeteries (almost all

Massimiliano Fuksas

that was being built in Italy at the time, he says), where he managed this Expressionism into a powerful, film-like suggestiveness. In the twisted walls of his Orvieto Cemetery (1990) – a broken ring half-sunk into the ground – and at the Civita Castellana Cemetery (1992), where a ring wall is perforated by a railway terminus with floorless buildings raised high above the ground, joke turns to elusive monument: the end of the line indeed.

Describing his process in the 1990s, Fuksas played up this wilful naughtiness: his architecture, he said, is 'very easy', based on painting, drawing, enjoying life – 'not like poor old Foster'. Designing a building, he says, takes 'ten minutes – perhaps five'. His lack of concern about down-pipe detailing made one builder ask if he was really an architect.

Yet he also makes serious studies on the city – particularly on the periphery – is urban consultant to Berlin, and by 2000 he was leading the Venice Architecture Biennale into the land of responsibility. 'Less Aesthetics, More Ethics' was a broad-brush manifesto for rebuilding idealism and the relationship with 'a town, a place, a family or whatever'.

Fuksas's confident, clever forms are intensely variable, from the Maison de la Confluence at Avoine (1989) – a mixture of greenhouse, church and windmill – to the Deconstructivist entrance emerging dragon-like from the prehistoric Niaux caves (1993), to the verdigris arts centre that closes its shutters to form a mute box in Bordeaux (1995), to the 'at-ease' Miesianism of his Wienerberg Twin Towers for Vienna (2001). But now he describes them idealistically – the Hong Kong Armani store (2003), with its glossy, sinuous clarity, in terms of Armani's personal, charismatic management (like his own); his Ferrari project in Maranello (2003) in terms of Italian craftsmanship. And he is working on an extraordinarily politically tricky peace centre in Jaffa. There is something to be said for ethical flexibility.

f

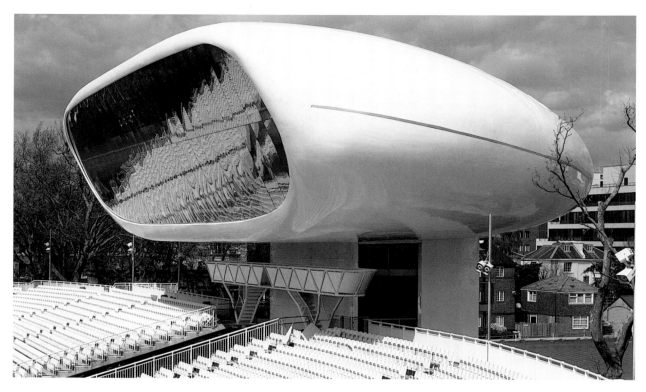

Architects have a habit of being called young until they are over fifty, but Future Systems take the biscuit. Their glamorous, space-age, curvy, day-glo Modernism with innovative technology is quintessentially young, fashionable, futuristic. When their Lord's Media Stand won the Stirling Prize in 1999, Jan Kaplicky was sixty-eight, Amanda Levete forty-four. They did not look it.

Future Systems established a powerful brand before they started building. It is based on technology transfer from other industries, proto-typing, mass production, technological innovation, inventive eco-thought. And absolute, consistent, gorgeous, sexy style.

In the 1980s recession they came up with a series of philanthropic speculative projects: low-cost folding emergency shelters for disaster areas; groundbreaking, glamorous eco-office buildings. Their lectures are punctuated with recycling and energy concerns but it was style that got their projects built. First, a small trolley for London's expensive Ivy restaurant (1990), then a series of projects dominated by luxury shops and houses.

Criticism of this combination of idealism and super-luxury is frequent but hardly fair. That's architecture. Their projects offer genuine prototypes – inevitably pre-mass production. And if anyone deserves exemption from such criticism for sticking to their guns through tough times, it is Future Systems. Kaplicky emigrated from Prague in the brief window of 1968, abandoning a hard-won small practice, and was ignored by London employers until Richard Rogers snapped him up. He later worked in Norman Foster's office. Many famous drawings of both Rogers' and Foster's key projects are his. He set up Future Systems with David Nixon in 1979, working on space satellite interiors and speculative projects like the Peanut Living Capsule, and also worked with Eva Jiricna. But it was when Amanda Levete – a young architect working in Rogers' office – came onto the scene (emotionally and professionally) that the practice really took off.

In the 1980s and early 1990s they produced a stream of competitions: the sensuous, split-double-mound Paris Library in 1989 – narrowly defeated by Dominique Perrault – and the glass-bubble Acropolis Museum, also in 1989. In an increasingly confident architectural world, their profile rocketed. A stream of smaller works began to be built: the lovely, fragile, tube-shaped marquee outside London's NFT (1992); the beautiful lime-green 'water skater' floating bridge at the foot of Canary Wharf (1994). And houses – notably, the glamorous Islington Hauer-King House (1994) and an earth-sheltered giant eye overlooking the Pembrokeshire coast (1998).

Future Systems continue to propose philanthropic schemes, but luxury projects have kept coming, rising to the scale of the revered Media Stand for Lord's Cricket Ground in London (1999) – a semi-monocoque aluminium shell, designed using boat-building techniques, overlooking the ground like a giant television – and the huge Selfridges in Birmingham (2003).

Some see Future Systems as space-age retro: theirs is a vision of the future people have been seeing for decades. But it is the first time this image has really been built – probably because building these ideas for real involves a huge amount of hard work.

f

Left: Guggenheim Museum,
Bilbao, 1997

Top right: DG Bank,
Berlin, 2001

Bottom right: Gehry House,
Santa Monica, 1978

Word has it that a local architecture critic hated the house that Frank Gehry built for himself in Santa Monica so much that he used to bring his dog along especially to crap on the lawn outside. Such trenchant criticism would easily slide off the shiny titanium skin of Gehry's Bilbao Guggenheim – if any came its way. The Guggenheim has met with near universal approval since it opened in 1997. Municipalities across the world have been after a similar 'Bilbao effect' to kick-start their cultural renaissance. Guggenheim central in New York has been quick to take advantage and are busy rolling out a series of signature buildings.

Success came late for the Canadian. He was born in 1929 and moved to his adoptive California in the 1950s, attending the University of South California. But apart from a 1972 house for one of his Californian artist friends, Ron Davis, he was busy producing forgettable corporate work and shopping centres until he built chez Gehry in 1978. Here he took a typical West Coast suburban villa and wrapped around it another house made of angular layers of corrugated metal, chain link fencing and rough wood. Its plan form may have been largely conventionally rectilinear but it pointed the way to the Gehry of the future.

A string of private houses for friends in the LA art community followed before a series of extraordinary buildings took his work to new levels: the Chiat/Day office building in Venice, California (1991), with iconic giant binoculars by sculptor Coosje van Bruggen at its entrance (Claes Oldenburg also worked on the artistic collaboration); and the 'Fred and Ginger' Nationale-Nederlanden Building in Prague (1994), where one of two corner towers grips its partner around the waist and polkas down the river front. Architecture is not supposed to be this much obvious fun.

Gehry, the architect as sculptor, went on to discover the computer-aided design and manufacturing software used to build Mirage jets. With it he found the tool to turn his consciously low-tech card-and-foamboard models (from which he derived his Easy Edge furniture) into realizable, curvaceous, cyber-Baroque buildings. His DG Bank project (2001), just across from the Brandenburg Gate in Berlin, appears to synthesize his commercial office buildings and his fanciful formal flights. Strict conservation controls meant that this time the shiny swoops were contained in a rectilinear box.

Gehry's work is extraordinary in its inventiveness but he likes to portray himself as straightforward, folksy even, in his approach to his work. He does not write theoretical papers and appears to be happy to let his three-dimensional collages be taken at face value. Critics are driven loopy trying to categorize his work. He would rather deal in amusing, self-effacing narratives, as biographically sketchy as his drawings. While building Bilbao, Gehry apparently examined an erroneous shape under construction from the vantage point of a café on the opposite bank of the river: 'Honestly, it looks fine to me,' he said. At the same time, he has compared the careful detailing of a corner window at his Santa Monica home to Marcel Duchamp's *Nude Descending a Staircase*. Nothing in Gehry's world – especially Gehry – is quite what it seems.

Frank O. Gehry

g

Michael Graves

It must be hard being best known for a kettle but Michael Graves has brought it upon himself. His conical design for Alessi became to the 1980s what Philippe Starck's tripod lemon squeezer was to the 1990s. It is one of hundreds of household products, pieces of furniture and ceramics to have emerged from his office. He is also an architect.

Before getting down to teapots, Graves' buildings ushered in Postmodernist historicism in all its floridity. The grandfather of these follies is the Public Services Building in Portland, Oregon (1983), an office block wrapped in the thinnest wallpaper of colour with vaguely Deco applied ornament. It outraged purists but its gaudily made-up face launched a thousand cheap and cheerful corporate imitators across the world. Grave's influence – for good or bad – has been incalculable.

He set up practice in Princeton in 1964 and has been a professor at the university there since 1972. His own education, however, was more wide-ranging. Born in Indianapolis in 1934, he attended the University of Cincinnati and Harvard before working in Rome at the American Academy for two years. When he returned to the US he became one of the New York Five group of architects and a protégé of Philip Johnson, gradually moving away from Modernism through historicism to pure kitsch, partly informed by his experiences of classicism in Italy. He also collaborated with Peter Eisenman on a much-publicized proposal for an imaginary city stretching from Manhattan to Philadelphia.

It seems a heavyweight background for the production of such lightweight material but Michael Graves is serious about his whimsy. He does it so well and with a sense of humour. This has made him the ideal architect to serve the needs of Disney, whom he supplied with a pair of hotels at Disney World, Florida, in 1990: the Swan, topped with Technicolor 2-metre-high swans, and the Dolphin, crowned with a 20-metre-high dolphin splashing in a waterfall. His classicism has been more to the fore, however, in buildings such as the dusty orange Clark County Library and Theater in Las Vegas (1994), with its pared-down historical forms.

This variegated approach has been commercially if not critically successful and Michael Graves & Associates' output includes museums, libraries, offices and academic buildings. Graves also still makes time to design private houses – which, to his chagrin, constitute his only imprint on Princeton, where serving staff are not allowed to build. Meanwhile, Graves Design, the product arm of his business, has been pumping out everything from lighting to charm bracelets. There is even a Graves Design Store. Graves has expressed surprise that his dabbling in the quotidian is seen as vulgar by some, referring his critics back to Bauhaus architects who extended their skills to all aspects of design.

Graves' first love was painting and drawing, at which he excelled, and it was his mother's advice to put this to a practical purpose from which he could make a living. His architecture, too, remains essentially painterly in concern; it is the images that seem to matter and if they are applied two-dimensionally to the façade of a building he does not much mind.

g

Main picture: Olympic
Stadium, Barcelona, 1992

Bottom left: ZEN housing,
Palermo, 1973

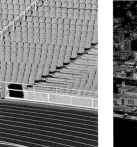

Bottom right: Belém Cultural
Centre, Lisbon, 1993

Vittorio Gregotti is one of the fathers of Neo-Rationalism in Italy, and to a large extent has become its scribe in addition to being one of its foremost practitioners. In 1965 he published his influential book *Il territorio dell'architettura*, which began a long and complex reaction against Modernist functionalism in favour of an architecture that is typological and interested in finding formal essences.

His mantra that 'architecture begins with the marking of ground', communicated through his editorship of journals such as *Casabella* and *Rassegna*, counters the view of architecture as the creation of a succession of objects on a surface. By Gregotti's formulation, the landscape is the primary datum in architecture and all building must engage with this.

Gregotti founded his practice in Milan in 1974, and early large-scale work revealed his ideas on urbanism, often using a megastructural approach, which he attempted to combine with a sensitivity to the fine grain of the city. This is particularly clear in his ZEN residential project in Palermo (1973) and his project for the Belém Cultural Centre in Lisbon, Portugal, which was completed in 1993. The Belém Centre, which hosted the European Union presidency in 1992, is arranged around a city block 400 metres in length, with a series of routes at different levels and functional blocks set perpendicular to the main axis. The idea is that the blocks give a morphological reminder of the complex urban fabric around the centre, while still appearing from the outside as an appropriately coherent institutional building.

Gregotti's refurbishment and extension of the Barcelona Olympic Stadium (1992) is one of his greatest buildings, despite the fact that it is almost invisible behind Domeneq y Montener's 1929 façade for the original. Inside, Gregotti's sensitivity to the existing structure is evident in the spectacular galleries underneath the stands. Circular openings allow light into these foyers, heightening the anticipation of the spectators. Gregotti's hugely expanded arena (his scheme increased capacity from 20,000 to 65,000 spectators) is overwhelming, the huge steel roof of the grandstand dominating proceedings.

Gregotti can perhaps best be considered as a 'scolding voice' for architects with a Modernist hangover, eloquently and almost dismissively rewriting the history of architecture for the last fifty years. In his address to the New York Architectural League in 1983, he said: 'The worst enemy of modern architecture is the idea of space considered solely in terms of its economic and technical exigencies indifferent to the ideas of the site... The origin of architecture is not the primitive hut, the cave or the mythical "Adam's house in paradise". Before transforming a support into a column, before placing stone on stone, man placed a stone on the ground to recognize a site in the midst of an unknown universe, in order to take account of it and modify it.' Poetically, he debunks functionalism, freeing the profession from the tyranny of structural honesty. It is perhaps for this that he has been called, by no less a fan than Kenneth Frampton, 'the most important architect, critic and intellectual writing today'.

Vittorio Gregotti

g

Main picture: Waterloo
International Railway
Terminal, London, 1993

Top right: The Eden
Project, Cornwall, 2000

Centre right: Sainsbury's
supermarket and housing,
London, 1988

There is something Victorian about Nicholas Grimshaw's work. It is a very straight expression of structure and envelope, 'skin and bones' – UK high-tech without refinements or aestheticism, based on a no-nonsense belief in nuts and bolts. There is no Foster-style classical purity here, no Rogers-style experimental play. Nor is Grimshaw particularly known for spatial dynamics. If some buildings have them, they are a gift that comes free with the structural logic.

You would have to read the small print of his books to find out, but Grimshaw famously set up in partnership with Terry Farrell in 1960s London. His earliest key buildings – the prefabricated service tower at Sussex Gardens student housing in London (1968), or the Park Road Flats, London (1970) – are products of this partnership. But Grimshaw's grasp of high-tech rules was totally different to Farrell's variegated lateral thought.

The best of their diverging style war was in Camden. Near Farrell's Postmodernist TV AM and just as expressive, Grimshaw's Sainsbury's super-market and housing at Camden Town (1988) took out-of-town high-tech servicing to a tough, tight, urban site, creating an inner-city scene, including a heavy, exposed-structure metal shed, workshops and a car park. And the adjacent north-facing canal-side houses, with rooflit sections snatching sunlight from the supermarket side, promoted proto-industrial lifestyles.

Grimshaw's work always seems to work best in relation to some kind of mechanical issue. The spectacle of the printing works for the *Financial Times* in east London (1988), where the huge presses are exposed to the busy surrounding area, depended entirely on the union of building and machine. The UK Pavilion for the Seville Expo in 1992 was another big high-tech box: it was the wall of water that drizzled down the glass to cool it in the baking heat, and the adapted container wall that held the water, that made it compelling.

Grimshaw's structures started to veer from the big shed into Expressionism – the *Western Morning News* Building, Plymouth (1993), for instance, with its huge boat-shaped shed with outrigger structure and central atrium and circulation yard in the middle; or the similar RAC Control Centre, Bristol (1994). But it is with real engineering challenges that Grimshaw is in his element: the Waterloo International Railway Terminal, London (1993) is by far his greatest work. It looks and works like a long thin airport – a deliberate, pedestrian idea, transcended by the lovely, asymmet-rical, curved roof, designed with Anthony Hunt. Its soaring forms are, again, functional: the curving length simply follows the tracks, the arch rising steeply to clear the trains at the single-track platform on one side. There have been high-profile technical problems with the glass, though.

The Eden Project in Cornwall (2000) is also a simple idea: a huge geodesic dome. The biggest greenhouse in the world, its scale and direct-ness win fans. Perhaps that is what gives Grimshaw's notable work his popular – sometimes more than critical – appeal: its direct, untheoretical functionalism which – when it hits the right combination of site, engineer and project – can simply take off.

Nicholas Grimshaw

g

Main picture: The Peak
competition painting, 1983

Top right: Vitra Fire Station,
Weil-am-Rhein, 1993

Centre right: Strasbourg
Tram Station, 2002

Bottom right:
Landesgartenschau Pavilion,
Weil-am-Rhein, 1999

Zaha Hadid exploded onto the world scene in 1983 with a spectacular series of paintings that won her the competition for the Peak Leisure Club in Hong Kong. The glamorous, dynamic, jagged forms, a deliberate shock to the white cubic formalities of Modernism, established a powerful imagery for the burgeoning Deconstructivist movement and a new icon in architecture's strange world where unbuilt projects can become architectural totems.

Hadid, architecture's formidable Issey Miyake-clad diva, was born in 1950 in Baghdad and studied maths at university there, moving to London and the Architectural Association, where she was taught by Léon Krier and Rem Koolhaas. Unsurprisingly, it was Koolhaas she went on to work with: she was a member of the Office for Metropolitan Architecture before opening her own office in London.

Her huge paintings show a seismic world suggesting speed, movement and Suprematism, with objects shattering and twisting. 'I almost believed there was such a thing as zero gravity,' she has said. The hundreds of paintings she makes for every project are published, exhibited, hugely influential and, she has said, 'larger than the ideas of the project', though elsewhere she describes building as her main drive.

Her first projects were small, most famously the Vitra Fire Station at the furniture company's Weil-am-Rhein factory (1993). A tiny lightning bolt of a building, it traced the activities of the fire engines like choreographic diagrams. Quickly converted to Vitra's Design Museum, it is now stacked with famous chairs – a function it suits admirably. Actually, the buildings have a tough act to follow in the super-famous paintings. As at Vitra's nearby successor, the sinuous, computer-age Landesgartenschau Pavilion (1999), Hadid's built forms are, inevitably (and surely rightly) sweeter, gentler and smaller-seeming than their parent paintings. They are loveable and luscious rather than suggesting a world of danger, but still masterly. At Strasbourg Tram Station (2002) the witty use of structure and car-park markings choreographs the moving trams, bikes and people into Hadid-esque form and movement.

Big projects were a long, hard time coming. Despite a string of major competition wins – Berlin Ku'Damm (1986), Dusseldorf Art and Media Centre (1993), the Habitable Bridge Competition for London (1996) are just a few – her reputation as one of the great visionaries who never got built was dramatically reinforced when her 'string of pearls' Cardiff Opera House (1994) was controversially scrapped.

Undaunted, unrepentant, Hadid has continued. She has designed major exhibitions (at the New York Guggenheim, the Vienna Kunsthalle and the Hayward, London); temporary pavilions and structures, notably the Mind Zone at London's Millennium Dome (1999); and interiors and furniture. Famous as a teacher, she has professorships in Hamburg, Harvard, Columbia, Ohio and Yale. And the bigger buildings – the Centers for Contemporary Arts in Cincinnati (2003) and Rome (ongoing) – have finally started to come through. But although her buildings are exquisite on their own terms, they are nowhere near as famous as her imagery, her impact and her profile. Yet.

Zaha Hadid

h

Bottom: Museum of
Fruit, Japan, 1995

Top left: Shonandai
Cultural Centre, Kanagawa,
1990

Top right: Sumida Culture
Factory, Tokyo, 1994

Centre right: Shonandai
Cultural Centre, Kanagawa,
1990

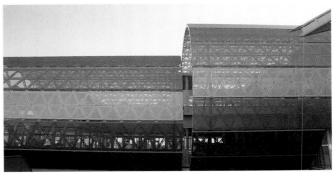

Japan's architectural profession is the most male-dominated in the world. While countries such as the US and the UK have a shameful record in encouraging women into architecture, Japan has almost no record at all. But the generation of Tadao Ando and Toyo Ito has one female voice that rises above all others – Itsuko Hasegawa. She is the first woman to gain a reputation in Japan equivalent to that of the best-respected male practitioners, and she has done so by following a path that is distinctively Japanese but all her own.

Born in Shizuoka in 1941, Hasegawa trained in Yokohama, working in the offices of Kiyonori Kikutake and Kazuo Shinohara, before setting up her own atelier in 1979, at the birth of the boom in the Japanese economy. She quickly won commissions, including her stationery shop in Yaizu (1979) – three metal-clad volumes with pitched roofs, echoing the surrounding low-rise roofscape while creating a public open space in a dense part of the city. Although this project hinted at a concern with context and the social effects of her buildings, it was hardly a forerunner of her later work, which quickly revealed itself to be at the opposite end of the spectrum from that of Ito and Ando. Where their architecture is concerned with the sublimation of material and technology, Hasegawa is interested in the way architecture can build connections and places of repose in the city, using a tectonic vocabulary inspired by forms from the Japanese landscape.

She is emphatically opposed to rational approaches to planning and architecture, and wrote in the introduction to her book *Island Hopping* (2000) that 'as a pursuit, architecture is similar to that of a poet dreaming of islands in the sea, or a composer creating music. My architecture pursues the creation of a rhythmic poetic machine, avoiding generalized approaches in favour of diverse concerns.'

Her breakthrough project was Bizan Hall (1986), which occupies almost an entire block in Shizuoka. This was followed by the Shonandai Cultural Centre (1990) in Kanagawa and the Sumida Culture Factory (1994) in Tokyo, both comprising compositions of blocks linked by walkways. These buildings featured her trademark perforated metal panels and were formally indebted in part to the Japanese Metabolists, with geometric shapes used, in the case of Shonandai, to create a model of the universe.

Her most famous work, the Museum of Fruit in the Yamanishi Prefecture (1995), presents three glass objects in the landscape, housing a museum and greenhouses themed around fruit – one of the most important contributors to the Yamanishi economy. These zoomorphic pavilions are intended to refer to seeds half-planted in the earth, or perhaps to the exotic fruits they contain. Inside, they give beautiful views towards Mount Fuji from elevated platforms, the elegant white steel structure and almost invisible glazing details adding to the futuristic drama.

Despite failing to win the few Western competitions she has entered (Cardiff Opera House in 1994 and Tower Hill masterplan in 1999), Hasegawa's legacy is secure as one of the greats of Japanese architecture of the second half of the twentieth century.

Itsuko Hasegawa

h

Top: Heinz Galinski
School, Berlin, 1995

Bottom left: Heinz Galinski
School, Berlin, 1995

Bottom right: Spiral
Apartment House, Ramat
Gan, 1989

Zvi Hecker's Judaism has been central to his life and work as an architect. This is hardly surprising as he was born in Cracow, Poland, in 1931 and survived the Holocaust.

After a year of architecture school in Poland he joined Diaspora Jews moving to Israel in 1950, where he completed his studies in architecture, engineering and painting. His work has been closely associated with the building of the Israeli state: housing, a new town centre, military museums and a military academy. More recently his buildings for the Jewish community in Germany have raised his international profile, particularly his Heinz Galinski School in Berlin (1995), the first Jewish school to be built since the Second World War.

Hecker has long been preoccupied with spirals and sunflowers (which formed part of his wartime diet) and the Heinz Galinski School is based on the petals of the sunflower with their spiralling 'celestial construction' – Hecker's take on design is part of Expressionism's return curve to Berlin. As with all his projects, the scheme evolved even as it was built and, as it grew, the Berlin school began to take on the form of the open pages of a book. A Talmudic debate ensued that confirmed the new image's appropriateness. After all, 'Beth-Sefer', the Hebrew word for school, means literally 'house of the book'. Hecker has since called it a 'friendly meeting of whales', and a city within a city of courtyards, culs-de-sac and alleyways, following the path of the sun.

Transformations such as this, regeneration and renewal, are part of his philosophy. The Tower of Babel form of Hecker's Ramat Gan apartments outside Tel Aviv (1989) is a spiral staircase writ large as a building that also changed form as it emerged. Other metaphors, inspired by nature, abound, especially crystal structures, their tightly wound cells expanding as incremental units evolve.

His significant earlier Israeli buildings include Bat-Yam City Hall (1963); a laboratory building at Haifa's Insitute of Technology (1967), where he trained; and the city centre of Ramat Hasharon (1989) – another design based on a sunflower. Later works include the Palmach Museum of History in Tel Aviv (2002), which rises out of the earth – 'a landscape of the dreams that have made Israel a reality'. Recent projects in Germany, Austria, Italy and Poland include a Jewish Community Centre in Mainz (1999), built around the ruins of a destroyed synagogue.

Hecker has described architecture as 'an act of magic', hiding more than is revealed, making spaces and silences for dramatic effect – but there is nothing flash about his work. On the contrary, he is concerned with the more essentialist aspects of human experience – fear, suffering, happiness. In his use of earthbound materials he has rejected the growing glassiness of architecture, where transparency is employed as a dubious 'alibi' for corporatism – 'soulless reincarnation' he calls it. Stones are preferable, he argues, if architecture is to express the ever-changing human soul and unchanging human emotions. For Hecker, architecture is both a psychological and a spiritual affair.

Zvi Hecker

h

Main picture: Wohnhaus,
Regensburg, 1979

Top left: Hall 26,
Hanover Expo, 2000

Top right: Expo
roof, Hanover, 2000

Thomas Herzog

As the sustainability agenda has moved increasingly to the fore following the Rio and Kyoto earth summits, eco-tech architecture has emerged out of high-tech. Whereas high-tech gives the appearance of being scientifically savvy through its exploitation of industrial and engineering elements, eco-tech wants actually to *be* intelligent in its use of technology to achieve ecological goals.

Something of a wunderkind – he became Germany's youngest professor of architecture at the tender age of thirty-two – Thomas Herzog has been at the forefront of these developments. Working from his home town of Munich (he was born there in 1941), he has been seriously engaged in developing the technology of architectural skins, building on research he began when he was a student interested in pneumatic buildings, membranes and the hands-on business of metalwork. Pneumatics were quickly rejected because of their heavy energy needs but Herzog has continued to investigate ways of making building envelopes cleverer in their response to climate and energy.

An early project was the Richter Residential Complex in Munich (1982), which had solar energy as a central concern. Since then experimentation has continued through his practice Herzog + Partner, established in 1983. His projects are not homespun green architecture but essays in innovative timber, glass and steel. That said, his Wohnhaus in Regensburg (1979), with its steep, ground-sweeping pitched roof, is content to get its summer shading from the tree canopy above. Bare branches allow winter sun to warm the perimeter conservatories.

On a much larger scale, Herzog's Design Centre in Linz, Austria (1993), is an exhibition hall formed as a giant cloche in the glass 'palace of industry' tradition. Here, however, the glass has a slatted sandwiched layer that allows light through but reflects direct sunlight back – a device that has been released as a new building product in its own right. Herzog is also one of a team of international architects working on Solar City in Linz, an ambitious green suburb where, in an ongoing project, he is building 400 housing units that will be the last word in solar and sustainable design. The Linz Design Centre additionally led to a commission to design a hall for the Hanover Expo in 2000. Hall 26 is a line-up of three great glassy tents, the roof of one swinging down to catch on the wall of its neighbour. Passive ventilation induced by the building form cuts energy use in half.

Herzog's output may be innovative and aesthetically competent but, as yet, it cannot touch the sublime heights of his high-tech equivalents (although he has expressed a desire to build an eco-tech skyscraper to show his flashier rivals how it can be done in a more sustainable way). However, another Herzog scheme for the Hanover Expo, the Expo-Dach, a permanent roof for an entertainment area, has more poetry about it. It consists of ten timber 'umbrellas' 20 metres high that support 40-square-metre crowns of laminated timber clad in self-cleaning membranes. Water flows off the roof down the middle of these pylons into a grid of canals that reflects the grid geometry of the roof. Eco-tech has come a long way in a very short time.

h

Left: Tate Modern,
London, 2000

Top right: Goetz
Gallery, Munich, 1992

Bottom right: Signal
box, Basle, 1995

To say Herzog & de Meuron are the masters of cool is not to diminish their absolutely serious architectural status. By the early 1990s they had already achieved international critical respect with their Ricola storage and Goetz Gallery buildings. But it was a measure of their absolute assurance when, as a relatively young practice, they beat the world's greatest – including Rem Koolhaas, Renzo Piano and Tadao Ando – to win the competition for Tate Modern, intended to be the best art gallery in the world.

Jacques Herzog and Pierre de Meuron, both born in Basle in 1950, have always worked with – and as – conceptual artists: before they set up practice in 1978 they paraded a controversial Joseph Beuys artwork round the Basle Carnival wearing Beuys' trademark felt suits. Like minimalist or Arte Povera artists they abstract and remake found and familiar forms and materials, transforming them into high architecture.

The 1993 Ricola Storage Building in Alsace – essentially a shell to wrap a metal container in a quarry – became an extraordinary object. Modelled on timber stacked on pallets, it uses a range of Renaissance and art tricks in standard Eternit boards: inverted golden section proportions diminishing towards the base; panels sliced in two and leaning at different angles. Op Art also figures in their copper-band-wrapped railway signal box in Basle (1995).

The exquisite Goetz Gallery in Munich (1992) was the building that convinced the Tate clients. The delicate glass box seems to float on the ground, just supported by two huge concrete channels. In fact, it is sunk a half-level: its grass-level windows are at clerestory height inside, and its pure plan and classical elevation mask a sophisticated circulation. Typically, it is much cleverer than its visual simplicity might suggest.

The remaking of the monumental 1950s power station on London's Bankside as Tate Modern (2000) was essentially a huge conversion yet, as always, Herzog & de Meuron seemed to make the old building their own. The exteriors were stripped of landscape so that they seem even more brutal. Visitors enter down a huge ramp into a rough, massive volume, the Turbine Hall, which acts as public space and 'outside' gallery, into which glass 'cloud' boxes protrude from the upper galleries. The Beaux-Arts sequence of linked galleries have rough, untreated floors and range, with the slightest variation, from the grand to the informal. The 'light beam' added on top of the build-ing illuminates both upper galleries and restaurant levels. It met expectations.

Herzog & de Meuron's buildings are never the same yet the work has strong characteristics: beautiful proportions, familiar forms, cheap materials treated as precious; cunning but underplayed circulation and structure; pro-portional and perspectival illusion; the quality of the skin – printed with photographic images and textures in many buildings, as at Pfaffenholz Sports Centre in Alsace (1993), or faintly iridescent, as at the disingenuously brilliant Laban Centre in Deptford, London (2003). And fantastic, dry, Arte Povera-type jokes: the fireplace in the chimney of the Tate; the vanishing corridor at Laban. Ordinariness camouflages the extraordinary – to the point of genius.

Herzog & de Meuron

h

Main picture: Simons Hall
student residence, MIT,
Boston, 2003

Bottom left: Kiasma
Contemporary Art
Museum, Helsinki, 1998

Steven Holl

In 2002 Steven Holl was named 'America's Best Architect' by *Time Magazine*, which benediction asserted his status as the highest-profile US architect of his generation. Born in 1947, Holl studied at the University of Washington and in Rome before pursuing postgraduate study at London's Architectural Association in 1976, when Rem Koolhaas, Bernard Tschumi, Nigel Coates and Zaha Hadid were tutors. These auspicious beginnings were followed by a series of publications including the foundation of the influential *Pamphlet Architecture* journal.

He began his career in practice in California, but opened his office in New York in 1976. Early projects included a few good-taste interiors, but his first truly influential building came with the remarkable Berkowitz Odgis House in Martha's Vineyard, Massachusetts (1988). This single-storey building reinterprets the balloon frame, with a veranda playing vertiginous games with views out to the ocean and back to and through the house itself.

An eclectic portfolio of housing followed, including his Void Space/Hinged Space housing in Fukuoka, Japan (1991); the Stretto House in Dallas (1992); and the Makuhari Housing in Chiba, Japan (1996). A major breakthrough was the Jesuit Chapel of St Ignatius at Seattle University (1997), where Holl created a series of geometric volumes, each bringing a different quality of natural light into the chapel to dramatize the various aspects of the Jesuit ritual. Holl used coloured glass to create a concept he describes as 'seven bottles of light in a stone box'. These bottles not only create amazing effects within the interior, but shine out across the campus at night as coloured beacons. His big break – the Kiasma Contemporary Art Museum in Helsinki, won in an open international competition – was to continue in this vein. Completed in 1998, Kiasma made Holl the first US winner of the Alvar Aalto Medal – one of Finland's highest architectural honours – and confirmed his reputation as a creator of theatrical and intense interiors in a building that also dealt with an incredibly difficult site at a motorway intersection.

More recent work perhaps shows Holl's desire to place himself in context. His Simons Hall student residence at Massachusetts Institute of Technology (2003) is a bold perforated megastructure with a disorientating scale worthy of Rem Koolhaas. Perhaps most significantly, in the 2002 competition for the reconstruction of the World Trade Center, he formed a team with three members of the 'New York Five' group who dominated US architecture in the 1950s and 1960s – Peter Eisenman, Charles Gwathmey and Richard Meier. Their scheme was not shortlisted, but Holl became an outspoken critic of the process, showing that he is one of the least parochial practitioners in the US, calling for US architecture to learn from the European model of procuring major public works – the open architectural competition with an informed jury.

Holl is still relatively young for an architect. What he lacks in Gehry-style bombast, he makes up for in his adaptability and invention. The question that remains is whether such a stylistic chameleon will ever have a coherent body of work. Perhaps it is best that he does not.

h

Hans Hollein seems to be that rare thing – an architect to whom Post-modernism in every sense comes utterly naturally. It may be 'PoMo' the style for which he is most famous internationally but his full, exploratory 'Postmodern' range – 'Everything is architecture,' he says – is best understood on his home ground. Born in Vienna in 1934, he trained there and in Chicago and Berkeley, eschewing the Ivy League for the toughness of the Midwest and the luxury and landscape of the West Coast, which he fused with the heritage of Adolf Loos and Otto Wagner. His architecture has a natural polemic, fun and toughness that is at home in dialectical atmospheres and survived the wild mood swings surrounding Postmodernism in the late twentieth century. 'To me, architecture is not primarily the solution of a problem, but the making of a statement,' he has said

His first built project was the tiny, comedic Retti Candle Store in Vienna (1965), just 3.6 metres wide, which set the scene with its elaborate, decorative, contemporary experiment – Secession meets West-Coast Free Modern. It won huge acclaim and a $25,000 prize – more than the value of the project. More tiny shops followed, notably the neighbouring jewellery store, where metallic tubes gleam out of a fractured Modernist façade.

Less architecturally famous are his fabulous artworks and collages: witty, surprisingly Arte Povera installations; collages of aircraft carriers or over-scaled Rolls Royce radiators in the landscape; brilliant, funny furniture like his revolving desk (1966). He has designed provocative exhibitions in many countries – notably the neon-signed 'Dream and Reality' (1985) and the tent-housed 'Turks Before Vienna' (1982).

But the architecture world has stayed fixed on his buildings. His decorative handling of tiny projects has stayed unusually intact as the buildings have grown bigger. The much-acclaimed Mönchengladbach Abteiburg Museum (1982) is curiously deceptive, comprising a substantial set of Post-modernist galleries – 'a sort of temple of art' – tucked into an apparently small, complex series of external volumes and materials. His Austrian Tourist Office in Vienna (1978), with palm trees, was iconoclastic and loved. Winning the Pritzker Prize in 1985, he was praised for his 'wit and eclectic gusto'.

Reaction to his Haas House (1990), a highly decorated shopping centre in Vienna, was somewhat more cynical. Opening at the height of anti-Postmodernism, the centre was described in Vienna as 'golden underwear'. Its elaborate, fanciful interiors provocatively took the then-debased shopping-centre interior to new decorative heights.

But Hollein's role in Vienna has been critical. Always culturally proactive, he is the father of Vienna's extraordinarily powerful place in late twentieth-century building and debate. At the height of the style wars, he seemed to shift from Pop Art to Postmodernism to Expressionism, but in fact his work has always been extensive – from the grid of caves proposed for the Guggenheim in Salzburg to his Vulcania Museum in the Auvergne (2002), which, with its tough, funny, expressive massing, is popular and confident. Looking back, his work looks extraordinarily coherent in its breadth of approach, its intelligent popularity and its experimentalism.

Hans Hollein

h

Looking at the colourful 1991 Team Disney Building in Orlando, Florida,
with its carved-out giant spherical sundial and Mickey-Mouse-ears entrance,
it is hard to imagine that its architect, Arata Isozaki, was once a collaborator
with the likes of Kenzo Tange and Kisho Kurokawa. He has moved a long
way from his roots deep within Japanese Modernism and specifically the
1960s Metabolism movement, under the aegis of which he produced influential projects such as the unbuilt Clusters in the Air (1962) – a vast housing
megastructure with units branching out from huge core trunks.

Like many of his contemporaries, Isozaki trained with Kenzo Tange
at Tokyo University and was a product of the post-war rebuilding years (he
was born in Kyushu in 1931). But of all of those contemporaries, he has
made the most significant break with a technocratic Modernism, embracing
Postmodernism with zest.

In the 1970s, Isozaki was in the Modernist mainstream, producing
buildings such as the Gunma Museum of Modern Art, Takasaki (1974),
based on a cubic grid reaching out over the surrounding parkland and
reflecting pool. As the decade progressed he struggled more and more

with orthogonal orthodoxy and began experimenting with new shapes, especially the circle, which he used in both plan and section. By the time he came to build the Tsukuba Civic Centre in the early 1980s at a new town outside Tokyo, which freely quotes everything from the neoclassical to Robert Venturi, he was clearly in a new phase of his life and work. It seemed full of irony but Isosaki would argue that all his work up to then had been about irony – his later work was instead irony-free 'wit'. Whether you get the joke depends on what you consider humour. Some things do not translate very well or become laboured in the process.

At the same time demand for Isozaki was growing overseas and he has constructed buildings all over the world. One of the most celebrated is the 1986 Los Angeles Museum of Contemporary Art – a tawny stone compilation of pyramids and domes arranged around a courtyard. Designed using principles of both the golden section and yin and yang, most of the museum's galleries are set underground and lit from above to address the planners' height limitations. Also in the US is the cartoon world of Team Disney with its vast multicolour cooling tower and mismatched grids.

Back in Japan, Isozaki's Kyoto Concert Hall (1995), composed of a cube and cylinder (Platonic solids were especially fashionable in the Japan of the 1990s), and the Mito Art Centre (1990), with its giant folded steel tower and Soane-like saucer domes, further demonstrated his new playfulness and expression of different volumes. The vast steel ellipse of the Nara Centennial Hall in Nara (1998), however, does the opposite, gathering everything neatly within its shiny carapace.

With such diversity, it has become impossible to know where Isozaki will go next and to decide whether he is a trendsetter still or a follower of fashion.

Arata Isozaki

i

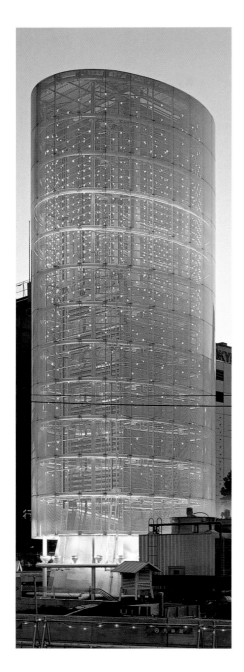

In the notoriously competitive and ego-ridden world of architecture it is rare to find an architect that almost nobody thinks is bad. Toyo Ito is one of these few, lauded by almost everybody for different reasons, and you will hardly ever hear a bad word said about him as an architect or a man.

Born in Seoul, South Korea, in 1941, he moved back to his father's native town of Suwa-shi Nagano in Japan soon after birth and graduated from Tokyo University in 1965. His ambition had always been to become a professional baseball player but he says that, as no university would give him a sport scholarship, he 'had no choice' but to study architecture. After his studies Ito worked for Japanese Metabolist architect Kiyonori Kikutake until 1969, before opening his own office in 1971.

His practice made its name with the introverted U-House in Tokyo (1976), clad in white masonry with no outward-facing openings. Instead the house looks into a central courtyard, with slits in the roof allowing a dramatic play of light in the minimal interior. Ito's work subsequently began to experiment more and more with diaphanous skins, holding lightness of structure and transparency as cardinal virtues. His own house, the Silver Hut in Nakano (1984), experimented with perforated and transparent screens in industrial materials to refer in a contemporary way to the lightness and translucency of traditional Japanese building methods. For Ito, industrial perforated aluminium can take on similar qualities to paper screens and movable walls, but the Silver Hut also has the qualities of an airship, with a taut, light skin stretched over a frame.

His most notable buildings after this period included the wonderful 'Tower of the Winds' in Yokohama (1986) – a light sculpture consisting of 1,300 flickering lamps configured to respond to the direction of the wind. His Old People's Home 'Hoju-ryo' (1994) and Municipal Museum (1991), both in Yatsushiro, were his first major institutional buildings. They launched a decade of success, including the Nagayama Amusement Complex in Tokyo (1993) and the almost completely transparent ITM Building in Matsuyama (1993), leading to his masterpiece, completed in 2001 – the Sendai Mediatheque.

Seldom has a building been so eagerly awaited. Widely trailed in the architectural press before, during and after construction, the media-theque was conceived as a seven-storey structure, clad in glass and held up by branch-like steel members arranged in thirteen tubular columns housing services and allowing light to penetrate the depth of the floor plate. It is spectacular, at once referring to the characteristic trees that line the roads of Sendai and providing a 22,000-square-metre space of incredible lightness. The mediatheque derives its diagram from Le Corbusier's 1914 Dom-Ino project, but also, again, refers to the movable screens and walls of the traditional Japanese house. The fit-out, with furniture and screens designed by Ross Lovegrove dividing the interior, has been criticized by some as being unsympathetic to Ito's structure, but it remains one of the most important buildings of recent years in Japan, and confirms Ito's place as the pre-eminent voice in contemporary Japanese architecture.

Toyo Ito

Eva Jiricna

Despite her well-deserved reputation for affability there is a steely strength to Eva Jiricna. There has had to be. Born in Czechoslovakia in 1939, Jiricna was on a trip to the UK when Soviet tanks rolled into Prague in 1968. The Iron Curtain clanked shut behind her and she found herself persona non grata in her home country.

For the following twenty-two years she built her career in London, bringing a Czech engineering tradition to UK high-tech. Like many an architect, her early work was mainly in interior design – but no cushion plumping for her. Jiricna handled the interiors of Richard Rogers' Lloyd's Building (1986) and, with former partner and fellow Czech émigré Jan Kaplicky, designed the influential metal-plated Way In department in Harrods (1985). Shops for fashion designer Joseph Ettedgui followed, spawning a reputation for building a mean staircase that established her independent career. The intricate web of engineered steel and glass treads she created in 1989 at the Sloane Street Joseph store was seminal, and even though the original is no longer there, it remains an icon of 1980s luxurious design. A whole flight of staircases followed, each with their own structural logic and often in the most glamorous locations for conspicuous consumption – Le Caprice restaurant and Legend's nightclub in London, for instance – and her spectacular skills with these materials have remained something of a signature even as the projects have become larger.

Although subsequently unlucky with a number of high-profile designs that did not make it off the drawing board, Jiricna went on to design a range of residential, commercial and public buildings in the UK and beyond. Most notable are an extension to a house designed by Ove Arup in north London (1994), and the Canada Water Bus Station (1999), which forms part of the Jubilee Line Extension's architectural pantheon.

The Velvet Revolution in Czechoslovakia in 1989 gave Jiricna, at last, the chance to build in her homeland, pulling out all the stops with a gossamer-light steel and glass orangery in the grounds of Prague Castle (1998). The commission came from President Vaclav Havel himself and the result is a show-stopping exercise in high-tech romanticism perched on a wooded terrace. Bringing her skills home has not been an easy task for this formidable perfectionist: when she started work on the project there was not even a nut and bolt in the post-Stalinist design lacuna that met her requirements, let alone the precision nodes needed for the Orangery. She persevered, however, and in the process, and through many subsequent projects and teaching, has given Czech design and product manufacture a significant confidence boost.

Jiricna is no longer the eternal exile. She divides her time between her London and Prague studios, designing museum interiors and a £4 million penthouse in London, offices in Warsaw, Moscow and Budapest, and a new university library for her Czech birthplace, Zlin. Glass, stone and steel, lightness and transparency, have a place in all of them. There is even the odd spectacular staircase, too. Jiricna is now that rare thing, an architectural prophet in her own country.

j

If anyone can be called the 'Grand Old Man' of architecture, there is no doubt that it is Philip Johnson. In the US Johnson has presided over the rise of the International Style, Postmodernism and, through his protégés, Deconstructivism. Along the way, he has designed some of the US's most recognizable landmarks. Powering towards a hundred years old, he shows no sign of relinquishing his position.

Johnson was born in 1906 but it was not until 1943 that he qualified as an architect. Six years later he had built the Glass House at New Canaan, Connecticut – a building that became an instant classic. Based on Mies's Farnsworth House, Johnson's house was finished a year earlier. Nine years after that came another high point: New York's Seagram Building, on which he worked with Mies van der Rohe himself. Later in life the Postmodern skyscraper was born with Johnson's AT&T tower (1983), which crowned Manhattan with an enormous broken pediment.

In many ways, however, it is not Johnson's buildings that have made him so influential (though of course they have helped) but his work as an educator and exhibition curator, which has changed the course of events. In 1932, as the first director of the New York Museum of Modern Art's Department of Architecture, he mounted, with Henry-Russell Hitchcock, the 'Modern Architecture' exhibition. This, together with its catalogue, *The International Style*, brought the Modern Movement from Europe, where it was soon to be stifled by Nazism and war, to his side of the Atlantic, where it flourished. Emigré architects followed.

In the mid-1950s Johnson finally left the museum to resume his building career with the Seagram Building. His conversion to Postmodernism in the 1970s was astounding to many: here was the man who had helped create the climate for Modernism dirtying his hands with flimsy historicism. Certainly his buildings since have never attained their former glory, even if, as with AT&T, they have made an impact. His Pittsburg Plate Glass headquarters in Pennsylvania (1984) is a glassy malnourished version of London's Houses of Parliament with spindly glass pinnacles. More recently, his town hall for Disney's idealized gated community, Celebration, Florida (1996), is like a stretched ante-bellum mansion where someone lost count of the portico columns. Horrible.

But under his tutelage at Yale, the witty East Coast patrician has fostered the talents of his 'kids' – Robert Stern, Peter Eisenman, Richard Meier and Michael Graves among others – who in turn have invested his own work with new twists. The Cathedral of Hope, Dallas, Texas, due for completion in 2004, could well be his last major building – a skin of Deconstructivist motifs, all angular tumbling volumes.

His stylisitic promiscuity has led to criticism that Johnson is simply a consummate follower of the 'next big thing' rather than an architect with his own *oeuvre*. It is easy to see why such mud sticks, given the eclecticism and patchiness of his output. But, even if it is true, his talents as a promoter of architects and architecture lend him greatness, like the host of an exceptional salon that has lasted several decades.

Philip Johnson

j

Bottom: Kunsthal,
Rotterdam, 1992

Top right: Villa
Dall'Ava, Paris, 1991

Centre right: *Flagrant Delit*
by Madelon Vriesendorp
from *Delirious New York*,
1978

If this book had a rating system, Rem Koolhaas would be number one. Incredible to non-architects ('Coolhouse? You're making it up'), he is the most influential architect in the world. What he does, generations will try ten years later. What he writes spawns a mass of imitators. What he studies forms the new avant-garde. This extraordinary feat – maintaining the cutting edge for over twenty-five years – has been achieved through venerable techniques: polemical projects, provocative buildings and books. Like Le Corbusier. Or Palladio.

Koolhaas's biography is critical. Born in Rotterdam in 1944, he spent part of his childhood in Indonesia, then worked as a journalist on the *Haagse Post* and as a freelance film scriptwriter before studying at the Architectural Association in London. His masterly handling of all media – the antithesis of architectural theory – is based on knowledge and an ability to write suggestively with utter lucidity. He formed OMA – the Office for Metropolitan Architecture – in 1975 with Elia and Zoe Zenghelis and Madelon Vriesendorp.

But he was sole author of *Delirious New York* (1978), one of the most brilliant and influential architectural books of the late twentieth century. Using Surrealist techniques, Koolhaas presents Manhattan as a spectacular architectural project, continuously swallowing earlier versions of itself, inventing the 'culture of congestion'. It is fantastically illustrated with New York history, interpretations of existing buildings like the Downtown Athletics Club, and OMA speculations like the Welfare Palace Hotel.

OMA's hugely discussed competition entry for the Parc de La Villette in Paris (1982) laid this Manhattan density on its side to form a stripe-planned park with a skyscraper's density of activities – but without the building. It won the jury's special prize but not the commission, though its forms and ideas are still copied in projects around the world.

But buildings came fast. In brilliant projects like the Kunsthal in Rotterdam (1992), the Villa Dall'Ava, Paris (1991), or his House in Bordeaux (1998), Koolhaas quoted, flipped and teased Modernism, overturning its structural logic and strait-laced ethics, reconfiguring it to become ironic and lovely. His ramped spaces, folded floors, juxtaposed programmes and mix of cheap and expensive materials have percolated the world. Even in his buildings he remains an architect of ideas. In some cases – the masterplan and congress building for Lille (1994) – the ideas are stronger than the buildings.

'Bigness' became a key concept in his books as well, outdoing Deconstructivist distress as the new generation both embraced and criticized the commercial world. Most famous of his increasingly massive later books was *S,M,L,XL* (1995). Part polemic, part project resume, part diary, its scope and graphic collage style were extensively imitated.

Koolhaas is sometimes criticized for cynicism, for acknowledging the failure of the Utopian project and embracing its popular commercial vanquisher, for making brilliant analyses of the Pearl River Delta or shopping and then swanning off to design Prada a flagship. But his razor-sharp self-awareness and proactive exploration of exactly these changing conditions of the world order keep him way ahead of the game.

Rem Koolhaas

k

120-121

Léon Krier is architecture's King Canute, vainly attempting to hold back the sea of Modernism, of modernity even. He has saved himself from drowning by setting up little islands of toytown classicism, helped in his task by a powerful patron – the future King Charles III of England.

Although Krier has built, he is much more of a polemicist, promoting the virtues of the traditional city and history in place of the 'kill the street' instincts of the high moderns. He maintains his position through small exemplars, ideal projects, writing and wonderfully evocative sketches.

Krier was born in Luxembourg in 1946 but moved for some time in London circles, teaching his 'New Urbanism' at the Royal College of Art and the Architectural Association. His architect brother, Rob Krier, has been following a similarly traditional path although his forms are not as directly classical. In the early 1970s Léon worked in James Stirling's office (not such an unlikely combination when you look at Stirling's No. 1 Poultry), before putting his own (unbuilt) proposals forward for the centres of Leinfelden and Bremen in Germany, Warsaw, Washington, DC, and Rome.

In the UK Krier has had the chance to put his theories into practice at a large scale in the masterplanning of the new community of Poundbury in Dorset (1991), on land owned by Prince Charles. Poundbury is an attempt to create instant history, with twisting and turning streets and neoclassical and neovernacular houses built on the very front edge of the plot in order to recall traditional village morphology. But Krier's design for a Gothic

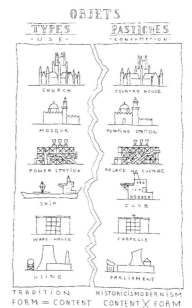

Léon Krier

market cross as the visual focal point of Poundbury is one of his many
thousands of paper schemes not to be realized.

This is probably less troubling to him than is his failure in the late
1980s to resurrect Atlantis on Tenerife in the form of a fantastical holiday
resort for a client there. Krier designed both the masterplan and the curious
mythological-looking buildings of the hill town – part-Italianate, part-Aldo
Rossi, and part something darker. The scheme was celebrated in full colour
images that are beguiling but rather frightening in their desire to control
the occupants' entire experience of their physical environment. It is for this
kind of totality that Krier has been highly critical of Modernism. Altogether
lighter are his buildings at Seaside, Florida, a similarly escapist community.
His charming clapboard belvedere (1988) is crowned by two timber loggias.

Krier may appear doomed to failure in his war with the moderns
but he has had more influence than he thinks, with contemporary architects
increasingly willing to look at traditional morphologies in their planning
even as they reject a historicist vocabulary for their buildings. Krier himself
has pondered whether to build a workable townscape using traditional
layouts but buildings that employ the grammar of Le Corbusier, Frank Lloyd
Wright or even Zaha Hadid to show the moderns how urban design should
be done. And although only one part of Poundbury is complete (Middle
Farm), the commercial success of the scheme suggests that more of Krier's
vision will be built.

k

Top left: Housing at St
Dizier, Marnaval Sud, 1997

Top right: Utrecht
Academy, 1985

Bottom left: MéMé,
Louvain-la-Neuve, 1977

Bottom right: MéMé,
Louvain-la-Neuve, 1977

Lucien Kroll's work has been called 'the denial of architecture'. His ground-breaking participation project at Louvain University was called 'war surplus materials, discarded on the battlefield after the defeat of the avant-garde'. In the 1970s and 1980s he was one of the key radical figures challenging the ruthless militarism of Modernism and was the inventor of a whole series of methodologies for collaborating with users. If he is out of the limelight today, it is partly because he is still doing what he has always done.

Kroll is outspoken in opposition to 'barbaric modernity' where environments are regimented and dehumanized by the aggrandizement of mass production: 'The functional no longer functions,' he says, and 'repetition is a crime'. Born in 1927, he studied architecture and city planning in Brussels and set up practice there in 1957, his buildings quickly moving from informal Modernism to his fast-evolving methods of specific collaboration. His Benedictine Abbey in Rwanda (1963) and his early housing complex in Auderghem (1975), which includes his own house and office, immediately began to develop techniques for extensive collaboration.

But it was at Louvain University that this process attracted most attention, at the beginning of the 1970s. The students of the university objected to the rigid planning and lack of local integration of their new purpose-built campus. As a compromise, they were allowed to choose their own architect for the Medical Faculty Housing. An extraordinarily fluid collaborative process produced an equally extraordinary building, the MéMé (1977), with residential and welfare facilities including a primary school. The scheme was designed to be so flexible that residents could choose and adapt their room's size, shape, height, windows, and whether facilities were communal. (One tall student made a small room 7 metres tall.)

The building was planned on a 100-millimetre grid, corresponding to traditional masonry construction. Servicing had to be fixed, but Kroll only gave up the idea of flexible central heating because the engineers panicked. The 'wandering column' grid was essential – Kroll was adamant that structural rigidity repressed use and experience. The workforce, too, were drawn in, asked to pattern brickwork and blockwork however they liked. They had to turn off their radios to concentrate on their work.

Inevitably, the process was not all to the authorities' liking; Kroll was eventually fired by the university, though he was invited back years later. But others were keen. At the Utrecht Academy (1985) huge rough holes were cut through the interiors of two old schools, creating a cosy junkyard bombsite of an institution, transgressing and charming its parent building. Most of Kroll's projects have been housing – some gradually forming a whole new district, some attempting to make over – or, as he would say, 'dislocate' – the surrealist, brutal world of existing housing estates.

Aesthetically these projects are an oddity, though less shocking now than they were in their iconoclastic heyday. Some are decidedly picturesque, like the housing at St Dizier (1997); some are ugly; yet all, as commentators have noted, are recognizably Kroll. This is curious in such a flexible process – but may be inherent in the nature of architecture.

Lucien Kroll

k

Kisho Kurokawa, still, at nearly seventy, one of Japan's most prolific and successful architects, began his career in the destruction that marked the beginning of the nuclear age and swiftly emerged into the creativity of the space age. While in the UK of the 1960s the Archigram group theorized about plug-in cities and buildings, Kurokawa actually built some of these dreams. His astonishingly avant-garde Nakagin Capsule Tower in Tokyo (1972) has detachable pods like giant washing machines clipped to a double core, designed to be updateable and replaceable as the building grew and changed. The tower remains an icon of its time and of the Metabolist movement that he jointly founded.

Born in Nagoya in 1934, Kurokawa trained in architecture at Kyoto University, graduating in 1957, and then, during his studies at the University of Tokyo, became a protégé and collaborator of Kenzo Tange. He was involved in Tange's fantastical project to extend the city of Tokyo into its bay on a series of artificial islands, and went on to promote his own ideas in projects such as Helix City and Space City at the beginning of the 1960s. The Metabolism movement had arrived.

Metabolism may have had aesthetic and functional similarities to the nascent high-tech movement in Western Europe but it was something different. In his philosophical writings Kurokawa has been keen to separate himself from the building-as-a-machine approach that informed mainstream Modernism. His work looked to the organic and even the mystical – the Age of Life Principle, which saw buildings and cities as living organisms with a life cycle, rather than as extensions of the industrial machine. Like Tange and other post-war Japanese architects, he was searching for a distinctively Japanese attitude to modernity.

Although the Metabolists as a formal group did not survive the early 1970s, Kurokawa has maintained his distinctive approach, building on these early principles. His book, *The Philosophy of Symbiosis* (1987), moves Metabolism on and takes the view that buildings and cities should 'enhance the ambivalent, heterogeneous nature of man', looking to history, culture and technology in the search for 'intermediacy' or *engawa* – the space in between: the overlap of artifice and nature, the past and the future. If that sounds like a recipe for anything goes, it sort of is. Buildings from this later phase are either agglomerations of disparate elements (the 1988 Nagoya City Art Museum, which looks like a marriage of Richard Meier's framework grid and James Stirling's Postmodernism) or amorphous forms and geometric solids such as cones and cubes ('abstract symbolism' he calls it) as seen at the Ehime Museum of Science (1994). Both buildings are in Japan and the bulk of Kurokawa's work remains there but he has worked across Asia and Europe producing varied projects such as the 1999 extension to Amsterdam's Van Gogh Museum, the Japanese-German centre in Berlin (1998), and, now at an early stage, a new capital for the former Soviet republic of Kazakhstan.

Although his theories may be becoming more impenetrable, it appears as if computers are allowing a closer connection than ever between Kurokawa's spiralling thoughts and their expression through architecture.

Kisho Kurokawa

k

There is something of the prodigal son about Peter Davidson, one half
of the duo who make up Lab Architecture Studio. Davidson and Donald
Bates, a Texan then fresh from working on Daniel Libeskind's Jewish Museum
in Berlin, formed the practice in London in 1994, grafting away on a series
of small-scale projects while both of them taught at London's elite
Architectural Association.

Then they achieved the sort of big break that is now becoming
increasingly rare for unproven practices: they won the Federation Square
project in Melbourne – a vast arts complex on a new deck above train tracks
that links the city's grid with the River Yarra. In 1997 they upped sticks and
set up practice in Melbourne. It was home in a blaze of glory for Davidson.
It must have helped having Libeskind on the Federation Square jury (what
luck!) but Lab have justified the award by their own achievement.

Peter Davidson, born in Australia in 1955, trained at the New
South Wales Institute of Technology in Sydney before moving to London,
while Bates, born in 1953, trained at Houston and then Cranbrook under
Libeskind. The influences of the latter, as well as European engineering,
fine artists and the theoretical hothouses of the London architecture schools,
have made themselves felt and Federation Square is the result. Its galleries,
cinemas, restaurants, atrium and television studios are wrapped in a crystalline skin of zinc, glass and stone panels with a pattern generated by fractal
geometry. Completed in 2002, it is one of the best buildings Australia has
seen in many years and brought Deconstructivism Down Under.

Like Zaha Hadid, Lab are part of a deeply theoretical generation of post-Postmodernist architects who have finally been able to build their ideas. The pair have already come close to winning two other major projects that would have confirmed their reputation: a new art gallery in Queensland, Australia (2002), and a BMW plant in Leipzig, Germany (2002). Both schemes have much in common with Federation Square: chromosome filaments of structure weave in and out of each other to create spaces and interstitial spaces; at Queensland, Federation Square's crystalline face becomes a prism.

Some critics have argued that the beauty of the work is skin deep, proffering façades that bear little relationship to the spaces within. But for Lab this is a conscious decision. They have rejected the orthogonal, the expression of the interior and the exterior, and also hierarchical elevation composition as a pattern book of pseudorationality imposed by the high moderns. There is barely a vertical or horizontal line to be seen in their work. The comparison they make is with the human body – 'a fabulous mask' that conceals the viscera within. Lab pursue more painterly concerns – flow, collage, uncertainty – as well as the more abiding architectural preoccupation with sequential spatial experience.

Federation Square in many ways reflects a desire in Melbourne for an icon that rivals Jørn Utzon's Sydney Opera House. Lab are too subtle for that, and their fragmented scheme can be seen as an anti-icon. They are not interested in offering the easy comfort of a coherent whole. Life is more complex than that.

Top left: House at Lège-Cap-
Ferret, 1998

Bottom left: House at Lège-
Cap-Ferret, 1998

Bottom right: Latapie House,
France, 1993

Top right: Palais de Tokyo,
Paris, 2002

Lacaton Vassal is one of the best French architecture practices working today. This may not be the highest accolade in the world, with French architecture languishing a little behind its intimidating neighbours in Switzerland, Spain and Belgium, but Lacaton Vassal is a truly individual voice and truly world class.

Characterizing their architecture is difficult, but every building has in common a desire to do the most possible with the smallest resources, budgetary or material. Born in 1955 and 1954 respectively, Anne Lacaton and Jean-Philippe Vassal met at architecture school in Bordeaux, where they both graduated in 1980. Their formative experience was the five years they spent in Niger, Africa, working as town planners. There they learnt how to make a building function in extremes of temperature, but also how to appropriate technologies for other uses.

On their return, their first jobs of note were one-off houses, all of which had extremely tight budgets. One of the first of these was the Latapie House at Floirac (1993), a low-budget project comprising a simple volume on a square base. The metal frame is part-clad in PVC sheets, forming a kind of conservatory and providing generosity of space on a budget. The house is also open to the landscape with large sliding doors at each end.

This oneness with the natural context was further explored in a house at Lège-Cap-Ferret, completed in 1998 on a densely wooded site. The architects resolved to fell no trees during construction. Thus the house is built around the trees, with trunks rising through the living areas. It has the look of an elevated Miesian box, but with a certain impermanence and sensitivity lent by the cheap corrugated perspex cladding.

Their house in Coutras (2000) is also a great example of their willingness to use unconventional technologies, in this case greenhouse frames and glazing. For using ready-made components unaltered, this approach has been called minimalist by some critics; for Lacaton Vassal these materials offer a solution that is 'as simple as possible, but not more so', to borrow a quote from Albert Einstein.

The practice's most high-profile project, the reconditioning of the Palais de Tokyo in Paris (2002), is an object lesson in how to do a lot with a little. Overlooking the Eiffel Tower, the building was almost derelict. Lacaton Vassal had just 2,500 francs per square metre to make the space into a venue for art. The then Bordeaux-based practice moved its office into the Palais, the design team gradually growing as artists, curators and collaborators joined them among the dust and dereliction. Their experience of the bustling square of Djemaa el-Fna in Marrakech was the inspiration for a space that is required to allow a constant state of improvisation. To this end, Lacaton Vassal retained an open floor plate that is intended to facilitate a live laboratory of contemporary art.

It would be fascinating to see what Lacaton Vassal might do with a bigger budget. They consistently maintain, however, that they have no interest in generous budgets. It seems that for a while yet their work will remain the architecture world's version of thrift-store chic.

Lacaton Vassal

l

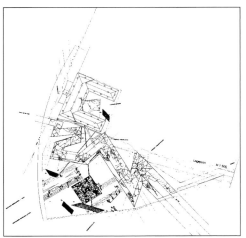

Daniel Libeskind's Jewish Museum in Berlin has redefined how architecture can appeal to the emotions as well as the senses. Libeskind is the consummate architect of memory and the symbolism of memory. That he is skilled at the drawing out of emotion should be no surprise. His earliest career was as a child prodigy virtuoso accordion player. Born in 1946, in the aftermath of the Holocaust, into a Jewish family in Lodz, Poland, Libeskind emigrated as a child to Israel and then New York – he still recalls arriving by boat and being greeted by the Statue of Liberty. He trained in music in Israel then graduated from New York's Cooper Union architecture school in 1970.

In the quintessential path of the avant-garde, he spent many years as a theoretician and educator. His famous early drawings remain mind-blowing classics. In 1989 he won the competition for the Jewish Museum and set up his practice in Berlin. His early talks described its relationship to Arnold Schoenberg, the vanished names of the Holocaust, the houses of famous Jewish Berliners. His later talks waxed eloquent about window details. The project took many years to complete but even before any exhibits had been moved in the building had 300,000 visitors and became a critical and popular sensation. Its central void, complex ramps, angles and disorientating spaces, generated in plan by the symbol of a fractured Star of David, defined Deconstructivist shape-making as something essentially profound. The yawning chamber that is its climactic element is a haunting evocation of imprisonment, totalitarianism, fear and loss.

The success of the project, which officially opened in 2001, led rapidly to other commissions: the Felix Nussbaum Museum in Osnabrück, Germany (1998), and the Imperial War Museum's northern outpost in Salford, UK (2002). Here too, there is one overriding symbol: a shattered globe. The building is made up of interlocking shards of a world destroyed by conflict. In the hands of a less skilled architect such an imposing metaphor could easily have become a one-liner.

But his conceptual intensity is not confined to traumatic commissions: he has designed an extension to the Denver Art Museum and one of the planet's biggest shopping centres outside Berne in Switzerland, the latter with a commercial zest that rocked some of his fans and amused his critics. The philosophy and mathematical beauty of classical music inform his project for the Victoria & Albert Museum in London, with its fractal tiling, just as Modernist twelve-tone music informed his Jewish Museum.

Libeskind was the (almost cynically) perfect architect to lead the rebuilding of the World Trade Center after the 11 September attacks. His response is a 1,776-feet-high lacy spire – he is always one for good mathematical content – to be the world's tallest building, with a sunken memorial garden created out of the foundations of one of the destroyed towers. He is fiercely ambitious and fought hard (some would say dirty) to win the job.

With his childlike, explosive, theoretical, enthusiastic persona, Libeskind is a top favorite with the world's highbrow media. Performer, thinker, communicator and battler, he remains the same performer he was as a child prodigy playing on Polish television at the age of six.

Daniel Libeskind

L

There are prodigies and then there is Maya Lin. In 1981, as a twenty-one-year-old undergraduate at Yale University, Lin was the winner against over 1,500 entrants of the high-profile competition to design the Vietnam Veterans' Memorial in Washington, DC. This was an event equivalent in the art and architecture world to child stardom for a movie star. Despite the substantial body of work she has produced since, Lin will be remembered always as the designer of the Vietnam memorial.

The design is a right-angled slash in the earth, with two retaining walls 247 feet high in polished black granite inscribed with the names of the 57,661 US service personnel who died in the Vietnam War. The names are arranged in the chronological order in which the individuals died – 'like a thread of life,' Lin says – and the text is justified ragged right like the pages of a book.

This understated and profoundly moving memorial, widely praised today, caused huge controversy at the time. A campaign was led to replace the monument with a conventional cenotaph or to alter its stark black stone to white. From the moment she received the commission in 1981,

Lin faced racism, sexism and a host of leftfield objections, but the strength of the project prevailed, despite the authorities' decision to construct an additional, traditional monument to assuage the vocal minority.

Lin did all she could to escape this bitterness, even going to work as a student architect at a low-profile practice in Boston in 1983, but could not be out of the limelight for long. She made a series of other memorials in the 1980s and 1990s, including the 'Women's Table' monument at Yale University and the Civil Rights Memorial in Montgomery, Alabama, before turning her back on memorial making. Her subsequent body of work – both art and architecture – is influenced by her eclectic background as a daughter of Chinese immigrants to the US, brought up in the Midwest, studying architecture and sculpture at university and working in the offices of Richard Serra – the quintessential architect's sculptor – and Frank Gehry before graduating in 1986. Lin says that architecture and art to her are two sides of the same discipline: 'Sculpture to me is like poetry; architecture is like prose,' she says.

Her architectural work ranges from some very average good-taste interiors – the nice but dull Norton Apartment in New York (1998) – to audacious architectural interventions, such as Langston Hughes Library in Clinton, Tennessee (1999). This project took a hundred-year-old barn and literally lifted it on top of two timber supports, making a strangely twisted bit of vernacular. The interior is clad in maple and is carpeted, a treatment that has little relationship to the exterior.

Lin is perhaps one of the most prominent people currently making both art and architecture and being taken seriously in each discipline. Her art remains more engaging than her buildings, and the Vietnam Veterans' Memorial is the US's most popular piece of public art, launching a whole new way of thinking about memorializing death and destruction. It would be staggering if she were not called upon again when memorials are commissioned for the 11 September bombings. Her brand of minimalism would be a fitting memorial to those highly emotive events.

Maya Lin

L

134-135

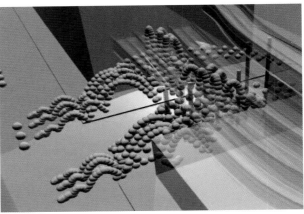

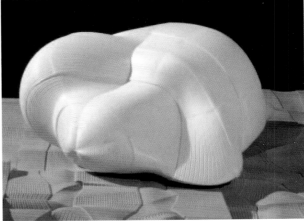

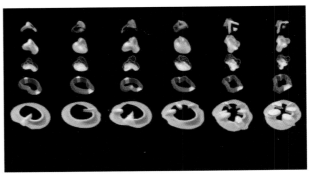

Left: Kleiburg
housing renewal project,
Amsterdam, ongoing

Top right: Port Authority
Gateway project,
Manhattan, 1995

Centre right: Embyrological
space, ongoing

Bottom right: Embyrological
space, ongoing

Greg Lynn glories in the title of Professor of Spatial Conception and Exploration. Well, that is when he is teaching in Zurich, rather than at Columbia University, New York, or one of his many other teaching positions. He also thinks that 'architecture remains as the last refuge for members of the flat-earth society'. Lynn is entitled to have an opinion or two, as one of the sharpest minds in architecture today while still under forty (he was born in 1964). He graduated in philosophy and environmental design before training as an architect at Princeton until 1988. Following stints in the offices of Peter Eisenman and Antoine Predock, he has been stretching and bending forms as only a computer-age Californian can.

Architecture, he argues, is too static and does not make use of the abilities of animation – movement, growth, change (in biological models for instance) – to formulate its spaces, sticking instead to gravity-bound Cartesian grids. Boat builders, he points out, deal with forces such as turbulence, flow and viscosity. This is way beyond the shape-making of Frank Gehry, which uses computers to generate new static forms: Lynn is looking at buildings that live and breath like organisms. The discipline, Lynn suggests, needs to start making use of the virtual in order to conceive of the possible. Crucially, though, Lynn marries this to a pragmatic exploration of the techniques of industrial design and fabrication – moulding for example. Technology now allows us affordable bespoke and adaptable solutions rather than fixed and depersonalized mass production – the myriad forms of training shoes are a favoured analogy. Architecture can literally push the envelope and use techniques such as continuous single-surface skins.

It has been hard for Lynn to put these developing ideas into practice, however. The Korean Presbyterian Church of New York (1999), an adaptation of an old laundry on which he worked in collaboration with McInturf and Garofalo Architects, is hardly demonstrative. He did do a refit for a now defunct dot.com business in Sweden (pglife.com) in 2000, but other projects such as the Hydrogen House in Vienna (1996) have yet to bear fruit. Apart, that is, from coffee and teapots for Alessi.

Instead, his ideas have been explored through competition entries such as the 1995 Port Authority Gateway project in Manhattan, which used modelling of pedestrian and vehicle flows to generate a set of force fields that gave rise to tensile enclosures around the existing ramps of the bus station. Lynn also developed a domestic house type in the mid-1990s with a wood particle and plastic surface comprising thousands of panels digitally connected so that when one changes the others adapt accordingly. This 'embryological' space uses a flexible skin that has adaptable openings, more like orifices than conventional doors and windows. More prosaically, Lynn is working on the remodelling of a block of Modernist flats in Amsterdam, using a series of escalators to reconnect them to the city. Although the project looks exciting, it is hard to see how Lynn's more advanced ideas can be retro-fitted to an existing building.

It is no wonder Lynn has begun exploring his ideas through writing science fiction: they may soon become science fact.

Greg Lynn

L

Top left: Hillside, Tokyo,
ongoing

Top right: Gymnasium,
Fujisawa, 1984

Bottom: Tokyo Metropolitan
Gymnasium, 1990

There is a big difference between how you might see Fumihiko Maki's buildings from a distance – huge, dramatic, monumental, or Expressionist – and Maki's sensitive, psychological descriptions of them. In his writings he explores the shared consciousness of form in Modernist and traditional architecture, and even the largest of his many huge projects enact these ideas. 'Perhaps the architect is pursued by his own inner landscape and spends his life constructing the scenery for it,' he says.

The first layer of Maki's inner landscape comes from his childhood in Tokyo where he was born in 1928: low wooden houses, the shadows of trees, the smell of earth, dark vacant properties. His Modernism is infused with Japanese ideas of change and accretion, adopting half-remembered configurations, adjusted to its culture, specific to its place. Yet he is also seen as a strong proponent of international Modernism in Japan, undoubtedly influenced by his years at Harvard.

Maki's first and longest-running job does demonstrate a Modernism of accretion. He started work on the Hillside Terrace project in Tokyo in 1967 and was still adding to it thirty-five years later. His original residential area of small-scale white units with its complex sequence of spaces has been extended in size and scale with changing materials and zoning laws but retains its 'non-assertive' identity. It has become more mixed in programme, gaining shops, a gallery and concert hall as well as the neighbouring Danish embassy. Maki's office and his daughter's home are there too.

But larger, more dramatic buildings brought Maki to international prominence. He was a founding member of the Metabolists, where he coined the term 'megastructure.' His larger projects are consistently integrated into the urban fabric, fusing new technology with rationalism. Many of the most famous buildings he went on to design are vast yet their great scale is founded on traditional and human models, and always meticulously detailed. Despite this, in some cases it is the expressive forms that grab the attention. His gymnasium in Fujisawa, with its huge, stainless-steel roof, evokes both medieval knights' helmets or a spaceship. The Tokyo Metropolitan Gymnasium (1990) is an elegant composition of massive forms with a vast, iconic 'beetle' roof over the main arena.

Despite the vast scale of the projects – still mainly in Japan although he has built the Yerba Buena Center for the Arts in San Francisco (1993) and a floating pavilion in Groningen, the Netherlands (1996) – Maki's descriptions sound ephemeral. He sees architecture as a visiting 'presence' that can take up residence but also leave a building if culture, values and the collective unconscious change. In the West, his larger expressionistic works remain less known, and critics' reactions range from critical regionalism to mannered functionalism. But Maki calls himself a Modernist – in Japan, Modernism was not divorced from tradition and the allusions reintroduced in the West through Postmodernism were always present. 'The ultimate aim of architecture,' he says, ' is to make spaces to serve society.' While the size of some projects may seem antithetical to these sensitive aims, to Maki such concerns are never left behind.

Fumihiko Maki

m

Top left: Roman Catholic
Church, Paks, 1990

Main picture: Farkasrét
Mortuary, 1975

Bottom right: Hungarian
Pavilion, Seville Expo, 1992

Western critics (with some exceptions) are not normally into deeply symbolic spiritual architecture, so Imre Makovecz does not figure heavily in Western publications. In Hungary he is simply the most famous architect there is, responsible for the rebirth of a whole new version of Hungarian romantic, organic and genuinely weird architecture.

The Makovecz story is extraordinary. Born in 1935, he trained and worked in Hungary's Soviet era, when architects could practise for the state alone and the only architecture on offer was Russian-prefabricated inter-nationalism. Yet even his early work is definitively organic, anthropomorphic and very idiosyncratic. This did not give him an easy ride. Countering Soviet internationalizing of Hungarian villages, he worked for free to ensure that Zalaszentlaslo village centre (1982) was a vision, as he says, of what might have been. He built the project, lost his job and architect's licence but won a completely unexpected freedom. As contractor for the Visegrad Forest Centre (1982), working with local craftsmen, he designed an extraordinary range of buildings – notably ablution rooms based on the Hungarian *yurt* – with layers of symbolic complexity. Interlocking forms open to a heart-shaped hole in the roof, with totems of male and female organs triumphantly aloft, the female side buried in grass, a crown emerging from the top.

Makovecz's dark, unfettered symbolism became more and more popular as Hungarian economic and cultural freedom grew. He has built projects – churches, houses, community centres, hotels – all over Hungary. One of the most famous remains his Farkasrét Mortuary (1975), where the timber structure resembles a human ribcage in which the funerary bier is placed in the position of the heart. Another, the Siófok Church (1990), was conceived as the mask of God or an ancient Celtic warrior. The mask, Makovecz explains, allows the wearer to undergo a transubstantiation.

Makovecz's uncensored expression is always meaningful. He uses trees, sometimes structurally, and eagles, angels and helmets. In his church at Paks (1990) the spire suggests the heart emerging from the body. The main building is seen as a huge pregnant belly, with door as vagina through which the population emerge reborn. His biggest international outing was the Hungarian Pavilion for the Seville Expo in 1992. The characteristic humped spine of a roof was slit diagonally and pierced with seven towers, the symbolic crossings from East to West expressed inside and a dead tree, roots and all, suspended in the glass floor. He was proud that his Hungarian craftsmen were poached to sort out high-tech problems elsewhere.

Makovecz cites Bruce Goff and Frank Lloyd Wright as sources, fused with a deeply indigenous Magyar and Celtic culture and the belief that his symbolism can evoke some kind of earlier version of the world. 'Our build-ings evoke an ancient, often dark atmosphere; the murmuring of long-dead beings can be heard from the walls; our domes cover us like sky; the plaster motifs of the folk art of our now-dispossessed ethnic group metamorphose into spatial frameworks; our ancestors, chased out of our consciousness, surge forward to speak to us,' he says (Edwin Heathcote, *Imre Makovecz: The Wings of the Soul*, Wiley-Academy, 1997). Not for the fainthearted.

Imre Makovecz

m

Top left: Vila Olimpica,
Barcelona, 1992

Top right: Guardiola House,
Argentona, 1955

Bottom left: Parque
de la Creueta del Coll,
Barcelona, 1987

Centre right: Europalma
Apartments, Majorca, 1964

From a distance, you might think that the only thing for which MBM are famous – and deservedly so – is the reworking of Barcelona for the 1992 Olympics, making the city one of the world's greatest cultural destinations and latterday planning models. But this was the apogee of a broad, influential career.

Josep Martorell and Oriol Bohigas graduated in Barcelona in 1951, setting up practice in 1958, joined by English–Irish David Mackay, who became a partner in 1962. The practice was almost the only exponent of Modernism under Franco's Fascist regime, establishing international connections and fostering many of the young architects who later made up Barcelona's strong design scene. The partners also wrote, edited, published and lectured, becoming strong exponents of critical regionalism – Modernism developed for local culture and conditions, in this case both the varied Spanish vernacular and the extraordinary Catalan Modernism of Gaudí's intricate fantasy work. MBM's work retained its rationalism, adapted to Spain's differing regions and climates, and built up a strong, varied strand of European Modernism. The Modernist Guardiola House in Argentona (1955) and many schools, libraries, churches and housing projects stand out. And when Franco died, MBM were in pole position, not just as architects but as key public figures in Barcelona's cultural and planning life.

Barcelona and MBM harnessed the Olympic development drive and ferocious time pressure to transform the city itself. In their civic role, MBM remastered Barcelona, cutting new squares into the crowded residential areas, adding major cultural facilities. As architects, they designed the Vila Olimpica and Olympic port, extending Ildefonso Cerdá's famous grid plan down to the Mediterranean coast to create a new area, planned as a residential and commercial district once the athletes had gone.

Barcelona's reworking was a spectacular success. Integrated with its main Olympic facilities, the city was left with better, more numerous public spaces, with a mass of cultural buildings animating the traditional areas, and housing, hospitals, offices and telecommunications facilities designed by big names – Norman Foster's telecommunications tower, Richard Meier's museum – or by local architects, including MBM. Sports facilities and parks regenerated the suburban areas – notably Enric Miralles' archery range and MBM's own Creueta dell Coll, one of the best of the new suburban parks.

Barcelona virtually invented the European urban renaissance of the late twentieth century as city after city tried to follow its lead. In 1999 it became the first city to win the RIBA's Gold Medal. For MBM it was part of an ongoing workload. They have built more than 500 projects all over the world, including the eccentric and technically amazing Gothic stone and tensile pavilion for the Seville Expo in 1992 and examples of their more classic regional Modernism. And, sensibly, they have been brought in to work on urban design projects all round the world – Bute Avenue in Cardiff (1995), Benidorm seafront (1996), Girona (2001), Rio de Janeiro (1997) and Salerno (1996). But it is for Barcelona that they will – and should – be remembered.

MBM

m

Getty Center, Los
Angeles, 1997

Richard Meier has now become one of the rotund elder statesmen of world architecture. He has won almost every honour there is to win and designed the major public facilities that are the plum commissions of a successful career. As is the way with many elder statesmen he was once a Young Turk – one of the 'New York Five', led by Peter Eisenman with Charles Gwathmey, John Hejduk and Michael Graves. Prominent in the late 1960s and 1970s, the group was nicknamed 'The Whites' for the clean, unadorned surfaces of their architecture and the classic white render they used as their principal exterior material. In contrast to the other members of the group, Meier remains the quintessential white-render Modernist.

On accepting the Pritzker Prize in 1984, he explained his enthusiasm for this non-colour: 'The whiteness of white is never just white; it is almost always transformed by light and that which is changing: the sky, the clouds, the sun and the moon' – a soaring, poetic pretension, but beloved of late-Modernist architects.

The key to understanding Meier's work is his interest in Le Corbusier, whose purist villas, such as the Villa Savoye, formed a starting point for buildings that are immensely complex and rich in plan. Meier's early houses – Essex Fells in New Jersey (1963) and the Smith House in Darien, Connecticut (1965) – are villas for architecture's sake and seminal US Modernist buildings.

It is Meier's museums that took him to prominence. The High Museum of Art in Atlanta (1983) and the Atheneum in New Harmony, Indiana (1979), are very different but both characteristic. The processional entrance ramp of the former and the prominent switchback stairs and ramps of the latter stress a functionally superfluous but formally expressive architectural idiom. Naturally, the exteriors are blinding white.

Meier was successful in the 1984 competition for the Getty Center in Los Angeles, considered by some at the time to be the most important architectural commission of the century – a judgement that has not entirely stood its ground. But this was Meier's big project. He confounded expectations and used a golden Italian travertine stone, creating a huge castle-like arts complex on a 45-hectare hilltop site overlooking the city. That a building on this scale was built at all, let alone with such complexity, is remarkable. It is not universally popular, but remains high-quality, heroic architecture.

Meier is now feeling older, he says. The youngest architect to win the Pritzker (forty-nine in 1984), at approaching seventy, he has seen an early building demolished: the Bronx Developmental Center, a futuristic, aluminium-clad mental health clinic in New York, completed in 1977 and hailed on completion as 'a consummate work of architecture – among the great complexes of our time', has submitted to the wrecker's ball. However, he is still very active, with prestigious commissions such as the Church of the Year 2000 in Rome confirming his enduring popularity. The objects he designs, white and shimmering, announce themselves as Architecture with a capital A. His Modernist vocabulary has spawned a hundred thousand imitators. But not many do it better.

Richard Meier

m

Top left: Igualada Cemetery,
Barcelona, 1992

Bottom: Olympic Archery
Range, Barcelona, 1992

Top right: Casa La Clota,
Barcelona, 1999

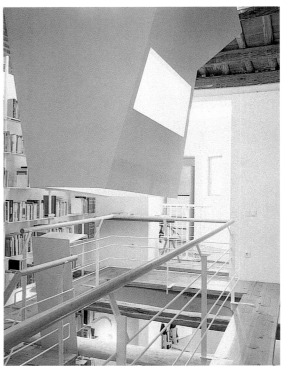

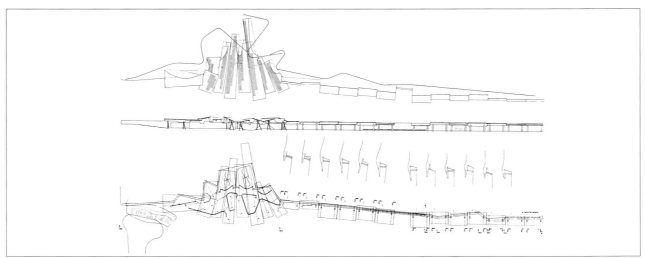

Enric Miralles' death in 2000 of a brain tumour was one of contemporary architecture's great tragedies. Almost the defining figure in Barcelona's extraordinary architectural efflorescence of the 1980s and 1990s, Miralles had moved from admired paper architect directly to internationally famous projects. The practice, now led by his second wife, Benedetta Tagliabue, is operating in the world league and is watched with extreme interest.

Almost every book on anyone 'Deconstructivist' starts by explaining why the label is inappropriate. Miralles had no theoretical extrapolations, violent anti-establishment angst or high critical theory. Yet his mass of exquisite drawings – which look ambiguous but are direct instructions on what to build – are in the Deconstructivist heartland. His projects are certainly not aggressive: they are unashamedly poetic and exuberant. But the swirling, jagged forms are the headline not the whole substance of the work.

Miralles was born in 1955 in Barcelona and studied at its Technical University, graduating in 1978. He worked with Helio Pinon and Alberto Viaplana from 1973 to 1984 on designs and competitions. And from the first his fantastic drawings became forceful physical objects – sometimes less refined than the drawings. His partnership with first wife Carme Pinós, from 1983 to 1990, produced iconic early works such as Els Hostalets de Balenyá Civic Centre near Barcelona (1994), with its extraordinary curved section, and, most famously, the Olympic Archery Range (1992) and Igualada Cemetery, near Barcelona (1992), where Miralles is buried.

The famous formal drama of the archery range, in a scattered, mountainous Barcelona suburb, is not actually its best feature. Its brilliance – like all Miralles' work – is in the translation of the spidery, ambiguous drawings to minute details of structure, tiles or concrete formwork markings. The slash-cut doors of the civic centre at La Mina (1985), the sloping gap between roof and handrail in the boarding school at Morella (1985), the relation of roof truss to mountain in the National Training Centre for Rhythmic Gymnastics, Alicante (1993) are what transfigure such projects.

Igualada Cemetery, in the countryside outside Barcelona, is probably the best loved of all these buildings. The traditional forms of the burial casket walls are cut into a kind of false quarry, tilted and twisted – surely one of the quintessential projects of its Expressionist, *fin de siècle* age.

Miralles' work remained spatially dramatic – a typically Catalan trait. One often longs for a good, thorough, edit, as in ongoing projects such as the monumental Scottish Parliament Building, Edinburgh, with its elaborate forms, or the extraordinary roofscape of Santa Caterina Market. Yet the later phase of his work, with Tagliabue, also gained some unexpected and wonderful historical richness – notably the creative gradual restoration of their own house in Barcelona, where layers of old painting and decoration were excavated to form a new composition. Or the Casa La Clota (1999), where old buildings were cut away with new section insertions to form an extraordinarily rich junkyard glory. Many of their exhibition installations also suggest this historical layering. It is this sensitivity to detail that we wait to see in the projects that Tagliabue is pursuing with so much verve.

People say Rafael Moneo is an architect whose work is so specific to the project that he does not have a 'style' at all. Looking at pictures of his work it is hard to credit this: they suggest a powerful aesthetic – a slightly man-nered, Postmodern rationalism. But visiting them, the experience is totally different. It is the setting, the circulation, the sequence of often simple, natural spaces that stays in your mind.

Take his lovely Bodega for the Chivite family's high-profile vine-yard in his native Navarra (2002): photos show the dramatic cubic gateway, the striking rooflines and canopy of the new buildings. Visiting, you are struck by the beauty of the whole place: the exquisite setting of the old buildings framed by the plain new ones, half-hidden in the woods; the drama of the route through the simple, varied spaces, often tucked behind undramatic doorways; and the occasional moments of luxury. It is a treat of unexpected modesty.

Moneo was born in 1937, trained in Madrid and Rome, and worked in Jørn Utzon's Hellebaek office as a young architect. He practises in Madrid and has taught in Madrid, Barcelona and Harvard, where he was chair from 1985 to 1990 and is still professor – one of architectural education's top posts. He won the Pritzker Prize in 1995. Most of his work has been in Spain, where he has built museums, airports, railway stations, banks, housing – you name it. Most famous are his exquisite Museum of Roman Art at Mérida (1986) – which one critic called 'the best European building of the 1980s' – the Miro Foundation in Palma de Majorca (1992); the Thyssen Museum in Madrid (1992); the Kursaal Auditorium and Congress Centre in San Sebastian (1999); and the dramatic canopies of Atocha Station in Madrid (1992). But

he has also worked abroad: the Architecture Museum in Stockholm (1998) and the new Catholic Cathedral in Los Angeles (2002).

The external plainness of many of his buildings is often credited to Nordic influences, and is useful for dealing with these large volumes. They contain highly complex sequences of spaces, specific to site and purpose and rarely visible from the outside. The sequence of interiors can come as a surprise. At the Museum of Roman Art, Moneo explains, the powerful outline helps to 'recover the idea of the vanished Roman town', but it also frames the two theatres on the site. The new arched brick building 'literally adopts Roman construction systems rather than applying moulding and orders', creating a suggestive juxtaposition, where the visitor moves down from the new building to the Roman pavement. In his Los Angeles Catholic Cathedral (2002), there are suggestions of the early buildings of the Spanish Mission, and (of course) an unexpected, dramatic sequence of spaces.

Moneo says that beauty is often ignored in favour of contemporary cultural reflection. This is, he says mildly, 'dangerously close to the arbitrary'. He offers a different, more fundamental architecture based on experience and understanding. His lack of dogma comes, like finding a soaring cathedral of barrels behind a plain door, as a fabulous surprise.

Rafael Moneo

m

148-149

Thom Mayne, co-founder of Morphosis, has been learning from Los Angeles since he set up practice with Jim Stafford in 1972. But it is Mayne's partnership with Michael Rotondi, who joined up shortly afterwards, that led to a famous collaboration. Their difficult split in 1992 (Rotondi went on to set up Roto Architects) gave the practice a new direction and there has been a seismic shift in the office's output since computers came onto the scene and led to exploding building designs by architects along the San Andreas fault and beyond.

Morphosis's detonation is a controlled one, however. The practice's later work (it dumped the drawing board and went over entirely to CAD in 1994) is technologically enabled rather than technologically driven – not the wilful curlicues of other tech-head Californians. Morphosis's beautiful drawings are now joined by beautiful computer renderings.

Their metamorphosis is one of form rather than intent. The practice's two best known earlier works – Cedar's Sinai Cancer Care Center in West Hollywood (1988) and the Crawford House, Montecito (1990) – look, with their ordered axiality, like the work of a different hand from the mouse-driven blades and angled planes of the Diamond Ranch High School in Pomona (2000) or even the earlier California Science Center School in LA (1992). But the work remains embedded in the local, engaged with the landscape and the cultural context of the site and the project – the essence of a place, its history, and the building's programme. The axiality and the orthogonal remain; they have just been digitally distorted to allow a closer orientation to the earth and the elements.

These are long-standing concerns for many architects, and taxonomists have a hard time labelling the practice, given that its formal expression is, well, constantly morphing. Morphosis is too engaged with the real – even if that 'real' is the fractured reality of Los Angeles – to be labelled Deconstructivist; too self-consciously architectonic to be lumped with Frank Gehry's free-reining computer-generated buildings. Morphosis keep the computer on the leash. A regional label is therefore bestowed – the LA school.

There remain familiar concerns: typically the idea of enclosing a site by wrapping the architecture around a central space, be it external or internal, rather than creating a solid block at the core of a site. This is as true of Cedar's Sinai as it is of Diamond Ranch, although the latter has hunkered down, loose-limbed, into the geology of its site, its various heads raised and looking out across the landscape.

The number of education projects is also telling; Morphosis is as much about teaching as learning. With Roto, Mayne helped establish Sci-Arc – the Southern California Institute of Architecture – and he often teaches in schools across the world, including his alma maters, UCLA and Harvard.

Now fifty-eight, Mayne has said that he sees himself as between two generations of architects – those who hold a pencil and those who sit at a keyboard. It is the ability of Morphosis to transcend these generations that results in an architecture that is the product of the computer age without flying off into the virtual and leaving the concrete behind.

Morphosis

m

Top: The Paramount,
Culver City, 1990

Bottom left: The Beehive,
Culver City, 1994

Bottom right: Samitaur
Building, Culver City, 1996

To build a dream building architects tend to need a dream client. Eric Owen Moss has been in dreamland for years with client Frederick Samitaur-Smith, who is as much a collaborator as a patron. Over more than a decade they have steadily been transforming down-at-heel Culver City, Los Angeles, into a showcase for the Moss vision and an exemplar of post-industrial urban regeneration.

Although he does not like the label, Moss is regarded as one of the LA school of architects, along with Frank Gehry, Morphosis and Roto, who coalesced around the Southern California Institute of Architecture (Sci-Arc), where Moss took on the role of director. His own education was at UCLA, Berkeley and then Harvard's Graduate School of Design. He completed his studies in 1972 and headed straight back to LA (he was born there in 1943).

The fateful meeting with Smith came in the mid-1980s. Moss was a tenant of the property developer in a low-rent industrial unit. Smith turned to Moss after a series of architects rejected Smith's proposals for reinventing Culver City by peppering architectural landmarks through the area. Moss said yes and what became known as the Ince Complex grew out of a group of 1940s factory buildings. Among the striking Deconstructivist designs – Moss is keen on chaos theory and likes his buildings ragged – are the Lindblade Building (1990), the Gary Building (1990), the Paramount (an old laundry, 1990), the Beehive (1994) and the Box (1994). The buildings retain their industrial aesthetic, transformed by arty accretions and subtractions around courtyards and under rooflights. The Box went an architectural stage further by thrusting a teetering concrete cube high above the existing building to house a new café. One corner is cut away, a glazed replacement helping to break down the angular form.

As Culver City has come up in the world, the budgets and the projects have got bigger and corporate clients have been led back into the area. The Samitaur Building for Eastman-Kodak (1996) is a case in point. Bridging the road, it is a raised, rectangular megastructure, broken up at one end, where it looks like a series of concrete enclosures that have been stacked on top of each other and had bites taken out of them. Moss's buildings have become less like organic agglomerations of everyday materials and more like refined pieces of architecture, and perhaps some of the quirky joy has been lost in the process. Or maybe it is the move from drawing board to computer (Moss apparently had to be dragged to CAD kicking and screaming) that has resulted in the loss of some of the charm of the earlier projects' rough edges. Or maybe because attempting to 'distress' a new-build scheme like a fake antique instantly destroys any authenticity.

The success of the Culver City experiment has created a platform from which Moss has reached out across the US (including a competition win for Queens Museum of Art, New York) and overseas in Vienna, Spain and France. Culver City is not a coherent whole – that is absolutely not the point – but it has become a singular environment in which to enjoy one architect's developing thesis of how a future city could grow: carefully controlled chaos.

Eric Owen Moss

m

Top: Magney House, Bingie
Point, 1984

Bottom left: Marie Short
House, Kempsey, 1975

Bottom right: Arthur and Yvonne
Boyd Education Centre, New
South Wales, 1999

There are countless thousands of architects who work on their own as sole practitioners, often from home, without anybody taking much notice. There are thousands more whose stock-in-trade is designing private houses in the countryside and suburbs and who have never built a major office building, opera house or shopping centre. You have probably never heard of them.

There is only one architect who fits this bill but also enjoys world-wide acclaim and has become almost synonymous with the architecture of his country: Glen Murcutt. Born in 1936 in London, Murcutt is a private person who unplugs the telephone for a bit of peace and quiet, eschews computers and has never built outside his native Australia or inside its major cities. Yet he has been lauded with all the major architectural prizes, including the 2002 Pritzker, and teaches all over the world.

No wonder people find him hard to work out. He is a Modernist and a rationalist but has an intense relationship with nature, the land and his personal spiritual journey. His work has been described as a 'synthesis of Mies van der Rohe and the Australian woolshed'. He is happy working on his own or with his wife and son – both architects. Murcutt's clients do not pick him: he picks them. And they might still have a five-year wait. Nobody appears to doubt that he is worth waiting for.

What they get is a meticulously crafted orthogonal building where everything down to the last screw head is aligned with the needs of the occupiers, the path of the sun and the moon, the sweep of the landscape. He is an architects' architect. His signature materials are lowly: corrugated iron sheeting, local timber, stone and concrete, transformed into something specifically of its place and of its time. The Aboriginal phrase, to 'touch the earth lightly' informs his ecologically minded buildings. He is in it for the 'joy of the path', describing himself as a 'discoverer' rather than a creator.

Although houses have been his staple since the 1960s, including the Magney House at Bingie Point (1984), the Marie Short House, Kempsey (1975), and the Ball-Eastaway House, Glenorie (1983), an artist's retreat, he recently completed one of his first public buildings for a decade – the Arthur and Yvonne Boyd Education Centre near Sydney (1999). It is the first time he has used *in-situ* concrete, although, of course, it is mounted on piers so that rainwater can soak away below. Its sculptural jutting blades provide shading and a strength appropriate to a public rather than a private building, and it is a long way from the shed stereotype.

Perhaps Murcutt's universal appeal is precisely his specificity. In some ways his work is the polar opposite of Finnish architecture, which he much admires, but the connections are there: when to make the most of the sun and when to keep it out; an architecture that has to address the power of nature in a climate of extremes. Murcutt works with the climate with screens and breezes rather than fighting it with air-conditioning and sealed boxes.

More personal influences are his father and Sigmund Freud, both of whose ideas crop up in his conversation. This is a family business after all even if it has a worldwide reach and imitators. Murcutt ignores it all and, like his beloved Henry David Thoreau, 'marches to the beat of his own drum'.

Glen Murcutt

m

MVRDV is a practice surfing the wave that began in the Netherlands in the early 1990s and it has enjoyed a decade of extraordinary critical hegemony. Its moniker is an abbreviation of the names of partners Winy Maas (born 1959), Jacob van Rijs (born 1964) and Nathalie de Vries (born 1965), and the practice was formed after Maas and van Rijs left Rem Koolhaas's Office for Metropolitan Architecture.

MVRDV's Koolhaas-style books, *Statics* (1992), *FARMAX* (1998) and *Metacity/Datatown* (1999), are bestsellers – full of typographical innovation, tables of statistics and long passages of manifesto-like, graphically glamorous explorations of serious problems like density and urban planning. They convinced many of MVRDV's intellectual rigour and exploratory intent as well as confirming them as young, modish and hungry for new commissions.

Their most significant early built project was the Villa KBWW (which was designed with Bjarne Mastenbroek in 1997). It shows MVRDV's passion for integrating divergent uses in one building envelope by breaking away from conventional multi-storey, cellular arrangements. In their career so far, though, it is an eye for the right aesthetic buttons to push that has guaranteed their success but doomed them in some eyes to the eternal label of OMA-lite – a kind of pale imitation of the master.

Their Villa VPRO building (1997), an office for a public television company in Hilversum, has the best and worst of MVRDV: an OMA-style play between plan and section, UN Studio-style folds, but the building seems to want to be many different things at once. It is wilfully eclectic: at various points raw concrete ceilings hang with Baroque chandeliers, a staircase pops up through a concrete hillock with half a tree-trunk as a banister, and giant staircases double into auditoria. It is this inventiveness that makes MVRDV one of the most exuberant and confident practices in Europe.

While MVRDV continues with the themes of VPRO in buildings such as the Silodam housing in Amsterdam (2002), their more polemical projects, such as their Hageneiland Housing Estate near the Hague (2002), have kept critics on the hop. These extraordinary houses look like a series of Monopoly pieces laid out in broken terraces. They are regular concrete-frame buildings, with conventional interior layouts, built at a high density. What sets them apart is their external skins, which are minimally detailed and clad in single materials – aluminium, black PVC, green ceramics, wood shingles – turning them into a multicoloured collection of iconic house shapes. Huge blank gable ends with a single window and no eaves or gutters have a disorientating scale, and the uncompromising use of materials is a witty comment on housebuilders' obsession with brick.

MVRDV are the most self-conscious of the Dutch architects of their generation. They are witty and creative and do things that not many others would have the gumption to try, in a way that can be disarming – such as the dramatic cantilevers at the WoZoCo housing block in Amsterdam (1997). Unbuilt projects like the high-rise farm 'Pig City' attracted swarms of student followers. However, their magpie tendencies mean that their *oeuvre* can feel more like a box of tricks than a coherent body of work.

MVRDV

m

Neutelings Riedijk is one of the most idiosyncratic and perverse of contemporary European practices. Inspired by the drawing methods of cartoonists, the work borrows heavily from architecture from the 1950s to the present. This eclecticism has been distilled into one of the most successful blends in Dutch architecture, mixing the pragmatism of many contemporaries with a pleasing note of whimsy, while making space for deep thinking about urbanism and planning. Born in 1959, Willem Jan Neutelings had already worked for Rem Koolhaas's Office for Metropolitan Architecture for five years when he graduated from Delft Technical University in 1986 and founded his own practice, Michael Riedijk (born 1964) joining him in 1990 as a partner.

Their best-known project is probably the Minnaert Building at the University of Utrecht (1997), characterized by its sensuous pleated skin and the integration of columns into supergraphics that give the building's name and hint at the monumental signage of 1950s industrial buildings. Minnaert is divided in plan and section into a 'net programme', including workrooms, lecture theatres, laboratories and a canteen, and a 'tare programme', which includes circulation and technical services, as well as a pool of water in the main hall that collects rainwater to cool the building.

The work combines a fashionable interest in the skin of buildings with a less fashionable interest in decoration. Neutelings claims the buildings are 'born naked', and the decision about what to clad them in is taken only after the programmatic requirements of the brief are decided. The Minnaert building's rust-coloured sprayed concrete is typical, reworking a technique used on the charming post office in Scherpenheuvel, Belgium (1997), which creates a sand-coloured building on two sides of a new urban square.

Their buildings are defiantly specific about their programmes. In his essay 'Town, Theatre and Tomatoes' (2002), Neutelings wrote that 'a building that is supposed to be adaptable to every situation in the end lacks character. Even a character actor does not play every role.' Thus the glazed façade of the Veenman printworks in Ede (1997) is intended to house typographic artworks, hinting at the activity inside, and the two fire stations in Maastricht and Breda (1999 and 1998 respectively) are different in character but each arranged entirely around the garages housing the magnificent fire engines.

The later work is promising great things. The Stuk Centre in Leuven, Belgium (2002), is one of the most convincing new arts complexes in Europe, making sense of a difficult sloping site. A dazzling set of auditoria is placed around a series of public spaces that can be appropriated for events or used as an outdoor cinema. The complex mimics a medieval hill town, with a campanile-like lift tower and viewing platform and endless characterful access ways and staircases hidden behind the homogenous brick façades.

Other projects under development include the prestigious Aan de Stroom City Museum in Antwerp, Belgium – an OMA-like cuboid with glazed sections cut out of it – as well as social housing on a canal in Ghent and a new home for the Dutch audiovisual archives. Neutelings Riedijk's buildings have a wit and character that should not disguise their serious social, environmental and urbanistic objectives.

Neutelings Riedijk

n

Oscar Niemeyer's name will always be synonymous with Brasilia, the very beautiful and very flawed new capital of his home country, on which he worked from 1956 to 1964. He created a sequence of astonishing, robust, concrete buildings that have since helped define the image of modern Brazil.

A year younger than Philip Johnson (he was born in Rio in 1907 and trained at the Escola Nacional de Belas Artas, graduating in 1934), Niemeyer too has had a powerful influence on New World Modernism. And, like Johnson, he worked early on with one of the luminaries of Europe's Modern Movement – in Niemeyer's case Le Corbusier, whom he joined on the Ministry of Education and Health in Rio de Janeiro in the late 1930s. The project transformed Brazilian Modernism and profoundly influenced Niemeyer, who had previously worked in a Modernist, purified form of Brazilian Baroque.

It is the consistency of Niemeyer's vision and his intrinsic creativity that sets him apart from his North American contemporary, however. He was wedded not just to the style of the Modern Movement but also to its Utopian political goals and he has remained largely untouched by succeeding architectural fashions. His belief in communism eventually forced him out of his role as chief architect at Brasilia and into exile in Paris, where he found the perfect commission – the Communist Party Headquarters (1972) – before returning to Brazil and Brasilia in the late 1960s once the political climate had improved. He collaborated again with Corb on the United Nations buildings in New York (1952).

For lovers of concrete, Niemeyer is the heir to Le Corbusier's Brutalism, engineering his material into brazenly sensuous forms that engage with his early formal concerns and marry the curvaceous to the Utopian. This is evident in his own house, Casa Canoas, in Rio (1954), with its light slabs and floor-to-ceiling windows, but reaches full expression in Brasilia, where Niemeyer was charged with implementing Lúcio Costa's plans. In urban-planning terms it has been problematic but the individual buildings Niemeyer created are glorious. The Crown-of-Thorns symbolism of the roof of the cathedral and the great saucer domes of the National Congress fully exploit concrete's plastic and sculptural properties. Niemeyer worked on other projects in the city, including the Palace of Justice and the university.

Although Niemeyer has worked in France, Italy and Algeria (where he designed the zoo), it is in his home country that his work achieves a continuation of tradition into the future while maintaining his lifelong concerns. The recently completed Museum of Modern Art at Niteroi, near Rio (1996) is nothing less than a flying saucer lifting off the top of the hill, hovering above the land in the same way that some of his buildings at Brasilia hovered above pools. Niemeyer is always trying to defy concrete's weightiness. Way before Frank Gehry made architecture as sculpture newly fashionable, he was defying rationalism in pursuit of beautiful abstractions.

As he said himself when he accepted the Pritzker Prize for architecture in 1988, it is reinforced concrete with its 'soaring spans and uncommon cantilevers' that gives flight to our imagination: 'Today's architecture is not a minor craft bound to straight-edge rules.'

Oscar Niemeyer

n

Bottom: Hotel St James,
Bordeaux, 1989

Top right: Institut du
Monde Arabe, Paris, 1987

Centre right: Cartier
Foundation, Paris, 1993

By the time you read this, Jean Nouvel's transition from one of Europe's
Young Turks to world architect should be thoroughly complete. What kind
of architect he will be by then is hard to predict. Born in 1945 in a small
village in south-west France, he studied at the Paris Ecole des Beaux-Arts
in 1968 during the Paris Evénements and worked for iconoclast Claude
Parent and philosopher-architect Paul Virilio. Encouraged by them, he
rejected the repressive architecture then current in France, inventing his
own varied, specific, lyrical – and cheeky – language.

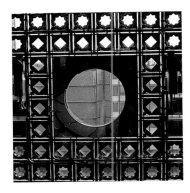

He set fire to the walls of an early school project (to the teachers'
consternation) and gold-leafed the ceiling. He lit a building to look as
though it were on fire. He daubed a gymnasium with paint and scraped
plaster in strips off Belfort Theatre (1980). He earned a role as one of the
cleverest of the *enfants terribles* – including Will Alsop and Massimiliano
Fuksas – of the 1980s and 1990s, inventing a way out of the atrophy and
Postmodernist style wars of the time.

His insistence on the parallels between architecture and film was
key during a boom of popular theory: 'Architecture exists, like cinema,
in a dimension of time and movement. One thinks, conceives and reads a
building in terms of sequences.' More aware than many followers of the
limitations of this analogy, he demonstrated it brilliantly. In the exquisite
Institut du Monde Arabe in Paris (1987), his first really iconic building,
dramatic circulation links the split volumes, leading from formal façade
to dark lifts, through a sequence of glass, mosque-like galleries, and down
the screen wall of the final, sharp-curved, riverside gallery with its juxtaposed, grainily diffused view of the Seine. The building is best known,
though, for its south wall – then the most expensive in the world – entirely

covered with metal lenses that open and close in response to the sun. The client wanted venetian blinds: he did not stand a chance. 'It is more expensive and it does not really work,' he told a delighted London audience in 1990. 'It is a completely poetic system.'

Nouvel's wit is always specific. His fabulous Hotel St James (1989), set on a hillside outside Bordeaux, stands in a field like its neighbouring tobacco warehouses. Behind its rusty metal louvres, the interiors are immaculate white and playful. His Nemausus Social Housing in Nîmes (1987) was pragmatic and cheerful. His unbuilt Tour Sans Fins for Paris (1989) played with invisibility, as did his Cartier Foundation, also in Paris (1993), with its illusory reflections of trees.

His variety attracts criticism of variable quality: the Galeries Lafayette department store in Berlin's Freidrichstrasse (1995), with conical atria cutting through a standard layout, is certainly not his best; his 1991 office–shopping centre in Rem Koolhaas's Euralille has mixed support. But his substantial Cultural and Congress Centre in Lucerne (1998) won high praise. He was awarded the RIBA Gold Medal in 1991 and, with projects in Denmark, Vienna, Mexico, Prague, Strasbourg and New York, he is in the generation set to inherit the world's really big prestigious projects. We need his wit and lyricism to survive the scale.

Left: Furniture College,
Letterfrack, 2002

Top right: Irish Pavilion
at the Frieslandhal, the
Netherlands, 1990

Centre right: Gallery of
Photography, Dublin, 1996

Bottom right: National
Photography Centre,
Dublin, 1996

John Tuomey and Sheila O'Donnell are two of the most talented architects in Europe and have formed a key part of an Irish architecture scene that has become the envy of much of the world. O'Donnell & Tuomey, founded in 1981, is one of a group of practices that achieved international recognition after they won the famous competition to redevelop Dublin's rundown Temple Bar area. A result of the enlightened regime of Irish president Mary Robinson combined with good economic circumstances, Temple Bar became the catalyst for a new Irish architectural generation and sparked a cultural renaissance. There are projects in this area by many good young Irish firms but one practice's work stood out – O'Donnell & Tuomey's.

Their Irish Film Centre (1992) and Gallery of Photography (1996), set either side of a pedestrian square, both won the Downes Medal and put them on the map. The Gallery of Photography is probably the most successful element, clad in Portland stone with a large central window at first-floor level that doubles as a screen for an open-air cinema. Despite its small size and shallow plan, there are clever games with levels and circulation that give the building depth and texture.

The partners' approach is forged from what they describe as a three-part education: their training in Dublin; their early work in London (including a stint working with legendary British Postmodernist James Stirling); and their autodidactic education in the buildings of Ireland – a process that continues today. Their work has been called rationalist, but this is tempered by an educated and instinctive knowledge of their home country. Sheila O'Donnell says: 'We found that Irish buildings were simpler and more primal than English buildings, that they sat as objects in strong contrast to the landscape.' This is joined with a brilliant interpretation of and adjustment to the buildings of Ireland's grim institutional history.

Before their success at Temple Bar, O'Donnell & Tuomey's projects included their house at Ballyweelin (1983), a courthouse at Smithfield (1987) and the Irish Pavilion at the 1990 Frieslandhal, Leeuwarden, the Netherlands, which housed twelve paintings by artist Bryan Maguire. Built of timber and corrugated metal, the pavilion sat in a courtyard and aimed to enhance the paintings by defining a narrative journey with catwalks and stairways, hinting at the same time at the barns and farmhouses of rural Ireland.

The most rural of their major buildings is the stunning furniture college at Letterfrack (2002), where they refurbished an existing industrial school and added a series of workshops and production facilities to create a village-like group of buildings in the beautiful Galway countryside. The concrete and green-oak buildings crouch into the site, offset by a campanile-like tower in fair-faced concrete – a triumph of contemporary yet vernacular design with genuine community amenity.

Other projects have proved the breadth of their interests, notably in the educational arena. The practice was shortlisted for the 1999 Stirling Prize for its Ranelagh School in Dublin (1998), and their Centre for Research into Infectious Diseases at University College Dublin (2003) shows they can work with stringent technical criteria while still creating a memorable form.

O'Donnell & Tuomey

O

Avant-garde architectural movements of the 1960s and 1970s are suddenly back in fashion. Archigram, Archizoom and Superstudio are referenced frequently as seminal influences on a range of practitioners. In the midst of this enthusiasm for old radicals, one name has been slightly forgotten, even though its prime movers are now some of Europe's most prolific and respected architects: Ortner & Ortner.

Laurids Ortner formed Haus Rucker Co. with Günter 'Zamp' Kelp and Klaus Pinter in 1967. This Austrian collective of artists and architects made work that was very of its time, and, like Archigram, concerned with issues that seemed at the time like the ones that would define the future – disposable and demountable architecture often expressed in such Utopian schemes as their Pneumacosm plan for the extension of New York (1967).

Laurids Ortner (born 1941) was the most vigorous member of the group, and it was not long before his brother, Manfred Ortner (born 1943), joined Haus Rucker in 1971. The group always had strong links with Germany, and so it was no surprise that when the two brothers broke away in 1987 to form Ortner & Ortner they chose Düsseldorf as their home.

Despite the partners' experience, Ortner & Ortner has a very young but extensive body of work that is quite different from the avant-gardist tendencies of Haus Rucker. Early projects included the Brüser Berg Centre in Bonn (1987), the restoration of the central bank of the Land of Nordrhein-Westfalen in Düsseldorf (1990), and the Bene office building and factory in Waidhofen (1989), which began to hint at the monolithic forms and geometric fenestration of later projects. The Bene project was widely published, and its striking 230-metre-long façade, with a use of proportion and scale that calls to mind O. M. Ungers, gives it a strong presence in its rural setting.

It is for two major public building complexes that the practice has become known in recent years. The Museums Quarter in the Ortners' home town of Vienna (2001) is a complex of buildings, old and new, based in the eighteenth-century court stables in the heart of historical Vienna. The Ortners' most visible interventions are the basalt-clad Museum of Modern Art, and the white limestone cuboid of the Leopold Museum. They flank the renovated Winter Riding School, which also serves as an exhibition space. The successful integration of austere and contemporary architecture into one of the great Baroque settings of Europe is a testament to a mature and confident architectural approach. The practice had more freedom with its Saxon Federal Library in Dresden (2002), where it created a three-storey podium containing a glass-roofed reading room, with two strongly geometric boxes placed above, clad in masonry and with irregularly spaced openings.

Though it horrifies their old radical contemporaries of the Archigram days, Ortner & Ortner now have a strong instinct for homogenous and high-quality masonry façades that lend their buildings a timeless image. Whether their work matches the compositional ingenuity of Swiss contemporaries such as Diener & Diener is unclear, but their contribution to modern European architecture is undeniable, and their handling of major public buildings is never gimmicky.

Ortner & Ortner

O

Top left: Neuendorf
House, Majorca, 1989

Bottom: Pawson
House, London, 1999

Top right: Model for Novy
Dvur Monastery, Czech
Republic, ongoing

John Pawson is known as the man who brought minimalism to architecture. It is not an unproblematic term, and Pawson has been accused of creating a style with no content – minimalism as a lifestyle choice rather than a serious and definable way of thinking about building. He has not helped to counter such claims, producing, as well as his buildings and interiors work, a range of books that are more catalogue than architectural monograph, including *Living and Eating*, which tells the world how to dine Pawson-style. While he has spawned a host of imitators, minimalism has not really become an architectural movement and resides more comfortably as a lifestyle for the rich.

Where minimalism in art developed in the 1960s as a reaction to Abstract Expressionism, minimalism in architecture did not really emerge until the 1980s, when it became the style of choice of the biggest and most fashionable brands of the day – a kind of inconspicuous consumption in the days of fat wallets and vulgar consumerism. Pawson's clients, such as Karl Lagerfeld, Calvin Klein and Jigsaw, have been able to commission one of his coolly reduced spaces and see their stock rise accordingly.

Born in Halifax in the north of England in 1949 and educated at Eton, Pawson spent four years teaching and studying with designer Shiro Kuramata in Japan. It is said that he seriously considered joining a Buddhist monastery before deciding to return to study at the Architectural Association, setting up his practice in 1981. His early work comprised residential fit-outs for the art world, including houses for Doris Saatchi (1987), Victoria Miro (1988) and Carolina and Hans Neuendorf (1987).

The Neuendorfs were to commission Pawson's best-known early work – a house in Majorca (1989), designed in collaboration with the Italian Claudio Silvestrin, Pawson's business partner between 1987 and 1989. A vision in terracotta-coloured render, the house owes a huge debt to Mexican legend Luis Barragán, with its enclosure of 9-metre-high walls, broken only by a projecting pool of water that reads as a floating pier in the landscape.

This austere monument stands out as one of the more colourful moments in Pawson's work, which is dominated mostly by acres of white render. He is a canny operator, however, detailing his spaces so that they retain their immaculate planes as long as possible, and using high-quality materials such as the wonderful limestone in his Calvin Klein store on Madison Avenue, New York (1995). While his interiors are all shadow gaps and recessed lighting, his exteriors are actually less austere than you might imagine. His Seoul Calvin Klein store (1996) is a simple masonry cube with a glazed opening at the bottom, but the human scale of the tiles and the wide steps up to the door temper its severity.

Pawson's most eagerly anticipated project is his Novy Dvur monastery in the Czech Republic, commissioned by a group of Cistercian monks who were inspired to approach him on the strength of Calvin Klein New York – the ultimate example of austere lifestyle meeting commercialism, perhaps. He said in a recent interview: 'People think I am making some judgement about the way they are living. I am not. It is not a hair-shirt thing.' You can make up your own mind whether you believe him.

John Pawson

p

Left: Bank of China,
Hong Kong, 1989

Top right: Extension to
the Louvre, Paris, 1989

Bottom right: East wing
of the National Gallery,
Washington, DC, 1978

The appointment of I. M. Pei to redesign the Louvre in Paris was one of architecture's big shocks. For any big French cultural commission to be awarded without a design competition was unprecedented. That François Mitterrand, the newly elected socialist president, should give France's greatest project to a Chinese-American known mainly for big-league commercial architecture was astonishing; that Pei managed to pioneer the scheme through political maelstrom and public outrage, building a steel and glass pyramid in one of Paris's great public spaces, even more so. But that is just what Pei is good at.

As Michael Cannell, author of Pei's page-turning biography (1995), explains, Pei is something of an enigma – a well-publicized, ever-smiling figure whose sophistication and accomplishment in difficult circumstances is manifest but who is privately elusive. Born in 1917, the son of a successful banking family, Pei grew up in Westernized Shanghai and was steeped in both Confucian beliefs and US cars and movies. He set out to study architecture at the University of Pennsylvania but quickly switched to MIT, where he flourished, describing Le Corbusier's visit as 'the two most important days of my architectural life'. Delayed from returning home by the Second World War, he moved to Harvard, where he was taught by Walter Gropius – who called his thesis project 'the finest piece of student work I've ever seen'.

But Pei's Harvard colleagues were shocked by his 'defection' to work for wheeler-dealer developer Bill Zeckendorf. His designs for Zeckendorf were expensive but groundbreaking. They were in the first wave of projects that cut high-rises and plazas through city after city's planning restrictions and low-rise nineteenth-century centres. These monumental changes to the workings of the modern city were controversial and sometimes problematic. Still, Pei's brilliance carried him successfully clear of Zeckendorf's financial collapse into his own practice in 1958 and big-league cultural projects.

Early among these were the romantic National Center for Atmospheric Research in Boulder (1967) – which leaked, but looked lovely – and the John. F. Kennedy Library in Boston (1979). This project was fraught with political, planning and location complications – not least because of Pei's monumental style – but the official approval generated a wave of public commissions, including the City Hall (1977) and Meyerson Symphony Center (1989) in Dallas. Pei won the Pritzker Prize in 1983, quoting Leonardo da Vinci: 'Strength is born of constraint and dies in freedom.'

Pei's architectural profile remains curious. He is thought of as essentially commercial, but his great projects are some of the most important of their time. The crisp geometric monumentality of the East Wing of the National Gallery, Washington, DC (1978), has been called the first late-modern building. The Louvre (1989), with its steel and glass pyramid and its rational reworking of the chaotic museum, is one of the sights of Paris. And the Bank of China, in Hong Kong (1989), with its triangular geometry, is one of the few really memorable super-high-rises. 'He's not a design influence,' said Philip Johnson, 'He's just Mr Success.' Yet from the fringes of high architecture, he has done more than most to shape the world.

I.M.Pei

p

Top left: Bibliothèque
Nationale de France,
Paris, 1997

Top right: SAGEP water
treatment plant, Ivry-sur-
Seine, 1987

Bottom: Olympic velodrome
and swimming pool, Berlin,
1999

When Dominique Perrault, then only thirty-six, won the hotly fought competition for the Bibliothèque Nationale de France in 1989, beating Rem Koolhaas among others, the press on both sides of the Channel exploded in disbelief. Readers to be housed underground while the books fried in huge glass silo towers with perversely fabulous views inaccessible to the public? And all this from an architect supposed to be the great exponent of functional form, the French answer to Norman Foster?

The fabulous success of the Paris library (even Koolhaas admits Perrault's cleverness – a real accolade) was to prove them wrong, setting a new figure at the forefront of French architecture. The greatest of the last wave of François Mitterrand's Grands Projets, the TGB – Très Grande Bibliothèque as the library was dubbed in a pun on the high-speed TGV trains – went at extraordinary speed, finishing in 1997 (when it won the Mies van der Rohe European Prize for Architecture), compared to thirty-six years for London's new British Library. It was also huge.

Born in 1953 with an office opened in 1981, Dominique Perrault had certainly shown a form of rationalism in his work so far. His ESIEE engineering school in Marne-la-Vallée (1987) and his Hôtel Industriel Berlier, Paris (1989), both demonstrated a masterly control of pure form and Modernist materials, appearing as objects of almost abstract purity. But the Bibliothèque was to show just how far this sheer simplicity was a poetic, imaginative device.

The building is full of perversely symbolic, romantic ideas. Four glass towers, lined with timber shutters against the sun, raise the books above the city, taking the form of open books themselves – a gesture much criticized, but successfully pared to minimalist invisibility. The readers, hidden under a huge stepped podium, look out into a strip of forest, painstakingly and accurately transplanted from Normandy (and inaccessible except in case of fire). Meanwhile the public, using the timber-stepped podium on top of the reading rooms, gains a new square overlooking the river. Though wilfully shorn of all overt rhetoric, the TGB is, idealistically, a castle of books, a hillside, a scrap of imprisoned forest.

The lyrical suggestiveness of pure form is always dominant in Perrault's work: the Hôtel Berlier box; the folds of the SAGEP water treatment plant at Ivry-sur-Seine (1987); and the wedge of ESIEE, cut around a traffic roundabout (Perrault loves explaining that the client chose the site by helicopter). It is most evident in the fabulous Olympic velodrome and swimming pool in Berlin (1999) – a huge square and a huge circle, laid out with expansive, mathematical totalitarianism.

Perrault says he never warmed much to Le Corbusier, drawn instead to Mies and Louis Kahn for their 'quasi-mystical exactingness', which he manages in his own work with consummate skill. His work is 'Monumental by the near non-presence of the incidental object,' said Peter Cook, and in moving into buildings of major international scale, such as the extension of the European Community Court of Justice in Luxembourg, currently in progress, he has found his true medium.

Dominique Perrault

p

'Why do you want to be just an architect?' Renzo Piano's father asked his seventeen-year-old son, 'You can be a builder.' In many ways, his son accepted the advice. One of the architectural world's greatest names, Piano remains utterly rooted in how things are made – the inventive, practical, craftsmanlike, evolution of tectonics, materials, structure and environment. He wants to be, US critic Paul Goldberger argues, not an architect of ideas, but of things. Ironically, his first, most iconic project is one of the greatest 'ideas' buildings of the twentieth century: the Pompidou Centre in Paris (1977), built in partnership with Richard Rogers. But while Rogers has remained committed to the great polemic of the technologically flexible anti-institution, Piano seems ambiguous about the triumph of its technical rhetoric. He calls it a 'joyful urban machine', but 'a parody of the techno-logical imagery of our time'.

Piano was born in Genoa in 1937 into generations of builders. He studied at Milan Polytechnic, worked for Louis Kahn in the 1960s, and was friends with the hugely inventive designer Jean Prouvé. His first commission, the Italian Pavilion for Osaka Expo in 1970 (built by his brother, Ermanno), drew Rogers' attention. This partnership was followed by another, with the immensely creative engineer Peter Rice. He set up Renzo Piano Building Workshop in 1980 with Unesco support. 'We not only design things here, we make and test them. Keeping some of the action together with the conception makes me feel a little less like a traitor to my family,' says Piano.

Renzo Piano

His many major international buildings fuse technological experiment with urban responsibility. Kansai Airport in Osaka (1994), built on an artificial island – one of the biggest projects in the world – draws air naturally under its aerofoil roof. The Menil Museum in Houston (1987) is a delicate celebration of structure with responsive sunscreens. He converted the famous 1920s Lingotto Fiat Factory, with its rooftop track (2002). The wonderful, prefab-shell Bari Football Stadium for the 1998 World Cup is the most dramatic in the world. He is also gaining a reputation for high-rise buildings, with the Aurora Place tower in Sydney (2002), and the planned 'glass shard' office block in London. But iconic power can be incidental and innovation more admirable than thrilling. In Piano's rebuilding of Berlin's Potsdamerplatz (1998), urban responsibility overwhelms architectural joy. He sees criticism of his lack of spatiality as misunderstanding his use of transparency.

His most delightful building is the least easy to visit: his wonderful cliff-top office on Italy's Ligurian coast (1991). Piano is truly international, with offices in Genoa, Paris and Berlin, but this is the best. Abandoned by taxi on the coast road, you take the glass funicular up the cliff to a series of terraces overlooking the Mediterranean under a single glass roof. Louvres flick as the sun comes out. People from all over the world work on projects all over the world, spilling out into the gardens for lunch. Underneath is Dante's workshop, where models and research and materials are tested. It is a manifestation of the pure joy of making things.

p

New Age architect Antoine Predock works extraordinary magic out of his
New Mexico home. Lines of energy, haunted spaces and emanations from
buildings are his thing. He once said that he would rather talk about UFOs
than Palladio and it is easy to believe him. That is not to say he is some
yoghurt weaver exploring hemp-built eco-huts (although he is not averse
to a grass roof): his buildings are crystalline, fragmented forms that typically
rise out tectonically from their sites.

Born in 1936, Predock studied at the University of New Mexico
and Columbia in New York and set up practice in Albuquerque in 1967.
From this epicentre he has steadily been extending his architectural aura
through the US south-west and beyond ever since. Perhaps as a response
to the demanding climate and often savage sites, his buildings tend to be
introspective and private – they are grounded in nature but the natural is
carefully mediated. He thrives in deserts where he can create his own worlds.

Throughout the 1980s, Predock created a series of private houses –
the Fuller House in Arizona (1987), the Zuber House, Arizona (1989), and
the Turtle Creek House, Dallas (1993) – but his output goes way beyond this.
He may be interested in counter-culture and have an image of himself skiing
down the roof of one of his buildings on his website but his clients take him
seriously. At sixty-seven his output includes museums, theatres, libraries, a
clinic and academic buildings.

His domestic work is an investigation of his clients' fantasies and
their interaction with the site. The Turtle Creek House is a 'theatre of trees'
that allows its birdwatching owner to pursue his passion among the giant
limestone ledges dominating its setting. An internal bridge, a sky-ramp
towards the tree canopy and other eyries are incorporated.

Predock is explicit about his sense of the theatrical. While studying
at Columbia he became involved in dance and was an admirer of Merce
Cunningham. 'I think of my buildings as processional events, as choreographic events,' he says. 'They are an accumulation of vantage points both
perceptual and experiential.' This is literally true of the Fuller House, with
its two pavilions to watch the sunrise and the sunset.

Predock is also interested in the earlier Indian civilizations of the
US south-west. His preference for adobe has had to give way to concrete
as his buildings have become larger and more complex, but the image of
a tepee is a recurring one. The Las Vegas Library and Discovery Museum
(1990) incorporates one of these cones, while the American Heritage Center
in Wyoming (1993) takes the form of a giant cutaway concrete tepee. Adobe
terraces and cubist boxes are evident in the wonderful Nelson Fine Arts
Center at Arizona State University (1989).

As Predock reaches further geographically, the locally appropriate
New Mexico symbolism dies away. A project for a sports centre at Ohio
State University (begun 1999) may be conceived as 'ravines, promontories,
towers and bridges', but the more abstracted dance steps of sport seem as
much an inspiration as landscape or the flakier end of his self-described
'cosmic Modernism'.

Antoine Predock

p

Magnet project, 1994

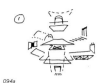

① 094a

Temporary protection
Length of linear – STEPS, STAIRS,
        – short-haul LIFT –

Steps &   – Resting AREA
  platforms   Observation AREA
Ease of access   – Hanging around
Ease of change of level Space – safety.
Threshold Safety – not much ground level
                congregation

STAIRWAYS

---

② 094b

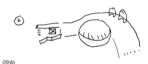

Ease of access
VIEWING & ENJOYING
Safety.
Ref. to small information

PROMENADE

---

③ 094c

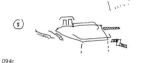

Platform observation – with SAFETY
Cross-routes. – Large volume of people
  ESCALATORS
Access to existing bldg.
VARIABLE secondary STAIRS

PLATFORM

MAGNET

---

④ 094d

ARCADE – Shelter, Protection
INFORMATION – advertising
SERIES of STRUCTURES
A second 'STREET' Threshold.

ARCADE

---

⑤ 094e

Series of MOVEABLE DECKS
WALKWAY + OBSERVATION
TEMPORARILY HOLDING –
  MOVING.

CAUSWAY

---

⑥ 099a

ROAD BRIDGE AS
THRESHOLD.
3 DECK
– open air Top FL.
'ISLAND' terminal.
SIDEWAYS access to;
    (Local interest)
POSSIBLE MAJOR
MOVEMENT (occasional)

PIER

---

⑦ 099b

STRESSES BRIDGE with 'TORSION'
VERTICAL DOMINANCE
Wide 'BASES' – observation
ACCESS WALKWAYS – interim

ARCH

MAGNET

---

⑧ 099c

ROOF LEVEL
WALKWAY +
CONTEMPLATION
cond. – access
& stability – helped
by EXISTING BLDGS.

CITY GRID CHANGE
A SECOND STREET – NEW
POSSIBLE CRANE SUPPORT
LONG TERM

TRANSPORTER

---

⑨ 099d

A SECOND STREET – NEW
POSSIBLE CRANE SUPPORT
LONG TERM
Neighbour
BLANKET
BROADWAY
at 90° to diagonal
Cond. for LAND
USE / NEW

'CITY' SQUARE

---

⑩ 099e

A NEW VARIED
LEVEL GENERATOR
of the entire AREA
A NEW
A CITY STARTER
varied directional
feeds. MAGNET

MAGNET

MAGNET

Cedric Price must be the most influential architect who has, consistently, over a forty-year-plus career, built almost nothing – and is not particularly famous for what he has built. His expansive, detailed, lateral projects are often tough to figure out – but they are the inspiration and conscience of decades of progressive architecture and have directly influenced some of its best-loved examples.

Though his detailed, quirky, comic drawings are world famous, it is almost impossible to envisage what the projects might look like. Normally they are unlike anything done by an architect. His work overturns our usual obsessions: appearance does not matter, he says; what matters is what a building does. His projects deal with time, delight, responsibility, change, social conditions, engineering. Almost by definition, most architects will propose a building as a solution to a problem. Price will tell his clients that what they need is a new computer. Or a divorce.

Born in 1934 and educated at Cambridge and the AA in the 1950s, Price set up office in London in 1960 and his influence was immediately and consistently felt by a whole series of younger generations. His legendary Fun Palace project (1961), where the whole structure acts as an adjustable stage set for theatrical and other activities, was the direct model for the Pompidou Centre. A tiny fragment of his South Bank plan (1983), which involved bridging the Thames from Westminster to Waterloo, was a viewing-capsule big wheel on Jubilee Gardens – the model for the London Eye.

Asked what he would do about York Minster, he replied 'flatten it'. He argues that all buildings should be capable of removal when no longer needed: the Fun Palace was to last for ten years only; the Aviary at London Zoo (1961) – one of his few built buildings – is designed to be folded up and taken away. He campaigned for the demolition of his own Inter-Action project in Kentish Town (1971). He says architecture should anticipate change, suggesting new social activities and means of occupation rather than ossifying those we have as permanent buildings inevitably do.

His Magnet project (1994) is a prime example of 'anticipatory' architecture. The provocative temporary structures made from cranes and other rentable equipment ranged from a huge, curved town square that would roll over the North Circular road, linking severed communities and marking the roadside houses beneath as ripe for demolition, to a treetop viewing walkway to peep over the walls of London Zoo. The Potteries Thinkbelt (1964), another hugely influential early project, also proposed alternatives to 'institutions': faced with the industrial decline of his native Staffordshire and a boom in UK education, he proposed a roving university system, using the abandoned railway and industrial infrastructure.

His schemes involve immensely complex, inventive, often invisible engineering work and social provision, including work on labour relations. Yet his work is deeply romantic, infused with a kind of poetry – sometimes lyrical, sometimes unbearably tough. His prolific projects slowly percolate through books and exhibitions and magazines, expanding and challenging our structure of belief of what architecture is and what it could be doing.

Cedric Price died in 2003 as this book was going to press.

Cedric Price

p

Bottom left: Concertgebouw, Bruges, 2002

Main picture: Boijmans van Beuningen Museum, Rotterdam, 2003

Bottom right: Aue Pavilions, Documenta, Kassel, 1992

Although it may be a little hackneyed to ask for the name of a famous Belgian, it is an easy question to answer in terms of architects and designers. This culturally diverse and politically tense country is currently in the throes of an explosion of design creativity. Antwerp has become a global centre of fashion design, and Belgium's furniture and architecture is characteristically serious and confident. Ghent-based Robbrecht & Daem is at the heart of this renaissance and is increasingly respected as one of the most credible practices in all of Europe.

Partners Paul Robbrecht and Hilda Daem were both born in 1950 and trained at Ghent's Hoger Architectuurinstituut. They set up practice together at the tender age of twenty-five, entering a series of competitions such as the Godecharle social housing project in De Muide, Ghent (1978), and completing one-off houses such as the Robbrecht-Van Heule House in Wetteren Ten Heede (1979) and the Wijfels Ven Den Broecke House in Ballieul (1979).

Their fascination with contemporary art increasingly came to the fore in a variety of galleries and exhibition halls, including the Aue Pavilions for the 1992 Documenta art festival in Kassel, Germany. These temporary steel buildings sat on black stilts and, with their vaulted ceilings, seemed to hint at a vernacular that informs the practice's work without ever becoming obvious aesthetically. The pavilions were a huge success and have since been re-erected in Almere, the Netherlands, for the display of art. Robbrecht & Daem have also collaborated with many of the top names in European art including Gerhard Richter, Cristina Iglesias and the late Juan Muñoz, for whom they designed a house.

Two large buildings completed in 2002 and 2003 have cemented their reputation. Their Concertgebouw in Bruges, erected for the city's stint as European Capital of Culture, was the first – a tile-clad edifice near the city's waterside, dominated by the 35-metre fly tower of the main stage and the 30-metre tower containing the chamber music hall. The building was conceived with reference to the other major landmarks of historical Bruges, but its terracotta-clad façade has something of the industrial character of the sheds that line the roads into the city.

The commission to build a major new extension for the prestigious Boijmans van Beuningen Museum in Rotterdam, one of the most important of the Netherlands' cultural institutions, might have cowed lesser architects. Robbrecht & Daem responded brilliantly; their new wing faces the street with a layered façade of clear glass, large panels of cathedral glass acting as a rainscreen, and the steel structure exposed but not overbearingly so. In plan the new wing creates a new entrance courtyard for the museum, respecting the original and making a genuinely civic façade to the street. It also complements Rem Koolhaas's Kunsthal, sitting on the other side of the museum park, and deals with its roadside context in an equally assured way.

Robbrecht & Daem have plenty more projects in them yet, and major housing masterplans in the Netherlands (Utrecht and Amsterdam) should see them add a social dimension to the more ceremonial architecture they have completed so far.

Robbrecht & Daem

r

Top: Pompidou Centre,
Paris, 1977

Bottom left: Lloyd's
of London, 1986

Bottom right: Lloyd's
of London, 1986

Richard Rogers must be one of the most beloved architectural superstars. Pioneer of the UK's architectural renaissance, architect of two of the best-loved buildings of the late twentieth century, benevolent godfather of a whole generation, his greatest buildings straddle the ethical abyss between radical thought, humanitarian inclusiveness and big institutions.

Born in 1933, Rogers' love of society and teamwork is fundamental. He is open about his alienated, liberated childhood as an Italian in Surrey, the bust-up of his practice with Norman Foster in Team 4 and with first wife Su, his second marriage to Ruth, who took the firm's canteen, the River Café, to gastro-stardom. And partners John Young, Mike Davies and Marco Goldschmied are unusually well-acknowledged.

His early work – Team 4's romantic Creek Vean House of 1966 – shifted to a kit-of-parts approach with colour, flexibility and a concern for the way people live, in the Zip-Up House project (1968) and a house for his parents in Wimbledon (1968). The Inmos Factory in Newport, Wales (1982), was a totem of exposed servicing. But it was with the Pompidou Centre in Paris (1977) – or Beaubourg as Rogers calls it, unwilling to glorify politicians – that the firm began to soar. In partnership with Renzo Piano the young unknowns stormed the 1971 jury.

Partly based on the adaptablity and oil-refinery anti-aesthetic of Cedric Price's Fun Palace, the Pompidou gradually adopted its world-famous characteristics: the external panoramic escalators and the super-expressed structure and services were to become the banner of high-tech, forming a new Paris icon. Less famously, the public square was a major urban success.

Rogers has built prodigiously throughout his career, but is utterly defined by the Pompidou and Lloyd's of London (1986). An astonishing example of enlightened patronage at the peak of UK anti-Modernism, Lloyd's was an iconic hit and remains one of the greatest buildings of the late twentieth century. A surprisingly clear, rational, open plan is serviced by a battlement of external stainless-steel service towers exploiting the irregular, demanding site, holding bathroom capsules, fire-escape stairs, services and panoramic lifts, and giving the building a Gothic exuberance. Window-cleaning cranes remain as if under construction, an eighteenth-century Adam interior is collaged against a high-tech, high-rise skyline.

None of Rogers' many other international buildings manages this brilliant mix of institutional credibility and cheeky fun on anything like the same scale. It is Rogers' forte: wearing first knighthood, then peerage casually, combining left-wing campaigning with a big, highly commercial practice. His plans for London – self-government, public space, access to the river, active mixed use – helped to form Labour government policy and were influential in 1990s London's increasingly animated public realm.

Intellectually, his can-do optimism and his willingness to deliver commercial work while arguing left-wing ideals may weaken his rationale. But his best work is the brilliant apotheosis of this profoundly architectural compromise. And his liberal loosening of the UK establishment is an achievement in itself.

Richard Rogers

r

Top left: Khalsa Heritage
Memorial Complex,
Anandpur, ongoing

Top right: Hebrew Union
College, Jerusalem, 1989

Bottom: 'Habitat' housing
complex, Montreal Expo,
1967

Humanism infuses Moshe Safdie's work. From his early experimental housing schemes to his later cultural complexes and additions to the Holocaust Memorial, Yad Vashem, in Jerusalem, there is always a desire to promote the civic and the civilized. Many of his projects feel like cities in miniature rather than homogenous lumps of development. He is an urbanist as much as an architect.

Born in Haifa in 1938, Safdie moved to Canada aged fifteen, and Quebec and Israel remain the two ends of the multicultural axis along which he principally works from his practice in Boston. He trained at McGill University, Montreal, and spent two years in the offices of Louis Kahn before setting up practice in Canada in 1964, just after he had won the project that was to make his name – the 'Habitat' housing complex for the 1967 Montreal Expo.

In a housing climate of rational grids and point and slab blocks, Safdie pursued a cellular concrete building system that allowed more informal private layouts at higher densities, likened to Italian (or Israeli) hill towns. It proved an expensive approach but in later schemes in the US Safdie demonstrated its feasibility, even if Habitat '67 is now a high-salary enclave rather than the resource for those on lower incomes that was envisaged. Habitat '67 is something of a megastructure but it strives for intimacy – an approach evident in his subsequent work.

Safdie has built a great deal in Israel, including the Hebrew Union College campus (1989), with its courtyards and connecting arcades – an example of the meeting of the contemporary and the neovernacular that charaterizes his work. Other projects around Jerusalem include the mixed-use Mamilla Centre masterplan, begun in 1972 and still being developed. On the cusp of the Old and New cities, the development is intended to act as a shared space across the ethnic divide, with squares and landscaped routes designed to reconnect this fractured section of Jerusalem. In part it resembles the stacked apartments of Habitat '67, although here the vernacular elements are to the fore.

Back in Canada Safdie has been responsible for building some of the country's foremost cultural complexes. Quebec's Musée de la Civilisation (1989) demonstrates his skill at making parts of cities rather than simply set-piece buildings. Its different elements are connected by a courtyard route through the site that leads up to a rooftop garden and lookout tower. Gardens, he notes, began in the scriptures: 'Man's ideal is to come back to the state of nature,' he has said, and his buildings are indeed a combination of natural outcrops and a Modernism informed by local cultural traditions.

An ongoing project that brings together these consistent themes is the Khalsa Heritage Memorial Complex – a museum of Sikh history in the Punjabi holy city of Anandpur. Both intimate and monumental, the complex is divided into two and joined by a bridge over a ravine. Organized around a central courtyard and pools that will reflect the stone-clad concrete galleries with their gleaming stainless-steel roofs, it promises to be a perfectly Safdie juxtaposition of civilization and oasis.

Moshe Safdie

S

Top left: computer rendering of the
Toledo Museum of Art Glass Pavilion,
Toledo, due to open in 2006

Main picture: O Museum,
Nagano, 1999

After the wilful bashing out of ever-wilder organic metal shapes that has characterized much recent Japanese architecture, the work of SANAA – the partnership of Kazuyo Sejima and Ryue Nishizawa – offers a welcome measure of serenity, characterized by rational light boxes that recall the more minimalist moments of Herzog & de Meuron. Sejima is also one of an emerging generation of women architects who are finally getting attention at an international level.

Sejima was born in Japan in 1956 and after graduating from the Japan Women's University she set up Kazuyo Sejima Architect & Associates in 1987. Nishizawa was born in Japan in 1966 and set up the Office of Ryue Nishizawa in 1997 after graduating with a masters degree in architecture from Yokohama National University. Since 1995 they have teamed up under the practice name SANAA, winning a clutch of important competitions around the world. These have included a project for the regeneration of Salerno, Italy, two buildings in the Netherlands and a Manhattan art gallery.

It is the series of pristine and beautifully detailed luminous glass boxes – the O Museum in Nagano Prefecture (1999), and the 130-metre-long strip of the Day Care Centre for Elders in Yokohama (2000) – that has caught the eye of international juries. The approach has been carried through even on a domestic scale: Sejima's Small House in Tokyo (2000) is a doll's-house skyscraper on a landlocked site, its façade a screen of opalescent glass that mediates between glowing light within and the changing daylight outside.

All of SANAA's projects suggest the delicate play of Japanese shadow theatre. The shifting of light animates the austere choice of materials and ensures that SANAA is to glass what Tadao Ando is to concrete. If the façades are not translucent, they are reflective, porous or perforated filters that seem to make the skin of the buildings dissolve in certain lights.

It is appropriate, then, that a 2002 competition win is for the Toledo Museum of Art Glass Pavilion in the US. The project, with a budget of $25 million, will house a stunning collection of glass artefacts in a building created almost entirely out of glass – these days, one of architecture's most tech-nologically advanced materials. 'Housing glass in glass suggests contextual relations turned inside out,' they say. The project will blur physical borders and, as with all the practice's work, will play with the divisions between interior and exterior.

Another competition win – an extension to the New Museum for Contemporary Art in Manhattan – will double the size of the museum's building, located in the Bowery. At the Las Palmas warehouse in Rotterdam – soon to be the Beeld Instituut (for visual culture) – glass gives way to acrylic to create a roof-garden retreat that also acts as a beacon on top of the building. Some of the concave interior spaces will be hollowed out of transparent solid acrylic.

Understated is an understatement in describing SANAA's work – it is an architecture that is almost not there but leaves a residue of richness in its wake. This is a neo-Miesian architecture for a new millennium.

SANAA/Kazuyo Sejima + Ryue Nishizawa

S

Main picture: GSW
Building, Berlin, 2001

Top right: Experimental
Factory, Magdeburg, 2001

Bottom left: Photonics
Centre, Berlin, 1997

Architects are often judged in their early careers on where they studied and who they worked for. On these terms Matthias Sauerbruch and Louisa Hutton have a very strong pedigree. Sauerbruch was born in Constance, Germany, in 1955, and Hutton two years later in Norwich, UK. The pair met at the Architectural Association in London, where they studied and taught together between 1984 and 1990, forming Sauerbruch Hutton Architects in 1989 after Sauerbruch had worked for a stint at Rem Koolhaas's Office for Metropolitan Architecture in Rotterdam, and Hutton for legendary British Brutalist Peter Smithson.

When they won the job of rebuilding a whole city block in Berlin for property company GSW in 1991, it was obvious that the practice would become a major player. Their victory was assured by the boldness of their approach to scale. In contrast to the other competition entries, Sauerbruch Hutton proposed that the block – situated at the join of the two overlaid grid systems of the German capital – should not only react to the scale of Berlin's surrounding classical 22-metre blocks, but should also retain an 85-metre-high office tower on the site, integrating it into a massing strategy that also deploys a 110-metre-long podium, providing a grand but comprehensible scale to the main façade. A striking reworking of the existing façade of the curved block – a riot of coloured sunblinds – also allows the building to be efficient thermally, combining with natural ventilation to provide a 40 per cent energy reduction compared to a conventional block. This ecological interest remains an influential part of Sauerbruch Hutton's work and they are perhaps one of the most credible architects in the world dealing in a committed way with making green buildings.

The GSW building took a decade to build and was nominated for the Stirling Prize in 2001. Meanwhile, the practice carried out a number of projects, including influential schemes in London such as the L-House (1991), a refurbishment of a Victorian terraced house; the H-House (1995), a refit of a 1960s house; and the N-House (1999), which converted a six-storey house in west London by retaining the details of the original historical building and providing a series of new floor surfaces – rubber, screed, gravel, carpet, leather – to make new atmospheres.

It is their buildings in Germany that are perhaps better known, including the sinuous take on Mies van der Rohe that is their Photonics Centre in Berlin Treptow (1997) and their candy-striped Experimental Factory in Magdeburg (2001). For some critics the obsession with colour in these buildings has masked their seriousness, but Sauerbruch Hutton's work continues to deal in a very sophisticated way with environmentally responsive skins and rational internal plans.

The seemingly unstoppable rise of this Anglo-German pair was checked in 2003 by the cancellation of their project for the Museum of Contemporary Art in Sydney (scuppered by local opposition to the demolition of the original Art Deco building). However, with the completion of GSW still fresh in the mind, Sauerbruch Hutton will not have to wait long for their next chance to shape a city on a grand scale.

Sauerbruch Hutton

S

Main picture: Rose Seidler
House, Sydney, 1948

Top right: Horizon
Residential Tower,
Sydney, 1998

For an architect still embedded in the International Style it must be strange to be associated with just one country – Australia. Few architects practising today have Harry Seidler's pedigree when it comes to high Modernism. And he is very aware of it – patrician is a frequent description of the man. Born in 1923, he left his native Vienna before the Second World War, trained in Canada then Harvard under Walter Gropius, and worked with Marcel Breuer in New York and Oscar Niemeyer in Rio before setting up his own practice in Sydney in 1948. He wears this history with obvious pride.

With his first project, a house for his mother (1948), the twenty-five-year-old brought his credentials to bear on the staid architectural scene of Sydney with a gleaming glass and white-concrete box hovering above the landscape. It made a huge impact. And despite his repeated reference to the inscription on Joseph Olbrich's 1898 Viennese Secession pavilion – 'To each era its art and to art its freedom' – he has stuck doggedly to his masters' voices ever since.

Early in his Australian career he was credited with bringing innovative living spaces and construction techniques Down Under. Seidler had a long collaboration with Italian engineer Pier Luigi Nervi, one of the most important products of which is the Australia Square office tower, Sydney (1967), which brought together poured and pre-cast concrete and introduced the US pocket plaza to the city. The double-height, open-plan spaces of his houses and apartment blocks also brought a more casual style of living to a region that had previously been rather too wedded to British antecedents.

Seidler's continental models of Le Corbusier and Breuer, often tempered by climatically appropriate external solar shading, made themselves felt. In a reprise of his work with Breuer he built the Australian Embassy in Paris (1977), which shows a common heritage with the Brutalism of Breuer's Whitney Museum in New York.

His most visible work in his adoptive home is the forty-three-storey Horizon Residential Tower (1998), sticking up a finger to the surrounding low-rise inner-city streets and commanding views of the harbour. It is now one of Sydney's flashiest addresses. Inside is nothing special but externally the curious piano-curve balconies recall Niemeyer's Modernist Baroque, if with a rather stolid heartiness. The block that houses his own office and apartment in north Sydney (completed in 1973 and augmented in 1988 and 1994), incorporating similar ideas, is, however, outstanding. Quadrant curves make frequent appearances in his work. Shell House, Melbourne (1989), is a case in point. His later output has included, in addition to the apartment and office towers, shopping, cultural and civic centres, such as the elegantly sculptural Waverly Civic Centre (1984).

Determinedly non-parochial, Seidler can be credited as a key player in the internationalization of Australian architecture and he remains a big fish in that smallish pond, despite never really making much of an international career for himself (the Paris embassy and a vast housing scheme in Vienna aside). However, he has never really left Europe. As a new generation of Australian architects get back in touch with the land, he is unchanging.

Harry Seidler

S

Top: Fondazione Sandretto
Re Rebaudengo, Turin, 2002

Bottom left: Armani
Store, Milan, 2001

Bottom right: Fondazione
Sandretto Re Rebaudengo,
Turin, 2002

Although Claudio Silvestrin's career is intimately connected with that of John Pawson, his former partner, there are big differences. These have been characterized in terms of the contrast between the 'London Minimal' of Pawson's early residences and interiors, and the 'Mediterranean Minimal' of Eduardo Souto de Moura and Silvestrin himself. But despite being born in Italy in 1954 and having a slightly more sensuous feel for materials than the white-render-obsessed Pawson, Silvestrin is nowhere near the class of the likes of Souto de Moura. What he is, is a wonderful stylist, creating super-stylish venues, boutiques and shops for some of the coolest names in the worlds of fashion and art.

First, he tackled art. An early project was the White Cube Gallery in St James's, London (1993), for art dealer Jay Jopling. It became one of the trendiest spaces in London, with a single room lit by two slot windows. Cooing art critics of the time described the experience as 'almost religious'.

In 1999, the ultimate name in understated yet expensive cool – Giorgio Armani – wanted to reinvent the identity of his shops. Naturally, he turned to Silvestrin, who took to the task with alacrity, and has since refurbished flagship stores in Paris, Milan, Düsseldorf, Moscow, Chicago, Boston and Tokyo, along with new-build projects in São Paolo and Seoul. These are more than just exercises in wide open spaces of expensive natural materials, and have a spatial interest that creates a subtly branded consumer experience, particularly in the long corridors of the Paris store, or the low benches of the Milan store.

Silvestrin's most important project so far is a new contemporary art gallery for the Fondazione Sandretto Re Rebaudengo in Turin, Italy (2002). Contemporary art is not exactly thriving in Italy at the moment, and one reason may be that this building is the first such gallery created in twenty years. As one critic wrote on its opening: 'Italian creativity today may have little to add to contemporary culture, but it will have a great space in which to explore its potential.' High praise indeed. The gallery is worth a visit in spite of the poor quality of what may be inside. Silvestrin's design is an elongated stone rectangle with huge pine doors that give larger art works access to the 1,000 square metres of display space. Long cuts in the building's envelope allow slots of light to enter, but the space is deliberately hermetic and contemplative, with minimal views out. Although Silvestrin claims it is 'not a polemic', its understatedness contrasts strongly with the current trend for showpiece cultural buildings with strongly expressive forms, such as those of Frank Gehry or Daniel Libeskind. It attempts to be a neutral presence internally and a quiet limestone background externally.

Silvistrin's stylistic palette has always lent itself perfectly to furniture – Cappellini and Dema have manufactured his work – and one feels that this will lead to the inexorable growth of the Silvestrin brand. But he has proved, perhaps even more so than Pawson, that a minimalist aesthetic, with all its perceived limitations, can manifest stand-alone buildings of quality, as well as the slick interiors that characterize the many boutiques and restaurants in his portfolio.

Claudio Silvestrin

S

Top: Santa Maria Church and
Parish Centre, Marco de
Canavezes, 1996

Bottom left: Swimming
pool, Leça da Palmeira,
1966

Bottom right: Boa
Nova Restaurant, Leça
da Palmeira, 1963

Alvaro Siza is a problem for the writer. While looking as natural as possible, his buildings do peculiar things – they lie or tell jokes, they are exquisitely beautiful or dull to the point of torpor. Yet he is one of a handful of the world's greatest architects. He is simply making architecture – not architectural theory. Born in Portugal in 1933, Siza completed his first famous project in 1963 – the Boa Nova Restaurant in Leça da Palmeira, with its luxurious, airy, vernacular late Modernism, designed down to the light fittings and ashtrays (only stable when upside-down). His concrete, open-air swimming pool nearby (1966) is similarly relaxed – and of a completely different language.

He is intensely well informed, using references widely – Le Corbusier, Alvar Aalto, Adolf Loos, the vernacular – without being defined by them. 'Architects', he says, 'are the great copiers...to copy one architect is not good...To copy a thousand is food for development.' But these references are often hidden – some even secret. Walk through the Chiado district of Lisbon and you would hardly notice anything. The area burned down in 1988. Siza rebuilt it faithfully, making new routes through the congested courtyards and streets. The area does not look different: it works differently. Pragmatic elements can be the most dramatic, like the service aqueduct in the housing at Evora (1997).

Despite some criticism of the Baroque Modernist whimsy of buildings like the Serralves Institute in Oporto (1999), Siza has become one of the most important Portuguese artists in any medium. Respect for his work and teaching is international: he won the Pritzker Prize in 1992. But the sheer range of type, idea, scale, manner and degree of expression defies categorization, from the elegant work at the University of Alicante (1998) to the Portuguese Pavilion at Lisbon Expo in 1998, displaying a simple Modernism yet with a visually perverse, sagging, reinforced-stone canopy. 'A builder of works of gravity', he is funny with it.

He is certainly not your average contextualist: 'I am not in favour of submitting to the context. The very idea fills me with a type of horror,' he says. New buildings must enter their context like a ballerina into a ballet, 'not creating something new but transforming something that already exists'. Despite its fragile context, his Santiago de Compostela Museum in Spain (1995) is powerful – a wedge-shaped granite form with simple, sophisticated circulation, its servicing housed in what looks like an upside-down minimalist table hanging from the ceiling. His 1996 Santa Maria de Canavezes Church and Parish Centre is a wonderful abstraction of Modernism and the Baroque.

Siza, like Aalto, is called an architect without theory – surely a huge compliment. His own brief, lucid descriptions blow theory away, suggesting a more personal understanding of architecture and its integration into life. In this, he is, incidentally, theory's best critic. 'Architects are modest if anyone is. In one way or another they wrap mantles around their own work. These mantles, very intricate and occasionally elegant, with a complex hang, stand up perfectly well when suitably starched and can be confused with the body of a theory' (quoted in Kester Rattenbury, 'Siza Matters', *Building Design*, 15 December 2000). He seems to see right through the emperor's new clothes.

Alvaro Siza

S

Top: Bibliotecha
Alexandrina, Alexandria,
2002

Centre left: Karmoy Fishing
Museum, Norway, 1998

Bottom left: Norwegian
Embassy, Berlin, 1999

Bottom right: Bibliotecha
Alexandrina, Alexandria,
2002

What's in a name? A lot when it comes to Snøhetta, one of the few young architectural practices whose moniker is neither an amalgam of surnames nor some fashionable abstracted techno-speak. Oslo-based Snøhetta take their name from a mountain in central Norway – not just a beautiful peak but also the seat of the Norse gods.

Mysticism, metaphor and mountain, indeed landscapes generally, come together in the work of the practice, established in 1987 for the competition to build a new library in Alexandria, Egypt – a building to replace one of the wonders of the ancient world. They won.

Completed in 2002, the library is, to date, their *magnum opus* – a giant 160-metre-diameter glazed disc that emerges out of the layers of history and tilts its face to a northern light. Its solid granite drum is inscribed with alphabets that represent 10,000 years and 500 cultures. The great amphitheatre of the reading room sits 2,000 readers. Next door a spherical planetarium is suspended above the ground so that, like Atlas, you can take the world on your shoulders. A bridge across the site invokes the streak of a comet. The library mediates between land and sea, earth and air, past, present and future.

This attempt to connect with the enduring is typical of all of the practice's deeply symbolic work. Their art museum scheme for a gallery dedicated to William Turner in Margate, UK, is similarly a harbour wall outcrop, a monolith duelling with the power of the sea. Their work also reveals a desire to connect the particular to the universal; from the screens woven from a native coastal bush on the flank of the Karmoy Fishing Museum in Norway (1998) to the building's concrete-framed glazed end wall, which gazes out to infinity.

Snøhetta reject society's artificial hierarchies in favour of the wider horizons of the natural environment. This is reflected in the organization of the practice, run by three partners: American Craig Dykers (born 1961), Christoph Kapeller (born 1956) and Kjetil Thorsen (born 1958). They work in an integrated way as landscape designers and masterplanners as well as architects. Everybody can work simultaneously on a web-based hyper-file that holds, updates and synchronizes the projects. Connection is central to their way of working.

It is hard to detect recurrent motifs in the buildings – while each creates its own topography, they are too attuned in both material and form to their own locale – although Snøhetta do have a knack for cornering spectacular edge-condition sites. The location for their Norwegian Embassy in Berlin (1999), just south of the Tiergarten, is more prosaic but they have made a Norwegian landscape of it. The embassy's south wall is a single, 120-ton, monolithic slice of grey Norwegian granite. Another wall comprises glass louvres designed to hint at the verticality of forests and the cool of glaciers.

A new landscape will emerge on home turf when Oslo's National Opera House is completed in 2008 – a fractured mountain of a building, rising diagonally out of the fjord. Again, for Snøhetta, landscape and building fuse into one universal whole.

S

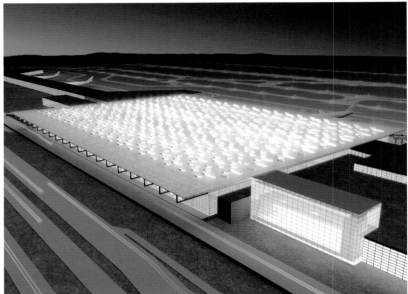

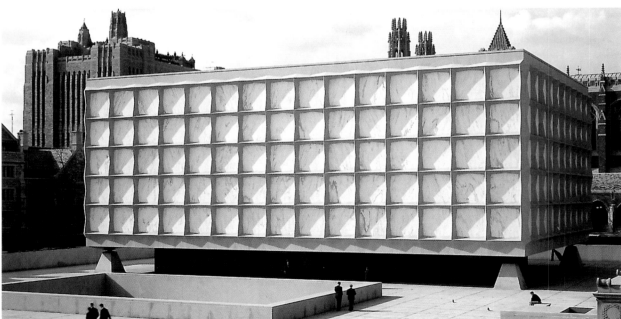

There are nearly 2,000 architects working in Skidmore, Owings, & Merrill offices all over the world. The firm has carried out over 10,000 architectural, engineering, interior-design and planning projects in its long history. These staggering statistics tell you almost all you need to know about this office.

Formed in 1936, SOM is almost single-handedly responsible for a model of practice that provides accommodation for the globalized corporation, wherever that might be in the world. It has produced buildings that remain unforgettable landmarks – the US's tallest building, the Sears Tower in Chicago (1974), springs to mind as an example – whatever their quality as pieces of architecture.

Rather than focusing on the ego of a single, named architect, SOM was founded as a collective of designers. This idea was perhaps laudable but did not work. If you know that SOM designed the famous, elegant, Miesian Lever House in New York (1952) or the Beinecke Library at Yale University (1963), then you probably know that the partner in charge was Gordon Bunshaft, the most prominent creative force behind SOM in the 1950s and 1960s and winner of the Pritzker Prize in 1988. Likewise, you might even know that it was Walter Netsch who designed the Colorado Springs Air Force Chapel (1962), and Bruce Graham who was responsible for the classic cross-braced skyscraper that is the John Hancock Center in Chicago (1970). Suddenly, the anonymity of the SOM initials starts to fracture.

Today this paradox continues. A firm the size of SOM cannot possibly maintain stylistic consistency, but it is clear that certain SOM offices produce far better buildings than others. David Childs of the New York office has been an outspoken voice in the efforts to reconstruct the World Trade Center site, as well as being the author of the plan to resurrect New York's Penn Station. Roger Duffy, design partner at the New York office, is the progenitor of the best of the work coming out of SOM at the moment. This includes the spectacular flat roof of Changi International Airport in Singapore (2003), with its 2,000 skylights, and the Libeskind-esque Training Facility for the Kuwaiti State Police (2003). Duffy himself has claimed that not identifying individuals with their work led to a 'shield of anonymity that permitted a decline in quality' in the 1980s and early 1990s.

Despite SOM's staggering commercial success, there are some indisputable dogs in their portfolio, such as the corporate Postmodernism of the Quaker Oats Building in Chicago (1986) and the sub-Cesar Pelli extruded section of the Lutheran Brotherhood Building in Minneapolis (1983). However, the classics are all there. Lever House is perhaps rivalled only by Mies van der Rohe's Seagram Building in New York as the most elegant of 1950s skyscrapers. The Beinecke Library, which had the most expensive façade ever constructed when it was completed in 1963, made of thin alabaster panels in a concrete honeycomb structure, stands today in the heart of the retro architectural melange of Yale University, a mysterious object illuminated internally by dappled light – a truly fantastic architectural experience. SOM's body of work is a palimpsest of mainstream architectural history.

S

Main picture: Casa das
Artes Cultural Centre,
Oporto, 1991

Top right: Silo Norte
Shopping Centre,
Lisbon, 1998

Centre right: Quinta do
Lago House, Oporto, 1989

Until recently, Eduardo Souto de Moura's name would rarely have been heard without Alvaro Siza being mentioned in the same breath. The two Portuguese architects' careers have been inextricably linked, Souto de Moura usually being mentioned as an apprentice of Siza or, at worst, as some kind of pale imitation.

This comparison is a little unfair, given that Souto de Moura is nineteen years Siza's junior, and although he did work in Siza's office for five years, he left in 1979 and has since firmly built his own credentials. Souto de Moura was born in Oporto in 1952 and graduated from the school of architecture there in 1980. He established his own practice the same year and started a ten-year stint as a professor at the faculty of architecture in Oporto in 1981.

Souto de Moura forms part of a regional school that grew up around Oporto when the architecture faculty was under the direction of Fernando Tavora, and his work has strong resonance not just with Siza but also with Adalberto Dias, Maria de Graca Nieto and Jose Manuel Soares. However, his work has a minimalist bent that some critics attribute to the influence of US artists such as Donald Judd and Sol LeWitt and others see as a distillation of such architectural references as the filigree steel sections of Mies van der Rohe and the Tropical Modernism of Luis Barragán.

The vast majority of Souto de Moura's early work is in and around Oporto, including his Casa das Artes Cultural Centre (1991), his three Nevogilde houses (1988) and the extraordinary Quinta do Lago House (1989), which took strongly geometric shapes and tamed them within the perimeter of a single-storey bungalow. This white-render creation was the first suggestion that Souto de Moura was moving beyond the language of his masters and this is an impulse that has continued since.

More recent and significant work includes his row houses at Via Lugarinho in Oporto (1996), the renovation of the municipal market in Braga (1997), and the Portuguese Pavilion at the Hanover Expo in 2000 – a collaboration between Souto de Moura and Siza that drew almost universal plaudits for its spectacular covered outdoor space and the audacity of its sweeping suspended ceilings internally. His adaptability was also shown at the Silo Norte Shopping Centre (1998), where he created an exhibition space and gallery in the belly of an old cylindrical parking garage.

Now his portfolio is heaving with some of the most prestigious of the commissions that are transforming Oporto in time for the 2004 European Football Championships in Portugal. His project for a stadium at Braga sits in spectacular fashion in the dramatic topography, with two sweeping stands that allow views not only of the game but also of Portugal's countryside.

Various people and publications have, in recent years, searched for the next generation of Portuguese architects in a country dominated by Siza and Souto de Moura. The talent is there, but these two titans – mentor and younger master – are likely to remain on top of the heap for a while yet.

Eduardo Souto de Moura

S

Japan's cities had been reduced to ashes by the end of the Second World War – occupied and erased (utterly in the case of Hiroshima and Nagasaki). The country's insular culture, already crumbling under the forward-looking Meiji Restoration, had been broken down once and for all. Out of the carnage emerged Kenzo Tange, just graduated and in a perfect position to direct the rebuilding of the country on Modernist principles – even if these were largely alien to what had gone before. Tange's success was to bring something distinctively Japanese to the International Style's grasp for universality. His first great task was directly connected to the destruction: the creation of the Hiroshima Peace Centre (1950) and Hiroshima Peace Memorial Museum (1952).

Tange was born in Osaka in 1913 and brought up in Imabari, Shikoku Island, until, inspired by Le Corbusier (through an apprenticeship in Kunio Maekawa's architectural office), he began graduate studies at the University of Tokyo in 1942. Through his subsequent teaching and the establishment of the Tange Laboratory he helped mould the next generation of Japanese architects, including Fumihiko Maki, Kisho Kurokawa and Arata Isozaki. He established his own practice in 1961 but has remained a committed teacher both in Japan and, as a visiting professor, across the world.

It was Tange's pair of lotus-like elliptical gymnasia for the 1964 Tokyo Olympics that announced the first full flowering of his approach. Swooping semicircular roofs are held up by steel cables that create elevational curves to match the curves of the plan. The forms have been likened to samurai helmets.

Tange has also been linked with the promotion of megastructures and incorporated these in his 1960 Tokyo Plan, which proposed extending the city using linked artificial islands. Although never implemented it was hugely influential. Tange has since been invited to engage in planning projects in Bologna, Sicily (a 'new town' for Catania) and Paris. Such concerns with the larger scale and the interlinking of a city's transport and other networks appeared to ally Tange with Japan's Metabolist movement, which perceived buildings and cities as living organisms with life cycles, but he has always stood slightly apart from the group, looking for a 'union of technology and humanity'.

After producing a rich output of functionalist buildings across Japan, Tange flirted briefly with Postmodernism in the 1980s. The Yokohama Museum of Art (1989), with its decorated façade and overscale pyramid-topped porch, is a good example, although its Rationalist plan links the scheme back to his earlier Hiroshima project.

Kenzo Tange Associates has grown enormously and many critics consider much of the recent output of his office to be corporate fodder lacking the spark of his earlier work. But the oversized grids, struts and suspended polished sphere of the Fuji Television Building in Tokyo (1996), while gimmicky, still pack a punch, and the sheer scale of the paired towers of the 1991 Tokyo City Hall complex is staggering. Tange's practice is still building on a large scale across South-East Asia but appears increasingly marginal to the directions architecture is now taking internationally.

The description of TEN Arquitectos as international cutting-edge with deep Mexican roots can be confusing to the casual viewer. Their work looks so Northern European, with its cool, faintly witty skin jobs. But the skins allow clever climatic and spatial manipulations, their apparently seamless forms often remaking existing buildings or remnants of buildings. This is fusion architecture.

TEN (Taller Enrique Norten) was formed in 1985 by Norten and Bernado Gomez-Pimienta and is surely Mexico's biggest international star practice. Norten, born 1954, studied architecture at the Universidad Iberoamericano in Mexico City and at Cornell in New York and is visiting professor at universities in Mexico and at Sci-Arc, Rice and Columbia. He is also founding member of *Arquitectura* magazine (1991). Gomez-Pimienta, born in Brussels in 1961, studied at the Universidad Anahuao in Mexico and at Columbia and is visiting professor at Illinois Urbana, Champaign, Sci-Arc and at universities in Mexico.

Their work is formally varied – there are lots of clean and fairly dramatic shapes – but these are less important than the way they use the

dumb-looking skin to make and remake deceptively simple buildings. The best known of these is the Hotel Habita (2000) in Mexico City. Formerly a 1950s block, it is totally transfigured by its double skin of frosted glass, which screens old balconies and new circulation, forming a climatic, acoustic and visual buffer with horizontal patches of clear glass.

Looking random from the outside, these clear sections are carefully placed to edit views from the rooms – the best features of the Mexico City skyline are visible, sometimes at ankle height, while the worst are screened out. This continues in the frosted-glass balconies of the roof decks, which crop a dramatic skyline from the least promising surroundings. There is no sign of the mundane past yet the old building directly provides the sophistication of the new.

The Habita exemplifies ideas used in many of TEN's key buildings, though to different purposes and effects. The Princeton Parking Garage (1998) wraps a new skin round an old parking building. The Educare building in Jalisco (2001) and House 1A overlooking the lake at Valle de Bravo (2000) recompose irregular forms; House Le at Colonia Condensa (1995) makes clever use of tight-screened spaces. But often it is the shapes that first catch the eye, like the folded form of the Televisa Centre in Mexico City (1995), for which TEN won the first Mies van der Rohe award for Latin American architecture, or the huge, glowing bubble of the JVC Conference Centre scheme for Guadalajara (2000).

TEN's new and most major commission, the Brooklyn Library – part of an Office for Metropolitan Architecture/ Diller + Scofidio masterplan – looks set to be a classic demonstration of their architecture. Due for completion in 2007, the triangular site is, of course, screened, luminous, protected by double walls that lift like a curtain to open key views and skirt round a new public amphitheatre, formed from the ground like a piece of archaeology discovered on the site and taken into a new composition.

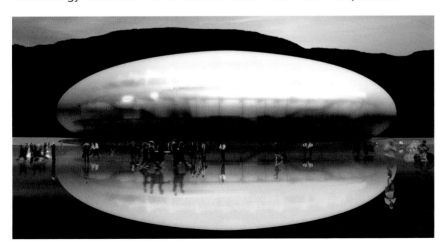

TEN Arquitectos

t

Top left: Parc de la
Villette, Paris, 1982

Centre right: Le Fresnoy,
Tourcoing, 1997

Top right: Parc de la
Villette, Paris, 1982

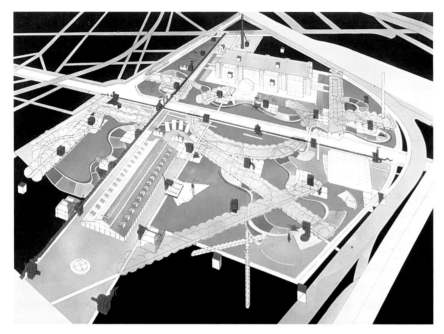

'To really experience architecture', reads Bernard Tschumi's 1976 *Advertisements for Architecture*, 'you may even have to commit a murder.' Tschumi's early experimental projects, like *The Manhattan Transcripts* – ambiguous, brilliant, funny storyboards of architectural drawing mixed with scene-of-the-crime reports – led a wave of 'manifesto' projects that proclaimed the essential relationship of architecture and event. Most of the rest of the 'narrative architecture' movement (which Tschumi more or less inspired) also made ambiguous 'event' drawings, but translated them into funny-shaped buildings – an allegory for the event – rather than manipulating the event itself. Tschumi's early work seemed to be leading this field – but the event not the shape was most important.

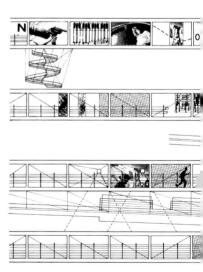

     Born in Switzerland in 1944, Tschumi was already established as a 'paper' architect when he beat the world's experimental field, including Zaha Hadid and Rem Koolhaas, to win the competition for a new Parc de la Villette on the Paris outskirts in 1982. Tschumi's scheme is, unusually, famous for both its speculative drawings and its built form. The drawn project is an extrapolated grid of manipulated red cubes, part Cartesian game, part space invaders, part axonometric, part planometric, further animated by a theoretical, funny text. As built, it is a huge grid of manipulated, choreographed red *folies* that are stages for events – Tschumi always illustrates the scheme with marching bands, cinema screenings and games of football.

Tschumi's study of event and form continued in buildings and books like *Event Cities* (1994), with drawings of firework displays or an ambiguous fusion of cinema storyboards with roof trusses for Le Fresnoy in Tourcoing, France (1997). This film and media centre covered and overlaid (rather than restoring or demolishing) a crumbling 1905 popular entertainment centre with a huge new roof. The collage of old and new includes extraordinary film locations – as in the roof – and looks oddly like the ambiguous drawings.

The clarity of Tschumi's building and writing is sometimes seen as a disadvantage. Some find his later work boring because it is no longer a funny shape. At Lerner Hall, Columbia University, New York (1999), he caused outrage by sticking with the Beaux-Arts plan and formal façades of the 1894 masterplan. The drama of the building comes from his arrangement of circulation and activity: a huge, glass ramp links library, media lounges, a cinema and pigeonholes into a vast, unpredictable, socially dynamic space.

Though Tschumi's recent computer images lack their predecessors' speculative iconic status, he continued to develop his theory as influential dean of Columbia and through prolific publications and exhibitions. At the turn of the century he landed a batch of major, fast-track buildings, including the Rouen Zénith concert hall (2002), and projects for the Acropolis Museum, Athens, the Museum of African Art, New York, and the Museum of Contemporary Art, São Paulo. All are designed to choreograph event, cityscape and unpredictable possibility within relatively modest forms – not allegories – exactly tailored to what the building might do. It is an admirable strategy even if it fails to satisfy those craving the early provocations.

Bernard Tschumi

t

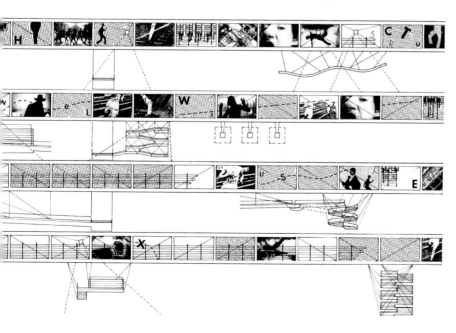

No post-war architect has come as close to articulating a truly German architecture as Oswald Mathias Ungers. He is the grand old man of German architecture, universally respected for his lifelong commitment to teaching, if not always for his buildings – their strongly Rationalist approach is not to everybody's taste.

Ungers was born in 1926 in Kaisersesch, Germany, and trained at the Technical University of Karlsruhe under Egon Eiermann, the man who kept alive the flame of International Modernism under Nazi rule. Eiermann's Modernist Rationalism generated the stylistic obsessions of much of Ungers' early work. After opening his own studio in Cologne in 1950, Ungers carried out large housing projects in the war-ravaged city, including influential schemes at Cologne-Braunsfeld (1951), Cologne-Nippes (1957) and Cologne-Seeberg (1966). He also built a series of one- and two-family houses in the Cologne suburbs, including his own house at Müngersdorf (1959) – a plain white rectangle with white-render façades that feature strong and regular series of full-height windows and conceal a rationally divided plan. His practice prospered in the 1950s, with industrial buildings in Cologne also in his portfolio, and his theoretical interests began to bear fruit, with his (albeit limited) involvement in the Team X group and his professorship at the Technical University of Berlin, which he held between 1963 and 1968.

Ungers then moved to the US, where he held many prestigious academic posts (including Cornell, Harvard and UCLA), but did not build much until the 1970s, taking his retrospective place at the top table of German post-war architecture. After opening an office in Frankfurt am Main in 1976, prestigious commissions arrived, such as his Deutsches Architektur Museum (1984). Sometimes seen as his masterpiece, this is famously a building within a building, inhabiting four storeys of galleries with an internal white-render tower complete with pitched roof. It is a mishmash of Ungers' Rationalism and his Postmodernist tendencies and is a horrendous place to look at an exhibition, with poor spaces at a small scale, an uncomfortable internal atmosphere, and a large sunken auditorium that photographs well but is badly out of scale with the room in which it sits.

His most famous project is most probably his huge office tower in Frankfurt, the Torhaus (1985), which expressed his obsession with the square as the predominant geometric shape in his work. This square has become almost a cliché and as a stylistic conceit perhaps conceals some of Ungers' importance as an urbanist. Rem Koolhaas has consistently praised Ungers' experimental urban planning work in Berlin in the 1960s, recognizing it as a kind of urban laboratory – Ungers' study presaged much of Koolhaas's own writing about post-Cold War Berlin.

But true to the form of most contemporary German architects, Ungers has hardly found popularity internationally. His only building outside Germany is in Washington, DC, and that is technically on German soil – the German Embassy and Ambassador's Residence (1994). As he reaches his dotage he continues to build on a huge scale, with projects such as the $270-million Pergamon Museum in Berlin underway.

Bottom: Möbius House,
the Netherlands, 1998

Centre right: SMART
Apartment Building,
Hilversum, 2003

Top right: Electricity substation, Innsbruck, 2002

UN Studio is the current name for the practice of Dutch pair Ben van Berkel
and Caroline Bos, who set up shop in 1988. Like Rem Koolhaas's Office for
Metropolitan Architecture, van Berkel and Bos's office has been the incubator
for a generation of new talent – Winy Maas and Jacob van Rijs, two of the
founders of MVRDV (see page 156) worked together at UN Studio – and van
Berkel is perhaps one of the only people that can rival Koolhaas in his enthusiasm to publish theoretical works and build a dazzling variety of architectural projects. This means that UN Studio has spawned a host of imitators,
good and bad.

By its critics the practice's work has been read as an architecture
of systems, taking arbitrary diagrams and making them form, coupled, of
course, with a Bond villain's taste in materials and scale. According to its
many supporters, the work has translated into a complex and information-
led architecture. Van Berkel, in his book *Mobile Forces* (1995), compares his
approach to that of Jeff Kipnis, Greg Lynn, Hani Rashid, Koolhaas, Bernard
Tschumi and Jean Nouvel – 'a commitment to open programmes, a thematic
interest in non-specific or residual spaces, a tendency towards highly flexible
or dynamic project processes'.

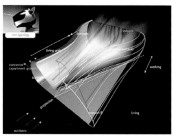

This vision of a nimble, information-led architecture is perhaps
ultimately impossible to build. UN Studio's remarkable Möbius House in
the Netherlands (1998) took the arbitrary diagram of the Möbius strip and
made a house out of it, ordering the spaces in succession around a route of

UN Studio

extraordinary complexity. This research into the house has continued with the more recent SMART Apartment Building project (2003), but while these diagrams deconstruct hierarchy and are reaching towards new housing typologies, they do not provide the flexibility of simpler diagrams.

The practice is perhaps most at home in its engineering projects. Two electricity substations, one in Innsbruck, Austria, and one in Amersfoort, the Netherlands, can be seen as physical manifestations of the forces at work in the project, be they electrical, urbanistic, political, aesthetic. At Amersfoort, the REMU substation (1994) is expressed as two interlocking volumes – one clad in conductive aluminium, one in insulating basaltic rock – referring to the invisible process of electrical transformation. The substation in Innsbruck (2002) moves these ideas on, using basalt and concrete for its cladding but making the seemingly hermetic envelope create one side of an urban square.

The difference between these two buildings, though, is slight, and the question arises – is UN Studio still progressing as quickly as it did in the late 1980s and 1990s? Have they passed their peak? The Innsbruck building and other recent projects are immensely stylish, but their work seems less diverse than it was. They have perhaps become victims of a stylistic palette they themselves had a hand in inventing.

It is undeniable, though, that any practice that can produce, in one decade, projects ranging from the famous Erasmus Bridge in Rotterdam (1996), to the Möbius House, to a teaset for Alessi (2003) is one with an immense range and motivation. Their production can only increase, with their profile now as high as it has ever been.

u

Top left: Soft and Hairy
House, Tsukuba, 1994

Top right: Poolhouse,
Sussex, 2001

Bottom: Truss Wall
House, Tokyo, 1993

Thatch is an unlikely contemporary building material, especially for architects with avant-garde pretensions, but in the hands of experts such as Ushida Findlay anything can happen.

The unlikely pairing of Scottish Kathryn Findlay and Japanese Eisaku Ushida has produced some extraordinary work – variously described as neo-Expressionist and organic Modernist – which at first glance seems to owe little to any antecedents and much to their powerful imaginations. The practice, which emerged out of the office of Arata Isozaki, was established in Tokyo in 1987 by Ushida (born 1953), who graduated locally, and Findlay (born 1954), who trained at London's Architectural Association. Now the centre of gravity has shifted to London, where Findlay works. Starting with their scheme for the experimental Houses of the Future programme, part of the Glasgow 1999 architecture festival, the practice has brought an inventiveness to the UK first made evident in Japan.

The thatch appeared on the roof of a glazed-wall poolhouse in the gardens of a sixteenth-century Sussex manor house (2001). A planted ridge-line brought an element of traditional Japanese building to the work. An earlier scheme, perhaps the practice's most celebrated project, is the Soft and Hairy House (1994) in Tsukuba which takes the planted roof to its logical conclusion – an edible garden above a courtyard home. A glass, speckled, blue blob pushing into the centre of this Surrealist dream-world is the bathroom. By constructing the house from a metal mesh armature sprayed with concrete the pair could create flowing bespoke interiors related to the human body, movement and the mathematically generated growth patterns of nature.

This is one of a series of private homes in Japan. The Spiral Wall House in Kobe (1994) is another, the Truss Wall House in Tokyo (1993) a third. The latter, on a tight urban site, has a series of internal spaces that relate only vaguely to the outside envelope, the walls being moulded into varying appropriate thicknesses and folded round to create a cocoon with a ramp up to a tiny roof terrace. Interiors and exteriors form one continuous surface – a non-hierarchical 'cluster within a cluster within a cluster'.

Grafton New Hall, designed in 2002 and as yet a paper project, is intended to be one of the most singular country houses built in the UK this century. It is a vast, sandstone-clad starfish heaving itself out of the clay of the Cheshire countryside. Like the Tokyo houses, a moulded-concrete interior is proposed that stretches and spirals and turns over itself to create a sequence of flowing interiors on a grand scale. The sandstone, partially worked and partially left rough, is another twisted way of using local vernacular crafts.

Ushida Findlay's buildings are increasingly bedded in the climate, too, with the passage of the sun and the desire to stabilize temperatures being incorporated into and generating the forms. A 2001 scheme for an art gallery in Brisbane, Australia, envisages a 'jelly' space – a double-skinned nimbus around the building – porous to light but moderating the surface temperature. Not since Antonio Gaudí have architects so wilfully departed from the rectilinear forms we expect from buildings. Strange fruit indeed.

Ushida Findlay

u

Left: Sydney Opera
House, 1978

Top right: Bagsvaerd
Church, Copenhagen, 1973

Bottom right: Can
Lis, Majorca, 1973

It is one of the greatest of architectural myths: the scribbled drawing plucked from the competition waste bin; the young architect unable to realize the unbuildable structure; the building nonetheless emerging as the most iconic in the world. And all of it is wrong – except the last. Jørn Utzon has been, until recently, the least acknowledged of all great living architects – a genius whose other extraordinary works remained largely unknown.

Utzon always worked like an artist or inventor. Born in 1918 in Copenhagen, his references and techniques are unusually broad, including Mayan, Islamic, Berber and Chinese sources as well as the modern greats. He studied at the Royal Danish Academy and went to Stockholm during the Second World War, returning to set up office and living off graphic and furniture design while entering architectural competitions. Exquisite product design and beautiful, ambiguous graphics – the roof plan of an exhibition or flow of goods through a factory – remain key in his work.

Even his earliest architectural work was rooted in experiment – as in his first, ruthlessly rigorous house at Hellebaek (1952), where he mocked-up on site without plans. His later houses and housing remain masterly, from his reworking of Danish suburban residential complexes to the manip-ulation of vernacular and minimalism and the framing of astonishing views in his 1973 house, Can Lis, in Majorca.

But it was Sydney Opera House that made his name. The story of the 1956 competition diverges from the myth. Utzon's radical submission, suggesting floating shells over the harbour, was noted by Leslie Martin as 'worth a second look'. Eero Saarinen, arriving late, picked it as a clear winner. The jury were unanimous. Far from being out of his depth, Utzon invented or adapted many of the extraordinary formal and structural tech-niques: the great Aztec-style platform over the harbour, built before the structure was resolved; the vaulted forms; their relation to a sphere, which allowed some prefabrication; the tiling of the shells to reflect the light. But internal politicking engineered his resignation in 1966. Architects and students took to the streets in protest – to no avail. The building was finished – internally compromised – in 1978.

Utzon arrived home in 1966, aged forty-eight, to be told he would get no further work from the Danish government – a tragic waste. His 1961 Silkebourg Museum has been called one of the greatest unbuilt projects of the twentieth century. Despite extraordinary smaller projects, like the curi-ous Bagsvaerd Church near Copenhagen (1973), he closed his office early and vanished into retirement in Majorca.

Sydney became the quintessential model both of the truly iconic building and of how a city might enter the world stage through architec-ture. Gehry was chosen for the Bilbao Guggenheim partly because his sketches suggested Utzon's. Yet Utzon was omitted from many classic works of architectural history, and there was no serious book on him until Richard Weston's fabulous *Utzon* of 2002. In the same year he was commissioned (with sons Jan and Kim) to renovate Sydney Opera House. Finally, in 2003, he won the Pritzker Prize, aged eighty-four.

Jørn Utzon

u

Bottom left: Benjamin
Franklin monument,
Philadelphia, 1976

Centre right: 'Duck and
Decorated Shed' drawing,
1972

Top right: National Gallery
extension, London, 1991

'A dangerous book' said the *Ohio Review* of Robert Venturi, Denise Scott Brown and Stephen Izenour's *Learning from Las Vegas* (1972). 'It threatens those things that we use to distinguish between us, the cultured, and them, the vulgar.' It was not the first time Venturi and his wife and partner (born 1925 and 1931 respectively) had challenged the orthodoxy – nor the last.

It started with the Vanna Venturi house in Pennsylvania in 1964. Countering wall-to-wall Modernist rigour, Robert Venturi's building was, as he says, both complex and simple, big and small, open and closed, good and bad. A big split capital was re-scaled as a little house, its Palladian planning distorted, stair and fireplace wrangling round each other for space. It was photographed, definitively, with Robert's mother, Vanna, sitting in Renaissance-Man centre stage. It is proto-Postmodernism at its most loveable. This was followed up in book form by *Complexity and Contradiction in Architecture* (1966). A 'gentle manifesto' against the prevailing Modernist purism, it welcomed the vernacular and historical back into the architectural repertoire. 'Main Street is Almost All Right', it said in one of architecture's most memorable slogans – arguably a turning point in architectural thought.

With *Learning from Las Vegas* things hotted up. Based on projects with the authors' Yale students, it argued that architects could draw from the commercial, the 'ordinary' and 'common' taste. A brilliant study of the

signs, decorations and typologies of the Vegas strip, notably the 'Duck and Decorated shed' – it suggested that Modernist buildings, eschewing ornament, had become their own decoration. Its pro-billboard embrace of commercialism was to remain controversial for at least thirty years.

Unsurprisingly, reaction to their complex workload was mixed. Their house-frame monument to Benjamin Franklin in Philadelphia (1976) was much loved – an early version of the urban regeneration that they have pursued (relatively unadvertised) ever since. Their Postmodernist vernacular houses – the paired Trubeck and Wislocki houses in Nantucket (1971) – were also popular; their public buildings sometimes less so.

The National Gallery extension in London (1991) entered a heated factional field (Prince Charles had damned a predecessor as 'a carbuncle on the face of an old and much-loved friend'). Their building's reaction – a thin classical stone wall visibly wrapped round the frame like a stage curtain – outraged UK critics. It took years for its contextual wit to be partly admired.

Despite their embrace of the popular, the firm works mostly in the classic grounds of high architecture. Their many buildings for big-league US universities range from boring to mannered, highly decorated to admired restoration work. Their museums are as varied. They have designed master-plans, major art exhibitions, community action and teapots.

And despite huge international fame, VSBA's work seems concentrated, almost isolated, in their native Philadelphia. Their current love affair is with Japan, resulting in the Nikko Kirifuri resort (1997) – as contentious as any project in the play of popular taste. The issues they have raised just will not lie down. Grudgingly, they are recognized as one of the most influential practices of the late twentieth century.

Venturi, Scott Brown & Associates

V

Top: Kimmel Center for
the Performing Arts,
Philadelphia, 2002

Bottom left: Tokyo
International Forum, 1996

Bottom right: Lincoln
Center Jazz Rooms,
New York, 2004

Concert pianist or architect? Rafael Viñoly could have been either. Like Daniel Libeskind, he is the personification of the much mused-on relationship between architecture and music. A designer of concert halls and the owner of five pianos, he has said there is no relationship between his two disciplines, but then given lectures on the subject. He has also designed an auditorium shaped like a cello and stresses the need to 'hear with your eyes'.

There are many other counterpoints to Viñoly: he is a highly commercial international architect who still takes time to teach at Harvard, Yale and Columbia; and he is the founder of what was the largest practice in South America but also an activist who set up an alternative architecture school following the 1974 military coup in his native Uruguay. Forever on the move, verbally, physically and geographically, he left Montevideo, where he was born in 1944 – to a father who was the artistic director of the Sodre Opera Theatre – and trained at the University of Buenos Aires. His practice built over nine million square feet of architecture before he moved to New York in 1979 to soak up its energy.

Stylistically he is constantly moving too. His pre-New York work, such as the 1978 Color TV Production Center in Buenos Aires, is squarely in the Modernist tradition, while some of his past US work, such as Princeton Stadium (1998), has something of a superficial Postmodern historicism about it. His work exploded onto the world stage with the Tokyo International Forum project (1996) – a vast crystal palace megastructure with a theatrical glazed oval atrium. All of his output has been informed by a nuts-and-bolts high-tech (even if not always expressed formally) and he shares a close working relationship – and New York and London offices – with British engineers Dewhurst McFarlane.

He is now a hugely successful architect with hundreds of millions of dollars worth of work, especially in the US, where he is designing offices, art galleries, laboratories and museums in a variety of idioms. This recent work includes the Kimmel Center for the Performing Arts in Philadelphia (2002), a project that defeated both Louis Kahn and Robert Venturi and that is home to his cello-shaped auditorium, treated as a free-standing building beneath another spectacular glazed roof.

In New York, as part of the Think consortium, he missed out (to Libeskind) in the 2002 World Trade Center competition. Viñoly envisaged a cultural space in the sky. An essential part of the New York experience, he argued, is the view of the city from above. He is still managing to build high in his adopted home, however, with his scheme for the Lincoln Center Jazz Rooms, which is expected to open in 2004 halfway up a skyscraper at Columbus Circle. It envisages a vast glazed backdrop for musical starry nights high above the lights of Manhattan. It could also be considered the archetypal Viñoly project if there were any chance of such a thing from such a versatile performer.

When the limelight gets too much he retires to his butterfly-roofed timber-clad home in the Hamptons, Long Island – custom-made for the sound of his Steinway.

Rafael Viñoly

V

It is impossible to overestimate the impact that Adrian Geuze and his office, West 8, has had on contemporary landscaping and urbanism. One of the most famous living landscape architects, Geuze has almost single-handedly re-established landscape on the agenda of Dutch urbanism and is now taking his influence global, with projects in the US as well as across Europe. He has also been involved in designing the open spaces in or around buildings by most of the best Dutch contemporary architects and he is at the heart of the 'Superdutch' generation.

Geuze was born in Dordrecht in 1960 and studied for his degree in landscape architecture at the University of Wageningen, graduating in 1987. Shortly afterwards, he founded West 8 in Rotterdam with Paul van Beek, who later left the practice. The practice has been an influential and provocative voice in the debate about Dutch urbanism. Its controversial Wilderness scheme of 1993 proposed that the Randstad (the Netherlands' sacred green heart) be populated with suburban development at ultra-low densities to allow housing to be built there without destroying the ecological balance of the area. This was anathema in Dutch architecture, which was spending its time arguing that what was needed was higher densities than the traditional Dutch suburb. The research was generated by Geuze's extreme sensitivity to a contemporary situation where society is increasingly a collection of individuals rather than a homogenous entity. His influential essay 'Accelerating Darwin' (1993) advocates not a tectonic or material improvement in the environment, but the encouragement of a 'sensation of spontaneous culture which the city dweller creates'.

West 8's best-known project, the Schouwburgplein in Rotterdam (1996), attempts to reconcile these motivations with the need to create a functioning urban square in between three of the city's cultural institutions. The square is a raised platform on a metal structure and is lit from below by green and blue lights. Crane-like structures, perhaps recalling Rotterdam's port heritage, support lights that can be controlled from below by passers-by who drop a coin in the slot, literally empowering the individual to light the square as they see fit.

The formal geometry of this square, defined by the context, is perhaps not the best example of West 8's work. On their Oosterscheldedam Flood Barrier (1994) the black-and-white stripes of mussel shells are as much pieces of land art as landscape, and their poetic transformation of the Carrascoplein in Amsterdam (1998) shows how romantic landscapes can spring from the most unlikely of places. The Carrascoplein project used the forgotten space beneath a series of viaducts to create a park, integrating car parking in abstract patterns with patches of green space. Lighting is used to illuminate the soffits of the viaducts, creating a magical, Ballardian urban park.

Geuze's office is now one of the largest in the Netherlands and West 8's ongoing masterplans at the Ypenburg Vinex near the Hague show that they can marshal large plots and world-class architects with assurance. The provocations also continue with the palm-trees-in-the-sky plan for Arroyo, Pasadena, designed in 2002, and a win in the 2003 competition for a new urban plan for Tromsø, Norway.

Tod Williams
Billie Tsien

Tod Williams and Billie Tsien are exceptional in the US. They could, perhaps, be called anti-American dream. They are unpretentious and call a spade a spade. They are not interested in fakery but make buildings that look like buildings not blobs, and objects that admit their mass rather than masquerading as floating, high-tech constructions.

This husband-and-wife team has worked together since 1977. Born in 1943, Williams spent his early career in the office of Richard Meier, launching his own practice in 1974. He is a prolific teacher, too, lecturing at Cooper Union for fifteen years as well as doing stints at Yale, Harvard and Sci-Arc. Tsien is six years younger. Her varied career adds something new to the partnership, having taken in graphic design and fine art as well as architecture.

'We don't believe in light architecture,' says Williams, 'Architecture can be light-filled, but it is always heavy.' This is borne out best by their stunning and multi-award-winning Museum of American Folk Art in New York (2002). Set on the edge of a much more opulent and high-profile building site – Yoshio Taniguchi's Museum of Modern Art, which will be completed in 2005 – it will eventually be overshadowed by the much larger building, but for now, this eight-storey tower has stolen the limelight, mainly because of its astonishing metal façade. Williams says: 'We like to think we are the jewel in the belly button of MoMA, but I don't think they see it like that.'

It is difficult to disagree with one critic's assessment that this is 'the most important façade since Jean Nouvel's Arab Institute in Paris'. Williams and Tsien describe the form as an abstracted open hand, but it is as much the material that has caught the imagination. Made of an alloy of copper, zinc and manganese, the panels were cast against rutted steel and concrete in a process that was deliberately uncertain, producing sixty-three pieces in varying consistencies and colours, which make an extraordinary presence on the street. Internally, this showpiece building has been criticized for its tight plan and excessive circulation. The site is only 12.2 metres wide but the plan still manages to squeeze in three staircases, leaving exhibition spaces at an intimate scale. Even so, it remains their most significant building and possibly the best in New York City for twenty years.

Although the American Folk Art Museum is Williams and Tsien's calling card now, their work is diverse enough to take in Feinberg Hall in Princeton (1986), New College at the University of Virginia (1992) and the athletics centre at Eliel Saarinen's 1930s Cranbrook Academy. This has a wonderfully integrated yet austere timber exterior and a rich and playful interior, with deep oculi in the roof above the swimming pool, which call to mind a night sky of shining stars.

Williams and Tsien are somewhat lonely voices in the US. They build austere yet civic exteriors that could take their place next to the best in Europe. However, whether their work displays the sophistication and clarity in plan and section that it has in material and site strategy remains to be proven. They are essential to the Stateside, though, and should be treasured.

W

Lebbeus Woods

'This man is an optimist – and craggy with it,' said Peter Cook of Lebbeus Woods. The optimism is a surprise – Woods' incredible scribbled drawings suggest a world under interplanetary war. But Cook is spot-on. Lebbeus Woods' extraordinary Gormenghast-meets-Piranesi drawings have enormous suggestive currency, although they are also probably hugely misunderstood. As a contentious paper polemic they were once apparently part of Deconstructivism, but now that this is an established style, they may constitute one of its strongest, if most obscure, critics.

Woods was born in Lancing, Illinois, in 1940, trained at the University of Illinois and worked in the conventional offices of Roche & Dinkeloo and for Eero Saarinen before he became the design director of a small firm in Champaign, Illinois. His early drawings, made at night, were somewhere between Giovanni Piranesi, Etienne-Louis Boullée, sci-fi comics and unravellings of Einstein. 'After a long time travelling across mythological landscapes, recording the architecture and cities I discovered, I wanted to build something of my own,' he said. His first paper project was the exploded Newtonian Epicyclarium (1985) – 'the cure for a fever to build', a sort of observatory with a thirty-foot electronic field projecting webs of light and energy.

But these extraordinary drawings are less famous than the sequence relating to sites of conflict – the 'Freescapes' of Berlin Free Zone and Zagreb Free Zone (both 1991), in which huge structures like hybrids of military hardware crash into or explode out of the forms of the city. Conceived as 'an architecture of liberation', they suggest violent interventions, exposing conflict and paradoxically offering new freedoms. 'Architecture is war. War is architecture. I am at war with my time, with history, with all authority that resides in fixed and frightened forms,' he said.

Woods argues that architects who monumentalize authority are part of authoritarian repression: 'Architecture is deeply implicated in the attacks on the World Trade Center and the Pentagon through the concentration of symbolic and pragmatic infrastructure.' But his drawings seem to suggest affiliation with the occupying power, rather than describing the alternative uses or occupations that the interventions are designed to provoke. Wilfully provocative in an age of Deconstructivist establishment-building (Daniel Libeskind's Twin Towers, for instance), it takes attention to discover the underlying criticism.

Woods has – unsurprisingly – not built much. But he is prolific in all kinds of other ways besides his continual drawing and publishing. His installation, La Chute (2002), at the Cartier Foundation in Paris was a hallucinatory fracturing of Jean Nouvel's hallucinatory building. He produces science fiction, consults on computer games and is a design consultant on movies – sometimes inadvertently: Terry Gilliam's *Twelve Monkeys* used a scene directly suggesting his 1987 Neomechanical Tower drawing. He is co-founder and director of the Institute for Experimental Architecture. *New York Metro* called him 'our resident visionary'. His images have worldwide circulation and this, perversely, perhaps disguises the less famous but equally eloquent text and messages behind them.

W

The hanging gardens of Ken Yeang have brought a new aesthetic to the design of skyscrapers. More than that, they have brought a new ethos of sustainable design to the building type. His 'bioclimatic' towers have had an impact around the world, fusing high-tech and organic principles that have grown out of a response to the harsh and humid climate of his native country – Malaysia.

Born in 1948, he established his practice in Kuala Lumpur in 1976 with royal prince T. R. Hamzah as his business partner. It was not a tower but his own house – the 1984 Roof-Roof House – that first made his name. Its concrete form shelters under a giant white curving screen that filters the sunlight and protects it from the rain. He had been working on such an approach for years – ever since his training at the Architectural Association and at Cambridge, UK – but it is one thing to design a house appropriate to climate (vernacular architecture has been doing it for years) and quite another to apply the technology to the hard-nosed commercial office world, which is not exactly known for its low-energy commitments.

Yeang has shown that these domestic measures can work at high levels, however. His most celebrated bioclimatic project is the fifteen-storey, louvre-clad Menara Mesiniaga tower (1992) in Kuala Lumpur, which houses IBM's office there. Skyscrapers, says Yeang, should be treated as cities in the sky and mapped in similar ways, looking at use, density, inhabitants and open spaces.

This approach reached new heights in the eighty storeys of the Tokyo Nara Tower (1994). Gardens climb up the building, providing a climatic filter in terms of air quality, temperature and noise. The spiralling floor plans shade the levels beneath and create double- and even triple-height floor spaces to contain the gardens. Louvres and screens similarly mediate the environment within the building, which incorporates the latest in low-energy-consumption technology. The result is a scaly, organic skin rather than a shiny, smooth corporate sheath.

Yeang has actively disseminated his vision through teaching (he holds posts in the UK and Australia) and through a series of books that are as concerned with the science of low-energy building as with the aesthetics of the end result. And it is not just equatorial extremes that are in his sights. He has designed a thirty-storey residential tower as part of the massive redevelopment proposal for Elephant and Castle, south London (a project whose future is uncertain). It envisages the usual sky gardens and is designed to be built of demountable and reusable elements as a way of conserving natural resources.

If Yeang's ideas take off, the twenty-first century will see the skyscraper cease to be an ecological bugbear and instead become an icon of green thinking. How this eco-tech architecture develops as built form remains to be seen: 'Total control means lack of freedom,' says Yeang. 'The environment does not provide a rigid set of rules but rather an inspirational basis.' Yeang, however, has done more than plant the seeds of ideas – he is nurturing and displaying proud specimens. Watch his garden grow.

Ken Yeang

y

There cannot be many architects who have a building listed as a protected piece of heritage in their own lifetime, let alone within two years of its completion. But Peter Zumthor is no ordinary architect and it was hardly surprising when his Thermal Baths at Vals won this honour in 1998.

For some, Zumthor is the greatest architect alive today. His works are few but achieve a transcendental and austere beauty that comes from the regional tendency in his work (the majority are around Graubunden, the easternmost canton in Switzerland) and an unmatched connection with material and the craftsmen who make his buildings possible. He is the most important figure on the Swiss architectural scene, despite having a fraction of the profile of the likes of Herzog & de Meuron. The main reason for this is his unwillingness to allow his buildings to be published internationally and his somewhat cantankerous reputation. And he has only recently begun to build outside his native Alpine context.

Zumthor was born in Basle in 1943 and trained first as a cabinet-maker. His father was a master joiner and had planned that Peter should take over the family business. Zumthor rebelled against this, continuing his education in design at the School of Applied Arts in Basle and then at the Pratt Institute in New York. In 1968, Zumthor got his first job as an architect in the Department for the Preservation of Monuments for the canton of Graubunden and set up his own office in 1979 in Haldenstein.

Early buildings included a school in Churwalden (1983), a two-family house in Haldenstein (1983), his own studio in Haldenstein (1986) and the enclosure for the Roman archaeological site at Chur (1986) with its austere timber façades – his first major public building. Real recognition came in the early 1990s with the Sogn Benedetg Chapel, Sumvitg (1989), and the Residential Home for the Elderly in Masans, Chur (1993).

The staggering Thermal Baths at Vals (1996) are his major work so far, catapulting Zumthor into the major league of world architecture. The rectangular building, cut into a steep mountain, is an adjunct to a 1960s hotel building. It is made from the dark black rock of the mountain above, carved into a cave-like set of thermal baths – a seemingly timeless presence on the hillside and a deeply introspective and moving building. It is at one with its context to the extent that the concrete slab of the roof has been allowed to grow with wild flowers, punctuated only by skylights that let shafts of light into the dark interior, animating the stillness of the stone blocks and forming another elemental presence alongside the splashing and gurgling of water.

Zumthor talks often about the need to 'do the thing that is obvious but difficult', and to produce buildings of this quality takes years of design work, meticulous supervision on site, an intimate knowledge of materials and real bloody-mindedness. Zumthor has all of this in spades. It has meant that two of his projects that have been planned for some time are still not complete: his Kolumba Diocesan Museum in Cologne, Germany, now on site; and his Topography of Terror Holocaust memorial in Berlin, projected for completion in 2005. We can be confident that they will be worth the wait.

Peter Zumthor

Z

Abalos & Herreros
Abalos, Iñaki, and Juan Herreros, *Areas of Impunity*, Actar, 1997
Abalos, Iñaki, and Juan Herreros, *Recycling Madrid*, Actar, 1999
Abalos, Iñaki, and Juan Herreros, *Abalos & Herreros*, with an introduction by Alejandro Zaera, Editorial Gustavo Gili, 1993
www.abalos-herreros.com

Will Alsop
Alsop, Will, et al., *Architecture, Projects, Drawings by the Studio of Will Alsop, Cliff Barnet and John Lyall*, Architectural Association, 1984
Alsop, Will, Bruce McLean and Jan Störmer, *City of Objects: Designs on Berlin*, Architectural Press, 1992
Gooding, Mel, *William Alsop, Buildings and Projects*, Princeton, 1992
Powell, Ken, *Will Alsop 1968–1990*, Laurence King, 2001
Powell, Ken, *Will Alsop 1990–2000*, Laurence King, 2002
Spens, Michael, *William Alsop: Le Grand Bleu, L'hotel du Departement*, Academy Editions, 1994
'William Alsop and Jan Stormer', *Academy Architectural Monographs*, 33, 1992
Alsop & Störmer Architects, *Alsop & Störmer: Selected and Current Works*, Master Architects Series, Images Publishing, 1999
www.alsoparchitects.com

Tadao Ando
Dal Co, Francesco, *Tadao Ando: Complete Works*, Phaidon, 1995
Frampton, Kenneth, *Tadao Ando: Buildings, Projects, Writings*, Rizzoli, 1984
Pare, R., T. Ando and T. Heneghan, *The Colours of Light: Tadao Ando Architecture*, Phaidon, 1996
'Tadao Ando 1983–2000', *El Croquis*, 44 and 58, 2000

Archigram
Cook, Peter (ed.), *Archigram*, Princeton, 1999
Crompton, Dennis (ed.), *Concerning Archigram*, Archigram Archives, 1999
Crompton, Dennis, et al., *A Guide To Archigram, 1961–74*, Academy Editions, 1994
Rattenbury, Kester, 'Informal Follows Dysfunction', *Building Design*, 1558, 29 Nov 2002, pp.18–19
www.archigram.net

Wiel Arets
Bock, Manfred, *Wiel Arets*, Uitgeverij 010, 1998
Costa, Xavier, *Wiel Arets: Works Projects Writings*, Princeton Architectural Press, 2002
Meuwissen, Joost, et al., *Wiel Arets: Architect*, Uitgeverij 010, 1989

Arquitectonica
Emanuel, Muriel (ed.), *Contemporary Architects*, 3rd ed., St. James Press , 1995
Dunlop, Beth, *Arquitectonica*, American Institute of Architects, 1991
Dunlop, Beth, 'Arquitectonica Brings Magic to NY Skyline', *Miami Herald*, 3 November 2002
www.arquitectonica.com

Ashton Raggatt McDougall
Day, Norman, 'Storey Hall', *Architecture Australia*, January/February 1996
Jackson, Davina, and Chris Johnson, *Australian Architecture Now*, Thames & Hudson, 2000
Taylor, Jennifer, *Australian Architecture Since 1960*, Royal Australian Institute of Architects, 1986
www.a-r-m.com.au

Asymptote
Couture, Lise Anne, and Hani Rashid, *Asymptote*, Rizzoli, 1995
Couture, Lise Anne, and Hani Rashid, *Asymptote: Flux*, Phaidon, 2002
Couture, Lise Anne, and Hani Rashid, *Asymptote: Works and Projects*, Skira, 2002
www.asymptote.net

Shigeru Ban
Ambasz, Emilio, et al., *Shigeru Ban*, Princeton Architectural Press, 2001
Ambasz, Emilio, and Shigeru Ban, *Shigeru Ban*, Laurence King, 2001
Ban, Shigeru, *Shigeru Ban – Paper Tube Architecture*, Junius Verlag, 2000
Ban, Shigeru, *Shigeru Ban*, with an introduction by David Buck, Editorial Gustavo Gili, 1997

Günter Behnisch
Blundell Jones, Peter, *Günter Behnisch*, Birkhäuser, 2000
Gauzin-Miller, Dominique, *Behnisch & Partners: Fifty Years of Architecture*, Wiley-Academy, 1997
www.behnisch.com

Mario Botta
Cuito, Aurora, and Cristina Montes (eds.), *Mario Botta*, teNeues Publishing, 2003
Jodido, Philip, *Mario Botta*, Taschen, 1999
Nicolin, Pierluigi, *Mario Botta: Buildings and Projects, 1961–82*, Rizzoli, 1984
Pizzi, Emilio (ed.), *Mario Botta: The Complete Works 1985–1990*, with a foreword by Jacques Gubler, Birkhauser, 1994
Sakellardiou, Irena, *Mario Botta: Architectural Poetics*, Universe and Thames & Hudson, 2001
www.botta.ch

Santiago Calatrava
Calatrava, Santiago, et al., *Calatrava: Public Buildings*, Birkhauser, 1998
Molinari, Luca, *Sanitiago Calatrava*, Skira, 1999
Tzonis, Alexander, et al., *Santiago Calatrava: The Poetics of Movement*, Universe, 1998
'Santiago Calatrava', *El Croquis*, 38, 1989
www.calatrava.com

Caruso St John
Caruso St John, *Knitting Weaving Wrapping Pressing: Caruso St John Architects*, Edition Architekturgalerie Luzern and Birkhauser, 2002
Smith, Deborah (ed.), *The New Art Gallery, Walsall*, Batsford, 2002
www.carusostjohn.com

David Chipperfield
Chipperfield, David, and Kenneth Frampton, *David Chipperfield*, Princeton Architectural Press, 2003
Rykwert, Joseph, and David Chipperfield, *David Chipperfield: Theoretical Practice*, Ellipsis, 1992
'David Chipperfield: Recent Work', *2G*, 1, 1994

Kees Christiaanse
Christiaanse, Kees, *Kees Christiaanse*, Uitgeverij 010, 1999
Christiaanse, Kees, *Astoc Architects & Planners/ Kees Christiaanse*, Deutschland Niederlande and Aedes, 1997
Christiaanse, Kees, and Angela Mensing Herausgeber, *Suburbia in Holland, Vinex Standort Arnhem*, Institut fur Stadtebau und Architektur an der Technischen Universität Berlin, 1997
www.kcap.nl

Henri Ciriani
Ciriani, Henri, 'Musée d'archéologie en Arles', *L'architecture d'aujourd'hui*, 1992, p.282
Miotto, Luciana, and Henri Ciriani, *Henri E. Ciriani*, Canal & Stamperia, 1998
Purini, F., H. Ciriani and M. Galantino, *Henri Ciriani: Architecture 1960–2000*, Skira, 2000

Nigel Coates
Coates, Nigel, *Guide to Ecstacity*, Laurence King, 2003
Glancey, Jonathan, *Nigel Coates: Body Buildings and City Scapes*, Thames & Hudson, 1999
Poynor, Rick, *Nigel Coates: The City in Motion*, Fourth Estate, 1989
Pearman, Hugh, 'Upwardly Mobile', *The Sunday Times*, 15 March 1998, available as 'The Power and the Oyster' on www.hughpearman.com
www.nigelcoates.com

Coop Himmelb(l)au
Boyarsky, Alvin, et al., *Coop Himmelblau: Blaubox*, Architectural Association, 1998
Cook, Peter, and Rosie Llewellyn Jones, *New Spirit in Architecture*, Rizzoli, 1991
Coop Himmelblau, *Architecture Is Now*, Thames & Hudson, 1984
Farrelly, E. M., 'Songs of Innocence', *The Architectural Review*, 180, August 1986, pp.17–24
Noever, Peter, et al., *Architecture in Transition*, Prestel, 1991
Prix, Wolf D., *Coop Himmelblau, Austria, Biennale de Venezia*, Art Data, 1997
Prix, Wolf D., *Coop Himmelblau*, Wiley-Academy, 1998
Werner, Frank, *Covering and Exposing – Coop Himmelblau*, Birkhauser, 2001
www.coop-himmelblau.at

Charles Correa
Belluardo, James, and Kazi Khaleed Ashraf (eds.), *An Architecture of Independence: The Making of Modern South Asia: Charles Correa, Balkrishna Doshi, Muzharul Islam, Achyut Kanvinde*, Princeton Architectural Press, 1999
Frampton, Kenneth, *Charles Correa*, Thames & Hudson, 1997
www.charlescorrea.net

De Blacam & Meagher
Ryan, Raymund, 'Shane de Blacam and John
Meagher', *A+U*, July 1999
10 x 10: 10 Critics, 100 Architects, Phaidon, 2000
www.debm.ie

Giancarlo de Carlo
Mioni, A., and E. C. Occhialini, *Giancarlo
de Carlo*, Immagini e frammenti, 1995
Zucchi , B., *Giancarlo de Carlo*, Butterworth
Architecture, 1992

Odile Decq Benoit Cornette
Melhuish, Clare, *Odile Decq Benoit Cornette*,
Phaidon, 1996
Tonka, Hubert, and Jeanne-Marie Sens, *Odile Decq &
Benoit Cornette Architectes: BPO Banque Populaire
de l'Ouest Montgermont, Bretagne, fotographies
de Georges Fessy, Le Editions du Demi Cercle*, Les
Editions du Demi Cercle, 1990

Xaveer de Geyter
de Geyter, Xaveer, Geert Bekaert and Ivan Nio,
After-Sprawl, Research on the Contemporary City,
Nai Uitgevers, 2002
Bekaert, Geert, *Xaveer de Geyter Architects,
12 Projects*, Catalogue-Ludion, 2001
www.xdga.be

Neil Denari
Neil M. Denari, *Gyroscopic Horizons*, Thames
& Hudson, 1999
Rattenbury, Kester, 'Philosophy and Application',
Building Design, 1158, 4 February 1994, p.2
nmda-inc.com

Denton Corker Marshall
Beck, Haig, et al., *Denton Corker Marshall*,
Birkhauser, 2000
Jackson, Davina, and Chris Johnson, *Australian
Architecture Now*, Thames & Hudson, 2000
Sudjic, Deyan, 'Australia Embassy Tokyo',
Blueprint Extra, 2, 1990
www.dcm-group.com

Christian de Portzamparc
de Bure, Gilles, *Christian de Portzamparc*,
Editions Pierre Terrail, 2003
de Portzamparc, Christian, *Genealogie des
Formes*, Dis Voir, 1997
www.chdeportzamparc.com

Diener & Diener
Diamond, Rosamund, and Wilfried Wang (eds.),
*From City to Detail: Selected Buildings and Projects
by Diener & Diener Architekten*, Architecture
Foundation, London, and Ernst & Sohn, 1992
Diener, Roger, and Martin Steinmann, *Das Haus
und die Stadt: Stadtebauliche Arbeiten von Diener
& Diener*, Birkhauser, 1995
Kieren, Martin, *Diener & Diener Architects: Buildings
and Projects 1981–1996*, with photographs by
Christian Vogt, Birkhauser, 2002
Strathaus, Ulrike Jehle-Schulte, Martin Steinmann
and Karl-Heinz Heuter, *Diener & Diener*, Rizzoli,
1993
www.dienerdiener.ch

Diller + Scofidio
Betsky, Aaron (ed.), *Scanning: The Aberrant
Architectures of Diller + Scofidio*, Whitney Museum
of American Art, 2003
Diller, Elizabeth, et al., *Flesh: Architectural Probes:
The Mutant Body of Architecture*, Princeton
Architectural Press, 1995
Diller, Elizabeth, and Ricardo Scofidio, *Blur:
The Making of Nothing*, Harry N. Abrams, 2002
Kellogg, Craig, 'Diller + Scofidio: Under Surveillance',
Architecture, 89, 6 June 2000, pp.128–47
www.dillerscofidio.com

Günther Domenig
Rattenbury, Kester, 'The Wings of Desire',
Building Design, 1159, 11 February 1994, pp.14–15
Domenig, Gunther, *Gunther Domenig: Stonehouse
in Steindorf*, Ritter, 2002
Domenig, Gunther, *Gunther Domenig:
Steinhaus/Stonehouse*, Architectural
Association, 1986

Balkrishna Doshi
Belluardo, James, and Kazi Khaleed Ashraf (eds.),
*An Architecture of Independence: The Making of
Modern South Asia: Charles Correa, Balkrishna
Doshi, Muzharul Islam, Achyut Kanvinde*, Princeton
Architectural Press, 1999
Curtis, William, and Balkrishna Doshi, *Balkrishna
Doshi: An Architecture for India*, Mapin
Publications, 1989
Steele, James, *Rethinking Modernism from the
Developing World: The Complete Architecture
of Balkrishna Doshi*, Thames & Hudson, 1998
www.indiabuildnet.com/arch/sangpath

Peter Eisenman
Benjamin, Andrew E. (ed.), *Blurred Zones:
Investigations of the Interstitial*, Monacelli, 2003
Eisenman, Peter, and Robert Somol, *Peter
Eisenman: Diagram Diaries*, Universe, 1999
Kipnis, J., P. Eisenman, T. Leeser and J. Derrida,
*Chora L Works: Jacques Derrida and Peter
Eisenman*, Monacelli, 1997
'Peter Eisenman', *El Croquis*, 41, 1989
www.eisenmanarchitects.com

Arthur Erickson
Erickson, Arthur, *The Architecture of Arthur
Erickson*, Tundra Books, 1975
Erickson, Arthur, and Edith Iglauer, *Seven
Stones: A Portrait of Arthur Erickson*, Harbour
Publishing, 1981
Erickson, Arthur, *The Architecture of
Arthur Erickson*, Thames & Hudson, 1988
Whiteson, Leon, *Modern Canadian Architecture*,
Hurtig, 1983
www.arthurerickson.com

Ralph Erskine
Collymore, Peter, *The Architecture of Ralph
Erskine*, Granada, 1982
Egelius, Mats, *Ralph Erskine, Architect*,
Byggförlaget, 1990
Pearman, Hugh, 'The Ark, London, Architect
Ralph Erskine', *Blueprint Extra*, 10, 1993
www.erskine.se

Terry Farrell
Amery, Colin, et al., *Terry Farrell*, Academy Editions/St Martin's Press, 1985
Farrell, Terry, *Buckingham Palace Redesigned: A Radical New Approach to London's Parks*, Andreas Papadakis, 2002
Farrell, Terry, et al., *Terry Farrell in Scotland*, Tuckwell Press, 2002
Maxwell, Robert, and Terry Farrell, *Terry Farrell and Partners: Sketchbook*, Right Angle Publishing, 1998
Pearman, Hugh, *10 years 10 cities: The Work of Terry Farrell & Partners 1991–2001*, Laurence King, 2002
Powell, Ken, *Terry Farrell: Urban Design*, Academy Editions, 1993
Tibbalds, Francis, *Making People-Friendly Towns: Improving the Public Environment in Towns and Cities*, Spon Press, 2000
More Plastic Form, Pidgeon Audio-Visual Library, 1983
www.terryfarrell.com

Fat
Bullivant, Lucy, et al., *Space Invaders: New British Architecture*, The British Council, 2001
Catterall, Claire, *Stealing Beauty*, ICA exhibition catalogue, London, 1999
Fat, 'Everything Counts in Large Amounts (the Sound of Geography Collapsing)', in Kester Rattenbury (ed.), *This Is Not Architecture*, Routledge, 2002
Greene, David, 'Fat', in Maggie Toy (ed.), *Architecture on the Horizon*, Academy Editions, 1996
Hill, Jonathan, 'Fat: Contaminating Contemplation' in *Occupying Architecture: Between the Architect and the User*, Routledge, 1998
Magayrou, Frederic, and Mari-Ande Brayer (eds.), *Radical Experiments in Global Architecture*, Thames & Hudson, 2001
www.fat.co.uk

Sverre Fehn
Fjeld, Per-Olaf, *Sverre Fehn on the Thought of Construction*, Rizzoli, 1983
Norberg-Schulz, Christian, et al., *Sverre Fehn: Works, Projects, Writings, 1949–1996*, Monacelli, 1998

Foreign Office Architects
Eriksson, Agneta, *Foreign Office Architects*, Eriksson & Ronnefalk, 2001
Ferre, Albert (ed.), *The Yokohama Project: Foreign Office Architects*, Actar, 2003
'Foreign Office Architects', *2G*, 16, 2001
www.f-o-a.net

Norman Foster
Jenkins, David (ed.), *On Foster...Foster On*, Prestel, 2000
Jenkins, David (ed.), *Norman Foster Works*, Prestel, 2003
Pawley, Martin, *Norman Foster: A Global Architecture*, Universe, 1999
Sudjic, Dejan, *Norman Foster, Richard Rogers, James Stirling: New Directions in British Architecture*, Thames & Hudson, 1986
Foster Catalogue 2001, Prestel, 2001
www.fosterandpartners.com

Tony Fretton
Diamond, Rosamund, and Wilfried Wang, *Reality and Project: Four British Architects*, 9H Publications, 1990
Frampton, Kenneth, Mark Cousins and Tony Fretton, *Architecture Experience and Thought*, Architectural Association, 1998
Turnbull, David, and Tony Fretton, *Tony Fretton*, Editorial Gustavo Gili, 1995
www.tonyfretton.co.uk

Massimiliano Fuksas
Fuksas, Massimiliano, *Frames*, Aldeasa, 2003
Lenci, Ruggero, *Massimiliano Fuksas: Oscillazione e sconfinamento*, Testo & Immagine, 1996
Welsh, John, *Recent Buildings and Projects: Massimiliano Fuksas*, Ellipsis, 1994
www.fuksas.it

Future Systems
Field, Marcus, *Future Systems*, Phaidon, 1999
Kaplicky, Jan, *For Inspiration Only*, Wiley-Academy, 1996
Kaplicky, Jan, *More For Inspiration Only*, Wiley-Academy, 1999
Pawley, Martin, *Future Systems: The Story of Tomorrow*, Phaidon, 1993
Pawley, Martin, *Hauer-King House*, Phaidon, 1997
www.future-systems.com

Frank O. Gehry
Dal Co, Francesco, et al., *Frank O. Gehry: The Complete Works*, Monacelli, 1997
Gehry, Frank, et al., *Frank Gehry, Architect*, Harry N. Abrams, 2001
Lindsey, Bruce, *Digital Gehry*, Princeton Architectural Press, 2002
www.frank-gehry.com

Michael Graves
Dobney, Stephen, *Michael Graves: Selected and Current Works*, Images Publishing, 1999
Powell, Kenneth, *Graves Residence: Michael Graves*, Phaidon, 1995
Eisenman, Peter, et al., *Five Architects: Eisenman, Graves, Gwathmey, Hejduk, Meier*, New York Museum of Modern Art and Oxford University Press, 1975
Wheeler, Karen Vogel, Peter Arnell and Ted Bickford (eds.), *Michael Graves: Buildings and Projects 1966–1981*, Rizzoli, 1983
www.michaelgraves.com

Vittorio Gregotti
Gregotti, Vittorio, *New Directions in Italian Architecture*, W. W. Norton & Co, 1968
Rykwert, Joseph, *Vittorio Gregotti & Associates*, trans. Renee Tannenbaum, Rizzoli, 1996
Tafuri, Manfredo, *Vittorio Gregotti*, Rizzoli, 1982
www.gregottiassociati.it

Nicholas Grimshaw
Amery, Colin, *Architecture, Industry and Innovation: The Work of Nicholas Grimshaw & Partners 1965–1985*, Phaidon, 1995
Kaplicky, Jan (ed.), *Nicholas Grimshaw & Partners: Process*, NGP, 1988
Kaplicky, Jan (ed.), *Nicholas Grimshaw & Partners: Product*, NGP, 1988
Pearman, Hugh, *Equilibrium: The Work of Nicholas Grimshaw & Partners*, Phaidon, 2000
Powell, Kenneth, and Rowan Moore (eds.), *Structure, Space and Skin: The Work of Nicholas Grimshaw & Partners*, Phaidon, 1990
www.grimshaw-architects.com

Zaha Hadid
Hadid, Zaha, *Planetary Architecture Two*, Architectural Association, 1983
Hadid, Zaha, *Zaha Hadid: The Complete Buildings and Projects*, Thames & Hudson, 1998
Hadid, Zaha, et al., *LF One*, Birkhauser, 1999
Hattenstone, Simon, 'Master Builder', *The Guardian*, 3 February 2003
Rattenbury, Kester, 'Big Bold Beautiful and Unbuilt', *Building Design*, 1 December 1995
Rattenbury, Kester, 'One Small Step for Zaha', *Building Design*, 19 March 1999
Sigel, Paul, *Zaha Hadid: Lines*, Editions Axel Menges, 1998
www.zaha-hadid.com

Itsuko Hasegawa
Goulet, Patrice, *Itsuko Hasegawa*, Birkhauser, 1997
Hasegawa, Itsuko, et al., *Itsuko Hasegawa: Recent Buildings and Projects*, Springer Verlag, 1997
Kira, Moriko, and Mitsuaki Furudoi, *Itsuko Hasegawa: Architect*, Netherlands Architecture Institute and Nai Uitgevers, 2001

Zvi Hecker
Feireiss, Kristin, *Zvi Hecker: The Heinz-Galinski-School in Berlin*, Distributed Art Publishers, 1997
Hecker, Zvi et al., *The House of the Book*, Black Dog, 1999
www.zvihecker.com

Thomas Herzog
Flagge, Ingeborg, et al. (eds.), *Thomas Herzog: Architecture and Technology*, Prestel, 2002
Herzog, Thomas (ed.), *Expodach: Roof Structure at the World Exhibition, Hanover 2000*, Prestel, 2000
Herzog, Thomas, *Sustainable Height*, Prestel, 2000
www.herzog-und-partner.de

Herzog & de Meuron
Mack, Gerhard, *Herzog de Meuron, The Complete Works*, vols. 1–3, Birkhauser, 1996–2000
Moore, Rowan, et al., *Herzog & de Meuron: Building Tate Modern*, Tate Gallery Publishing, 2000
Stungo, Naomi, *Herzog de Meuron*, Carlton, 2002
Ursprung, Philip, *Herzog & de Meuron, Natural History*, Canadian Centre for Architecture, 2002
Wang, Wilfried, *Herzog & de Meuron*, Monograph Studio Paperback, extended 3rd new edition, Birkhäuser, 1998
'Herzog & de Meuron', *El Croquis*, 60/84, 2000

Steven Holl
Frampton, Kenneth, *Steven Holl: Projects and Architecture*, Electa, 2002
Holl, Steven, *Intertwining: Selected Projects 1989–1995*, Princeton Architectural Press, 1996
Steiner, Dietmar, et al., *Steven Holl: Idea and Phenomena*, Lars Muller Publishers, 2002
'Steven Holl 1986–1996', *El Croquis*, 78, 1996
www.stevenholl.com

Hans Hollein
Emmanuel, Muriel, *Contemporary Architects*, St Martin's Press, 1980
Hollein, Hans, *Metaphores et Metamorphoses*, Pompidou Centre, 1987
Pettena, Gianni, *Hans Hollein, Opere, 1960–1988*, Idea Books Edizioni, 1988

Arata Isozaki
Isozaki, Arata, et al., *Masters: Arata Isozaki, Jean Nouvel, Legorreta Arquitectos, Steven Holl*, St Martin's Press, 1997
Isozaki, Arata, et al., *Arata Isozaki: Four Decades of Architecture*, Universe, 1998
Stewart, David B., et al., *Arata Isozaki: Architecture 1960–1990*, Rizzoli, 1991

Toyo Ito
Jencks, Charles, *Toyo Ito*, Wiley-Academy, 1995
Maffei, Andrea, *Toyo Ito: Works, Projects, Writings*, Electa, 2002
Schneider, Ulrich, Manfred Speidl and Hayakeyama Sakamo, *Toyo Ito: Blurring Architecture 1971–2005*, Edizioni Charta Srl, 2000
Witte, Ron (ed.), *Toyo Ito, Sendai Mediathèque*, Prestel, 2001

Eva Jiricna
Boyarsky, Alvin, 'Eva Jiricna Designs', *AA Files*, 15, Summer 1987, pp.76–82
Jiricna, Eva, *Staircases*, Watson Guptill, 2001
Pawley, Martin, *Eva Jiricna: Design in Exile*, Rizzoli, 1990
www.ejal.com

Philip Johnson
Jenkins, Stover, et al., *The Houses of Philip Johnson*, Abbeville Press, 2001
Johnson, Philip, et al., *The Architecture of Philip Johnson*, Bulfinch Press, 2002
Schulz, Franz, *Philip Johnson: Life and Work*, University of Chicago Press, 1996
www.pjar.com

Rem Koolhaas
Koolhaas, Rem, *Delirious New York: A Retroactive Manifesto for Manhattan*, Thames & Hudson, 1978
Koolhaas, Rem, et al., *S,M,L,XL*, Taschen, 1997
Koolhaas, Rem, et al., *Project on the City 1: Great Leap Forward*, Taschen, 2002
Koolhaas, Rem, et al., *Project on the City 2: The Harvard Guide to Shopping*, Taschen, 2002
Zaera, Alejandro, *Rem Koolhaas: Urban Projects (1985–1990)*, Quaderns, 1990
'OMA/Rem Koolhaas 1987–1998', *El Croquis*, 53/79, 1998
www.oma.nl

Léon Krier
Krier, Leon, *Architecture: Choice or Fate*, Andreas Papadakis, 1998
Krier, Leon, et al., *Leon Krier: Architecture & Urban Design 1967–1992*, St Martin's Press, 1993
Papadakis, Andreas, et al. (ed.), *New Classicism: Omnibus Volume*, Rizzoli, 1990
Porphyrios, Demetri, *Leon Krier: Houses, Palaces, Cities*, Academy Editions, 1984

Lucien Kroll
Jencks, Charles, *The Language of Postmodern Architecture*, Academy Editions, 1978
Kroll, Lucien, *Lucien Kroll: the Architecture of Complexity*, Batsford, 1986
Mikelledes, Byron (ed.), *Architecture for People*, Studio Vista, 1980
Morgan, Ann Lee, and Colin Naylor, *Contemporary Architects*, 2nd ed., St James, 1987
'Six Architects Across a Continent: Belgium, Lucien Kroll', Belgissche Radio en Televise, 1989

Kisho Kurokawa
Kurokawa, Kisho, *Millennium: Kisho Kurokawa Architect and Associates*, Images Publishing, 2000
Kurokawa, Kisho, *Kisho Kurokawa Architects and Associates: The Philosophy of Symbiosis from the Ages of the Machine to the Age of Life*, Edizioni Press, 2001
Kurokawa, Kisho, et al., *Kisho Kurokawa: From Metabolism to Symbiosis*, St Martin's Press, 1992
Kurokawa, Kisho, and François Chaslin, *Kisho Kurokawa: The Architecture of Symbiosis*, Rizzoli, 1998
www.kisho.co.jp

Lab Architecture Studio
Allen, Stan, 'Two Projects by Lab', *Assemblage*, 29, MIT, 1996
Bates, Ed, and Peter Davidson, 'Architecture after Geometry', *Architectural Design*, 127, 1997
Bevan, Robert, *Collage Education*, World Architecture, January 2003
10 x 10: 10 Critics, 100 Architects, Phaidon, 2000
www.labarchitecture.com

Lacaton Vassal
Ruby, Ilka and Andreas, and Dietmar Steiner, *Lacaton and Vassal*, Editorial Gustavo Gili, 2002
'Lacaton & Vassal', *2G*, 21, 2002

Daniel Libeskind
Libeskind, Daniel, *Daniel Libeskind: Between Zero and Infinity: Selected Projects in Architecture*, Rizzoli, 1981
Libeskind, Daniel, *Chamber Works*, Architectural Association, 1983
Libeskind, Daniel, *Daniel Libeskind, Radix-Matrix: Architecture and Writings*, Prestel, 1997
Libeskind, Daniel, *Jewish Museum Berlin*, G&B International, 1999
Libeskind, Daniel, et al., *Daniel Libeskind: The Space of Encounter*, Universe, 2001
Schneider, Berhard, *Daniel Libeskind: Jewish Museum Berlin: Between the Lines*, Prestel, 1999
'Daniel Libeskind 1987–1996', *El Croquis*, 80, 1996
www.daniel-libeskind.com

Maya Lin
Ergas, G. Aimee, *From Michelangelo to Maya Lin*, U*X*L, 1995
Lin, Maya Ying, *Maya Lin: Public/Private*, Distributed Art Publishers, 1994
Lin, Maya Ying, *Boundaries*, Simon & Schuster, 2000
Scruggs, Jan C., and Joel L. Swerdlow, *To Heal a Nation: The Vietnam Veterans' Memorial*, Harper & Row, 1985

Greg Lynn
Lynn, Greg, *Animate Form*, Princeton Architectural Press, 1998
Lynn, Greg, *Folds, Bodies and Blobs: Collected Essays*, La Lettre Volee, 1998
Lynn, Greg, *Architecture for an Embryologic Housing*, Birkhauser, 2003
www.glform.com

Fumihiko Maki
Maki, Fumihiko, Alex Krieger and Botong Bognar, *Fumihiko Maki, Buildings and Projects*, Princeton Architectural Press, 1997
Salat, Serge, and Françoise Labbé, *Fumihiko Maki: an Aesthetic of Fragmentation*, Rizzoli, 1988

Imre Makovecz
Heathcote, Edwin, *Imre Makovecz: The Wings of the Soul*, Wiley-Academy, 1997
Tischhauser, Anthony, *Bewegte Form: Der Architekt Imre Makovecz*, Urachhaus, 2001

MBM
Drew, Philip, *Real Space: The Architecture of Martorell Bohigas Mackay Puigdomenech*, Wasmuth, 1993
Martorell, Josep, Oriol Bohigas, David Mackay and Albert Puigdomenech, *The Olympic Village.Barcelona 92, Architecture, Parks, Leisure Port, LA Villa Olimpica*, Editorial Gustavo Gili, 1992
www.mbmarquitectes.com

Richard Meier
Brawne, Michael, *The Getty Center, 1997, Brentwood Hills, Los Angeles, by Richard Meier & Partners*, Phaidon, 1998
Goldberger, Paul, *Richard Meier Houses*, Thames & Hudson, 1996
Koshalek, Richard, and Dana Hutt, *Richard Meier: Architect*, Monacelli, 1999
Meier, Richard, *Richard Meier: The Complete Works*, special edition, Taschen, 1998
Rykwert, Joseph, and Kenneth Frampton, *Richard Meier, Architect*, Rizzoli, 1999
www.richardmeier.com

Miralles Tagliabue
Tagliebue, Benedetta (ed.), *Enric Miralles: Works and Projects, 1975–1995*, Monacelli, 1996
Zabalbeascoa, Anatxu, *Igualada Cemetery: Enric Miralles and Carme Pinos*, Phaidon, 1996
'Enric Miralles, Carme Pinos, Obra Construida 1983–1994', revised and extended edition, *El Croquis*, 30+49/50+72(II), 1994
www.mirallestagliabue.com

Rafael Moneo
Frampton, Kenneth (ed.), *Rafael Moneo*, Ellipsis, 1996
Thorne, Martha, *Rafael Moneo: Audrey Jones Beck Building, Museum of Fine Arts, Houston*, Edition Axel Mendes, 2000

Morphosis
Cook, Peter, et al. (eds.), *Morphosis: Buildings and Projects 3*, Rizzoli, 1999
Mayne, Thom, *Morphosis*, Phaidon, 2002
Weinstein, Richard, *Morphosis : Buildings and Projects 1989–1992*, Rizzoli, 1994
www.morphosis.net

Eric Owen Moss
Collins, Brad, et al. (eds.), *Eric Owen Moss: Buildings and Projects 3*, Rizzoli, 2002
Moss, Eric Owen, *Gnostic Architecture*, Monacelli, 1999
Steele, James, *Lawson-Westen House: Eric Owen Moss*, Phaidon, 1995
'Eric Owen Moss', *Academy Architectural Monographs* 29, 1993
www.ericowenmoss.com

Glen Murcutt
Beck, Haig, and Jackie Cooper, *Glenn Murcutt: A Singular Practice*, Antique Collectors Club, 2002
Farrelly, E. M., *Three Houses: Glenn Murcutt*, Phaidon, 1993
Fromonot, Francoise, *Glenn Murcutt: Works and Projects 1969–2001*, Thames & Hudson, 2003
Murcutt, Glen, *The Drawings of Glenn Murcutt*, Images Publishing, 2002

MVRDV
Maas, Winy, *Farmax: Excursions on Density*, MVRDV, Uitgeverij 010, 1998
Maas, Winy, et al. (eds.), *Costa Iberica: Upbeat to the Leisure City*, MVRDV, Actar, 2000
Maas, Winy, et al., *MVRDV*, Netherlands Architecture Institute and Nai Uitgevers, 2002
Salazar, Jaime (ed.), *MVRDV at VPRO*, Actar, 1998
www.mvrdv.archined.nl

Neutelings Riedijk
Neutelings, Willem, and Michael Riedijk, *Neutelings Riedijk: Minnaert Building*, Uitgeverij 010, 1997
'Neutelings Riedijk', *El Croquis*, 94, 1999

Oscar Niemeyer
Niemeyer, Oscar, *Curves of Time: The Memoirs of Oscar Niemeyer*, Phaidon, 2000
Salvaing, Matthieu, *Oscar Niemeyer*, Assouline, 2002
Underwood, D. K., *Oscar Niemeyer and the Architecture of Brazil*, Rizzoli, 1994
www.niemeyer.org.br

Jean Nouvel
Bosoni, Giampiero (ed.), *Jean Nouvel, Architecture and Design 1976–1995, A Lecture in Italy*, Skira, 1997
Nouvel, Jean, et al., *Nouvel: Jean Nouvel Emmanuel Cattani et Associes*, Artemis, 1992
Rattenbury, Kester, 'Nouvel Riche', *Building Design*, 1007, 12 October 1990, p.14
jeannouvelle.com

O'Donnell & Tuomey
O'Toole, Shane, et al., *The Irish Pavilion*, Gandon Editions, 1992
Quinn, Patricia (ed.), *Temple Bar: The Power of an Idea*, Gandon Editions, 1996
Rattenbury, Kester, et al., *O'Donnell & Tuomey*, Gandon Editions, 1997
New Irish Architecture 17, AAI Awards 2001, Gandon Editions, 2002
www.odonnell-tuomey.ie

Ortner & Ortner
Konig, Walther, *Ortner & Ortner: Three Buildings for European Culture*, Verlag der Buchhandlung Walther Konig, 1999
Ortner, Laurids, et al., *Ortner & Ortner: Primer of Architecture*, Birkhauser, 1999
Wipplinge, Hans-Peter, and Heide Linzer, *Ortner & Ortner: The Architecture of the MQ*, Triton Verlag, 2001
www.ortner.at

John Pawson
Pawson, John, *Minimum*, Phaidon, 1996
Pawson, John, *John Pawson Works*, Phaidon, 2000
Pawson, John, *Themes and Projects*, IVAM/Phaidon, 2002
www.johnpawson.co.uk

I. M. Pei
Cannell, Michael, *I. M. Pei: Mandarin of Modernism*, Carol Southern Books, 1995
Wiseman, Carter, *The Architecture of I. M. Pei*, Thames & Hudson, 1990
www.pcf-p.com

Dominique Perrault
Cook, Peter, et al., *Dominique Perrault*, Birkhauser, 1999
Favier, Jean, and Philippe Belavel, *Bibliotheque Nationale De France 1989–95: Dominique Perrault, Architecte*, Birkhauser, 1995
Perrault, Dominique, *Dominique Perrault: Selected and Current Works*, Images Publishing, 2001
Stalder, Laurent, *Dominique Perrault: Projects and Architecture*, Electa, 2002
www.perraultarchitecte.com

Renzo Piano
Buchanan, Peter, *Renzo Piano Building Workshop: Complete Works*, 4 vols., Phaidon, 1993–2000
Goldberger, Paul, *Renzo Piano, Buildings and Projects 1971–1989*, Rizzoli, 1989
Piano, Renzo, *Fondation Beyeler, A Home For Art*, Beyeler, 1998
Rattenbury, Kester, 'Dante's Workshop', *Building Design*, 10 October 1992
www.renzopiano.com

Antoine Predock
Baker, Geoffrey, *Antoine Predock*, Academy Editions, 1997
Predock, Antoine, et al., *Antoine Predock, Architect 2*, Rizzoli, 1998
Predock, Antoine, and Brad Collins, *Antoine Predock: Houses*, Rizzoli, 2000
www.predock.com

Cedric Price
Allford, David, et al., *Cedric Price (Works)*, Architectural Association, 1984
Barley, Nick, *Re:CP*, Birkhauser, 2003
Hardingham, Samantha, *Cedric Price: Opera*, Wiley-Academy, 2003
Price, Cedric, *Cedric Price: The Square Book*, Wiley-Academy, 2003

Robbrecht & Daem
Bekaert, Geert (ed.), *Paul Robbrecht and Hilde Daem: Works in Architecture*, Ludion Editions, 1998
www.robbrechtendaem.com

Richard Rogers
Appleyard, Bryan, *Richard Rogers: A Biography*, Faber and Faber, 1986
Gumuchjian, Philip, *Cities for a Small Planet: Richard Rogers*, Faber and Faber, 1997
Powell, Kenneth, *Richard Rogers*, Artemis, 1994
Powell, Kenneth, *Richard Rogers Complete Works 1*, Phaidon, 1999
Powell, Kenneth, *Richard Rogers: Complete Works 2*, Phaidon, 2001
Rogers, Richard, and Mark Fisher, *A New London*, Penguin, 1992
Sudjic, Dejan, *Norman Foster, Richard Rogers, James Stirling: New Directions in British Architecture*, Thames & Hudson, 1986
Sudjic, Dejan, *The Architecture of Richard Rogers*, Harry N. Abrams, 1996
Richard Rogers Partnership: Works and Projects, Monacelli, 1996
www.richardrogers.co.uk

Moshe Safdie
Safdie, Moshe, *Beyond Habitat*, Tundra Books, 1987
Safdie, Moshe, et al. (eds.), *Moshe Safdie: Buildings and Projects, 1967–1992*, McGill-Queens University Press, 1996
Safdie, Moshe, and Wendy Kohn, *The City After the Automobile: An Architect's Vision*, Basic Books, 1997
www.msafdie.com

Sauerbruch Hutton
Forster, Kurt, et al., *WYSIWYG: Sauerbruch Hutton Architects*, Architectural Association, 1999
Sauerbruch, Matthias, and Luisa Hutton, *Projects 1990–96*, Birkhauser, 1996
Sauerbruch, Matthias, and Luisa Hutton, *Sauerbruch & Hutton: GSN, A Building in Berlin*, Lars Muller Publishers, 2000
Sauerbruch, Matthias, et al., *Photonics Center*, Actar, 2001
www.sauerbruchhutton.de

Harry Seidler
Frampton, Kenneth, *Harry Seidler: Four Decades of Architecture*, Thames & Hudson, 1992
Seidler, Harry, and Stephen Dobney, *Harry Seidler: Selected & Current Works*, Master Architect Series, Images Publishing, 1997
Spigelman, Alice, *Almost Full Circle: Harry Seidler, A Biography*, Brandl and Schlesinger, 2001
www.seidler.net.au

Kazuo Sejima
Futagawa, Yuko, 'Richard Meier, Jean Nouvel, Tadao Ando, Norman Foster, Kengo Kuma, Kazuyo Sejima', *GA Document*, 64, 2001
Sejima, Kazuyo, and Ryue Nishizawa, *Kazuyo Sejima In Gifu*, Actar, 2002
Matter and Mind in Architecture, International Alvar Aalto Symposium, Alvar Aalto Foundation, Jyvaskyla, Ginko Press, 2001

Claudio Silvestrin
Bertoni, Franco, *Claudio Silvestrin*, Chronicle Books, 1999
Silvestrin, Claudio, *Eye Claudio*, Booth-Clibborn Editions, 2002
Silvestrin, Claudio, et al., *Claudio Silvestrin*, Birkhauser, 1999
www.claudiosilvestrin.com

Alvaro Siza
Frampton, Kenneth, et al., *Alvaro Siza: Complete Works*, Phaidon, 2000
Rattenbury, Kester, 'Siza Matters', *Building Design*, 15 December 2000
www.alvarosiza.com

Snøhetta
Dykes, Craig, *Snohetta*, Aedes, 1999
www.snoarc.no

SOM
Belmont, Kathryn, *Skidmore, Owings & Merrill*, Master Architect Series, Images Publishing, 1995
Bussel, Abby, *SOM Evolutions: Recent Work of Skidmore, Owings & Merrill*, Birkhauser, 2000
Krinsky, Carol Herselle, *Gordon Bunshaft of Skidmore, Owings & Merrill*, MIT Press, American Monograph Series, 1989
www.som.com

Eduardo Souto de Moura
Blaser, Werner, et al., *Eduardo Souto de Moura*, Princeton Architectural Press, 2003
Leoni, Giovanni, *Souto de Moura*, Phaidon, 2003
Riera Ojeda, Oscar (ed.), *Ten Houses: Eduardo Souto Moura*, Rockport Publishers, 1998
Trigueiros, Luiz (ed.), *Eduardo Souto Moura*, Blau, 1994
Wang, Wilfried, and Alvaro Siza, *Souto de Moura*, Editorial Gustavo Gili, 1990

Kenzo Tange
Boyd, Robin, *Kenzo Tange*, George Braziller, 1990
Tange, Kenzo, *Kenzo Tange 1946–1996*, Art Books International, 1997
'Kenzo Tange Associates', *SD*, 372 (9), September 1995
www.ktaweb.com

TEN Arquitectos
Norten, Enrique, et al., *Ten Arquitectos*, Monacelli, 1998
10 x 10: 10 Critics, 100 Architects, Phaidon, 2000
www.ten-arquitectos.com

Bernard Tschumi
Tschumi, Bernard, *Cinegramme Folie: Le Parc de La Villette*, Princeton Architectural Press, 1987
Tschumi, Bernard, *Architectural Manifestoes*, Architectural Association, 1979
Tschumi, Bernard, *The Manhattan Transcripts*, Academy Editions, 1981
Tschumi, Bernard, *Events Cities*, MIT, 1994
Tschumi, Bernard, *Architecture and Disjunction*, MIT, 1996
Tschumi, Bernard, *Le Fresnoy: Architecture In-between*, Monacelli, 1999
Tschumi, Bernard, *Event Cities 2*, MIT, 2000
www.tschumi.com

O. M. Ungers
Brown-Manrique, Gerardo, *The Architecture of Oswald Mathias Ungers: A Chronological Bibliography*, Vance Bibliographies, 1980
Dal Co, Francesco, and O. M. Ungers, *Oswald Mathias Ungers: Works and Projects 1991–1998*, Electa, 2003
Ungers, O. M., and Stefan Vieths, *Oswald Mathias Ungers: la citta dialettica*, Skira, 1997

UN Studio
Feireiss, Kristin (ed.), *Mobile Forces, Ben van Berkel*, Ernst & Sohn, 1995
van Berkel, Ben, and Caroline Bos, *Move*, UN Studio and Goose Press, 1999
van Berkel, Ben, and Caroline Bos, *UNFold*, Nai Uitgevers, 2002
www.unstudio.com

Ushida Findlay
Pearman, Hugh, *Contemporary World Architecture*, Phaidon, 1998
'Ushida Findlay', *2G*, 6, 1998
www.ushidafindlay.com

Jørn Utzon
Weston, Richard, *Utzon: Inspiration, Vision, Architecture*, Edition Blondal, 2002
www.utzon.dk

Venturi, Scott Brown and Associates
Venturi, Robert, *Complexity and Contradiction in Architecture*, MIT, 1977
Venturi, Robert, Denise Scott Brown and Stephen Izenour, *Learning From Las Vegas: The Forgotten Symbolism of Architectural Form*, MIT, 1972
www.vsba.com

Rafael Viñoly
LeCuyer, A. W., and Rafael Viñoly, 'The Making of Public Space', the 1997 John Dinkeloo Memorial Lecture, University of Michigan College of Architecture, 1997
Steele, James, *Architecture Today*, Phaidon, 1997
Viñoly, Rafael, *Rafael Viñoly*, Princeton Architectural Press, 2003
www.rvapc.com

West 8
Geuze, Adrian, *Adrian Geuze/West 8: Landschapsarchitectuur*, Uitgeverij 010, 1995
Molinari, Luca (ed.), *West 8*, Skira, 2000
van Dijk, Hans, et al. (eds.), *Colonizing the Void: Adrian Geuze, West 8 Landscape Architects*, Nai Uitgevers, 1996
West 8, *Engineer Meets Poet: West 8*, Aedes, 1999
www.west8.nl

Tod Williams Billie Tsien
Carter, Brian, and Annette W. LeCuyer (eds.), 'Tod Williams Billie Tsien: The 1998 Charles & Ray Eames Lecture', *Michigan Architecture Papers*, 5, The University of Michigan College of Architecture and Planning, 1998
Williams, Tod, and Billie Tsien, 'Tod Williams/Billie Tsien', *Studies in Modern Art*, 7, 'Imagining the Future of The Museum of Modern Art', 1998
'Tod Williams Billie Tsien', *2G*, 9, 1999/1.
www.twbta.com

Lebbeus Woods
Brown, Olive, and Peter Cook, *Lebbeus Woods: Origins*, Architectural Association, 1985
Woods, Lebbeus, *OneFiveFour, Lebbeus Woods*, Princeton Architectural Press, 1989
Woods, Lebbeus, 'Heterarchy of Urban Form and Architecture', *Architectural Design*, vol 62, no 3/4, March–April 1992
Woods, Lebbeus, contributions in *The End of Architecture: Documents and Manifestoes*, Vienna Architecture Conference, Prestel, 1993
Paper for Cooper Union at www.archleague.org.nyc.vidler.html

Ken Yeang
Hamzah, T. R., and Ken Yeang, *Bioclimatic Skyscapers*, Ellipsis, 2000
Yeang, Ken, et al., *T. R. Hamzah & Yeang: Selected Works*, Master Architect Series, Images Publishing, 1999
Yeang, Ken, *Reinventing the Skyscraper: A Vertical Theory of Urban Design*, Academy Editions, 2002
www.trhamzahyeang.com

Peter Zumthor
Achleitner, Friedrich, and Peter Zumthor, *New Kunsthaus Bregenz Building*, Hatje Cantz, 1999
Zumthor, Peter, *Peter Zumthor Works: Buildings and Projects 1979–1997*, with photographs by Helene Binet, Lars Muller Publishers, 1998
Zumthor, Peter, *Thinking Architecture*, Lars Muller Publishers, 1998
Zumthor, Peter, *Three Concepts: Peter Zumthor*, Birkhauser, 1998

Picture Credits

The author and Laurence King Publishing Limited thank the sources of photographs for supplying and granting permission to reproduce them. Photographs have been obtained from the architects responsible unless listed below. Every effort has been made to contact all copyright holders.

b=bottom; c=centre; l=left; r=right; t=top

8 main Bleda y Rosa, inset Jordi Bernardó
10 main © Paul Rafferty/VIEW
12tl, bl Mitsuo Matsuoka; 12tr Stephane Couturier; 12br Tadao Ando; 13 Kinji Kanno
14tl © 1964 Ron Herron; 14tr, b Dennis Crompton
16 Hélène Binet
18tl, br Arquitectonica; 18tr © Norman McGrath, used by permission; 19b © Robert Lautman
24 © Hiroyuki Hirai
28t, br Courtesy Archivo Mario Botta; 28bl Enrico Cano; 29 Marco D'Anna
30b Barbara Burg/Oliver Schuh, Palladium Photodesign, Köln/Germany; 30tr Paolo Rosselli
32 Hélène Binet
34t Richard Bryant/Arcaid; bl Richard Davies; 35 Nick Knight
36tl Jan Bitter; 36tr, b, 37 Courtesy KCAP
38tl, tr, br Jean Marie Monthiers; 38bl Michel Desjardins
40c © Graham Gaunt
42 main, tl © Gerald Zugmann; 42tr Margherita Spiluttini; 43 Alexsandra Pawloff
46tl Richard Beer; 46bl, r Peter Cook
52t Hans Werlemann; 52b Gilbert Fastenaekens
58 © Nicolas Borel; 59 © Gitty Darugar
60 inset Christian Richters
64l, tr Gerald Zugmann; 64br Karl Kofler; 65 Christian Jungwirth
66t, b, 67b © Yatin Pandya
70tl, bl Richard Weston; 70tr Nic Lehoux
74tl Richard Bryant; 74tr Nigel Young
78 ARKIFOTO/Norwegian Architecture Museum © Jiri Havran; 79 Stina Glømmi
80tl © Valerie Bennett
82tl Nigel Young; 82cl Dennis Gilbert; 82bl Ken Kirkwood; 82r Ian Lambot
84 main © Peter Cook/VIEW; 84 inset Hélène Binet
86t © A. Frudate; 86b © D.O. Mandrelli; 87l © A. Martinelli; 87r © Maurizio Marcato
88t Nicholas Kane/Arcaid; 88b Courtesy Selfridges
90l © Duccio Malagamba; 90tr Roland Halbe; 90br Richard Weston
92 main Proto Acme Photo; 92 inset G. Kopp; 93 Bill Phelps
94t, bl Mimmo Jodice
96 main Read & Peck; 96tr Herbie Knott; 96br Jeremy Cockayne/Arcaid
98tl Christian Richters Fotograf; 98cl, bl Hélène Binet; 99 © Steve Double
100tl, b, 101 Itsuko Hasegawa Atelier; 100cl Shuji Yamada
102 © Michael Krüger
103 © Hiepler-Brunier
104 Thomas Herzog
106l Nicholas Kane/Arcaid
106tr Richard Weston; 106br Margherita Spiluttini
108 © Paul Warchol; 109 Mark Heithoff
112t Yoshio Takase; 112b Hisao Suzuki; 113t Eiichiro Sakata; 113b Yasuhiro Ishimoto

114 © Shinkenchiku-Sha (Japan Architect)
116 Richard Bryant/Arcaid
118 main Norman McGrath; 118 inset Courtesy AT&T
120b Christian Richters; 120t, 121b Hans Werlemann (Hectic)
132l AKG London; 132ct © Miller Hare; 132r © Archimation; 133 © Luca Vignelli
134t Timothy Hursley; 134b The National Park Service; 135t Cheung Ching Ming; 135b Norman McGrath
138tl The Japan Architect Company Ltd; 138tr, b Toshiharu Kitajima
142tr Catala-Roca; 142bl, cr Lluis Casals
144 John Edward Linden/Arcaid
146tl © Hisao Suzuki
148b Timothy Hursley; 148t, 149b © Duccio Malagamba
150 © Atelier Kim Zwarts
154t Max Dupain Associates
156l Christian Richters; 156br © Nicholas Kane 2001
158 Christian Richters
160b Reto Guntli/Arcaid; 160tl, tr, 161 Courtesy S. Philippou
162t Richard Weston
164l Dennis Gilbert/VIEW; 164tr John Searle; 164c, b Hélène Binet
166 main Peter Cook/VIEW; 166 inset Stefan Müller; 167 Heribert Corn
168tl Christoph Kicherer; 168tr Richard Davies; 169 Cindy Palmano
170l Ian Lambot/Arcaid; 170tr © RMN; 170br © Robert Lautman
172tl, b Georges Fessy/© ADAGP Paris & DACS London 2003; 172tr Michel Denancé/© ADAGP Paris & DACS London 2003
174t Fregoso & Basatto; 174bl Hester Paul; 175t © Shinkenchiku-Sha (Japan Architect); 175c Berengo Gardin Gianni
176 Timothy Hursley
180 Kristien Daem
182bl, br Richard Bryant/Arcaid
186 main © Shinkenchiku-Sha (Japan Architect)
188 main © Annette Kisling; 186tr © Gerrit Engel; 186bl Bitter+Bredt Fotografie; 187 © Erik-Jan Ouwerkerk
190 main Marcell Seidler/Max Dupain Associates; Eric Sierins/Max Dupain Associates; 189 © Montalbetti+Campbell
192bl Matteo Piazza
194t © Duccio Malagamba
198tl Florian Holzherr; 198b © Esto
202 main © Shinkenchiku-Sha (Japan Architect); 202 inset Richard Weston
206tr J. M. Monthiers; 206cr © Esto
208 main K. Frahm/Artur; 208 inset Stefan Müller
210t, b, 211l Christian Richters
212tl Katsuhisa Kida; 212tr James Harris; 212b Kenji Shimizu
214-215 Richard Weston
216l Mark Cohn; 216tr Matt Wargo; 217l Rollin La France; 217r J.T. Miller
218t Román Viñoly; 218bl T. Waki/Koji Horiuchi, Kawasumi Architectural Photography
220-221West 8/Jeroen Musch
222 © Michael Moran
228 Christian Richters; 229 Hélène Binet

Text Credits

Kester Rattenbury:
Will Alsop, Archigram, Arquitectonica, Nigel Coates, Coop Himmelb(l)au, Odile Decq Benoit Cornette, Neil Denari, Günther Domenig, Ralph Erskine, Terry Farrell, Fat, Norman Foster, Tony Fretton, Massimiliano Fuksas, Future Systems, Nicholas Grimshaw, Zaha Hadid, Herzog & de Meuron, Hans Hollein, Rem Koolhaas, Lucien Kroll, Fumihiko Maki, Imre Makovecz, MBM, Miralles Tagliabue, Rafael Moneo, Jean Nouvel, I. M. Pei, Dominique Perrault, Renzo Piano, Cedric Price, Richard Rogers, Alvaro Siza, TEN Arquitectos, Bernard Tschumi, Jørn Utzon, Venturi, Scott Brown and Associates, Lebbeus Woods.

Robert Bevan:
Tadao Ando, Ashton Raggat McDougall, Santiago Calatrava, David Chipperfield, Henri Ciriani, Charles Correa, Denton Corker Marshall, Diller + Scofidio, Balkrishna Doshi, Peter Eisenman, Sverre Fehn, Frank Gehry, Michael Graves, Zvi Hecker, Thomas Herzog, Arata Isozaki, Eva Jiricna, Philip Johnson, Léon Krier, Kisho Kurokawa, LAB Architects, Daniel Libeskind, Greg Lynn, Morphosis, Eric Owen Moss, Glenn Murcutt, Oscar Niemeyer, Antoine Predock. Moshe Safdie, SANAA, Harry Seidler, Snøhetta, Kenzo Tange, Ushida Findlay, Rafael Viñoly, Ken Yeang.

Kieran Long:
Abalos & Herreros, Wiel Arets, Asymptote, Shigeru Ban, Günter Behnisch, Mario Botta, Caruso St John, Kees Christiaanse, De Blacam & Meagher, Giancarlo de Carlo, Xavier de Geyter, Christian de Portzamparc, Diener & Diener, Arthur Erickson, Foreign Office Architects, Vittorio Gregotti, Itsuko Hasegawa, Steven Holl, Toyo Ito, Lacaton & Vassal, Maya Lin, Richard Meier, MVRDV, Neutelings Riedijk, O'Donnell & Tuomey, Ortner & Ortner, John Pawson, Robbrecht & Daem, Sauerbruch Hutton, Claudio Silvestrin, SOM, Eduardo Souto de Moura, UN Studio, O. M. Ungers, West 8, Tod Williams, Billie Tsien & Associates, Peter Zumthor.